Routledge Studies on Gender and Sexuality in Africa

The Politics of Biography in Africa
Borders, Margins and Alternative Histories of Power
Edited by Anaïs Angelo

Gender, Judging and the Courts in Africa
Selected Studies
Edited by J. Jarpa Dawuni

Girls Negotiating Porn in South Africa
Power, Play and Sexuality
Deevia Bhana

Gendered Spaces, Religion and Migration in Zimbabwe
Implications for Economic Development
Edited by Ezra Chitando, Sophia Chirongoma and Molly Manyonganise

Fifty Years of Family Planning in the Democratic Republic of the Congo
The Dogged Pursuit of Progress
Jane T. Bertrand

Gender-Inclusive Higher Education in Tanzania
Transforming Academia
Edited by Susan P. Murphy and Perpetua John Urio

African Women in the Fourth Industrial Revolution
Change, Policies, and Approaches
Edited by Tinuade Adekunbi Ojo and Bhaso Ndzendze

COVID-19 and Gender-Based Violence in Zimbabwe
Women's Pandemic Experiences and Lessons for the Future
Edited by Isaiah Munyiswa, Pauline Mateveke and Ezra Chitando

For more information about this series, please visit: www.routledge.com/Routledge-Studies-on-Gender-and-Sexuality-in-Africa/book-series/GSA

COVID-19 and Gender-Based Violence in Zimbabwe

This book investigates the experiences of women in Zimbabwe facing COVID-19 and gender-based violence, arguing that the insights from this extremely tough period could be used as a springboard for positive legal, cultural, and policy changes.

In 2020, COVID-19 caught the world by surprise, and often the socio-cultural factors impacting the treatment and care of those infected by the virus were not fully considered. In Zimbabwe, the socially constructed role of women as caregivers left them particularly vulnerable. Not only this, but COVID-19 lockdowns coincided with particularly high levels of sexual exploitation and gender-based violence, with women again comprising the majority of victims and survivors. Authors in this book analyse the pandemic experiences of women in Zimbabwe, both in the workplace and at the home, with the hope of fostering positive cultural change, and sensitizing policy-makers to the need for legislation that protects women in moments of disasters.

The important lessons and discussion points raised by this book will be important to policy-makers both within Zimbabwe and beyond, and to researchers working on gender, public health, philosophy, sociology, and politics in Africa.

Isaiah Munyiswa (PhD) is Senior Lecturer in the Department of Philosophy at the National University of Lesotho. He teaches courses in political philosophy, critical thinking skills, and textual analysis. His research interests are in the capabilities approach to human development, citizenship studies, economic philosophy, and the philosophy of well-being.

Pauline Mateveke (PhD) is Senior Lecturer in the Department of English and Media Studies at the University of Zimbabwe. She is an African literature and culture scholar whose research interests include gender, sexuality, popular culture, and political and social themes on Africa.

Ezra Chitando (PhD) is Professor of Phenomenology of Religion in the Department of Philosophy, Religion and Ethics at the University of Zimbabwe. His broad research and publication interests include method and theory in the study of religion, as well as health, gender, security, politics, development, climate change, and sexuality, among others.

COVID-19 and Gender-Based Violence in Zimbabwe

Women's Pandemic Experiences and Lessons for the Future

Edited by
Isaiah Munyiswa, Pauline Mateveke and Ezra Chitando

Routledge
Taylor & Francis Group
LONDON AND NEW YORK

First published 2025
by Routledge
4 Park Square, Milton Park, Abingdon, Oxon OX14 4RN

and by Routledge
605 Third Avenue, New York, NY 10158

Routledge is an imprint of the Taylor & Francis Group, an informa business

British Library Cataloguing-in-Publication Data
A catalogue record for this book is available from the British Library

ISBN: 9781032799285
ISBN: 9781032799292
ISBN: 9781003494546

DOI: 10.4324/9781003494546

Typeset in Times New Roman
by Newgen Publishing UK

Contents

Boxes

Contributors

Makomborero Allen Bowa is Lecturer in the Department of Philosophy, Religion and Ethics at the University of Zimbabwe. Underpinning his social engagement scholarship is an overarching vision of fostering progressive social change through the creation of a more inclusive, equitable, and sustainable world, particularly for vulnerable and marginalized groups including persons with disabilities. His research, which often appropriates biblical themes, offers valuable insights and actionable strategies for promoting positive transformations that empower individuals and communities in the context of Africa's quest to achieve disability-inclusive development through the eradication of the disability–poverty nexus and other social injustices.

Lovejoy Chabata (PhD) is Lecturer in New Testament Studies at the Catholic University of Zimbabwe. He is also Research Associate at the University of Pretoria, South Africa. His research interests include Afrocentric interpretation of biblical texts; the Bible and gender studies; the Bible, politics, and human rights in Africa; the Bible and social transformation in Africa; the Bible, gender, and pandemics in Africa; New Testament ethics and leadership development in Africa; and theological education and social transformation in Africa.

Glory Ruvarashe Chirara is a renowned public relations practitioner and health communication researcher. With a distinction in research from the University of Zimbabwe, she has established herself as a leading expert in bridging mainstream media and health promotion. Her research and symposium presentations focus on harnessing media power for health awareness and wellness. Esteemed global organizations seek her expertise in developing effective health communication campaigns. Chirara's research investigates the impacts of media on health behaviours, develops evidence-based strategies, and informs policy and practice, shaping the future of health communication and media engagement.

Tracey Chirara (PhD) is Lecturer in the Department of Philosophy, Religion and Ethics at the University of Zimbabwe. Her research interests and publications focus on the interface between religion, gender, and contemporary themes such as ecology, climate change, health, and development.

Sophia Chirongoma (PhD) is an independent researcher. She is also an Academic Associate/Research Fellow at the Research Institute for Theology and Religion (RITR) in the College of Human Sciences, University of South Africa (UNISA). Her research interests and publications focus on the interface between culture, ecology, religion, health, and gender justice.

Nehemiah Chivandikwa (PhD) is Associate Professor at the University of Zimbabwe. He teaches theatre and development communication and play-making. His research interests are in performance and body politics, gender, disability, applied theatre performances, and media. He has published several articles on these areas in both regional and international journals. Chivandikwa has been involved in several projects in applied theatre on gender, political violence, disability, and rural and urban development.

Joyline Gwara (PhD) is Senior Lecturer in the Department of Philosophy, Religion and Ethics at the University of Zimbabwe. She is also a member of the Conversational School of Philosophy. She is a PhD holder from the University of KwaZulu-Natal Pietermaritzburg, South Africa. She also did her Master of Arts in Philosophy and Bachelor of Arts (Honours) in Philosophy at the University of Zimbabwe. She is the first woman to have a doctorate in philosophy in Zimbabwe. Her teaching and research interests include a wide range of themes in African philosophy.

Agber Thaddeus Igbalumun, SJ is a Jesuit from Nigeria. He holds a diploma in medical laboratory sciences and he is currently studying philosophy at Arrupe Jesuit University, Harare, Zimbabwe. He has a special interest in visual art, social justice, and promoting African identity.

Nyari Kachepa is a postgraduate student who has vast experience in writing and producing television programmes on development communication.

Elias G. Konyana (PhD) is Associate Professor of Philosophy in the Department of Ethics, Philosophy, Religion and Theology at Great Zimbabwe University. He is also Senior Research Associate at the African Centre for Epistemology and Philosophy of Science (ACEPS), University of Johannesburg.

Molly Manyonganise (PhD) is Senior Lecturer at the Zimbabwe Open University and Research Associate in the Department of Religion Studies, Faculty of Theology and Religion, University of Pretoria. She is an alumni of the Alexander von Humboldt Georg Forster Postdoctoral Research Fellowship. Her research interests include religion and gender, religion and politics, religion and sexuality, African Indigenous religion(s), as well as African Christianity. She has started to develop interest in the area of religion and decoloniality.

Tsiidzai Matsika (PhD) is Senior Lecturer in the Department of Creative Media and Communication at the University of Zimbabwe. She is a specialist in English language and literature/letters.

Chipo Musoko is Lecturer in Journalism and Media Studies in the Department of Creative Media and Communication at the University of Zimbabwe. She is also a journalist by profession, with over 10 years of work experience as a political, business, and financial journalist. She has worked for various national and international organizations including New Ziana and Reuters (The Source news agency in Zimbabwe) as a senior journalist and assistant news editor, respectively. She also worked for a German capacity-building organization, GIZ, as a communications specialist editing an alumni magazine for the SADC region. She has attended and presented papers at both national and international conferences in Ghana, South Africa, and Zimbabwe (UZ). She is currently studying a Doctor of Philosophy at the University of Zimbabwe focusing on social media and politics in Zimbabwe. Her research interests include media/ social media, communication, politics, gender, and business.

L. Uchenna Ogbonnaya (PhD) is a postdoctoral scholar at the African Centre for Epistemology and Philosophy of Science, Faculty of Humanities, University of Johannesburg and was a postdoctoral scholar at University of Pretoria, South Africa. He holds a PhD from the University of Calabar in Nigeria. His areas of specialization and research interest include African philosophy, epistemology, logic, metaphysics, and applied philosophy. He has published some articles and chapters in international journals and edited collections. Ogbonnaya has presented papers at some international conferences. He is a member of the editorial board for *Arumaruka* as well as an editorial assistant for *Filosofia Theoretica: Journal of African Philosophy, Culture and Religions.* He is a member and secretary of the Conversational Society of Philosophy (CSP) and serves as the coordinator of their Monthly Seminar Gathering (MSG).

Nomatter Sande (PhD) is Research Associate at the University of Glasgow (https://rastay.org/home/). He is also Research Fellow at the Research Institute for Theology and Religion (RITR) in the College of Human Sciences, University of South Africa (UNISA). His expertise lies at the intersection of religion, migration, transnationalism, disability, and youth.

Tabona Shoko (PhD) is Professor in the Department of Philosophy, Religion and Ethics at the University of Zimbabwe (UZ), Harare, since 1 January 1993. He lecturers in African Traditional Religion and Phenomenology of Religion.

Denise Shorayi is a television producer and presenter on current affairs, mainly focusing on crisis communication.

Beatrice Taringa (PhD) has a Doctor of Philosophy degree in Education, a Master of Education in Indigenous Language Education, and a Bachelor of Education degree in Indigenous Language Education, ChiShona, from the University of Zimbabwe and a Diploma Education specializing in ChiShona and History from

Gweru Teachers College. She is Lecturer and Research Fellow at Midlands State University National Language Institute. She is a Postdoctoral Research Fellow in the Department of Language Education, Arts and Culture at University of South Africa (UNISA). She is a consultant for curriculum issues in Education in the area of language, culture, gender, and human rights.

Acknowledgements

We would like to thank the contributors for their patience and support. We would also want to sincerely thank the Humboldt Research Hub at the University of Zimbabwe represented by Professor Ezra Chitando for funding the conference that resulted in this compilation.

Introduction

COVID-19 and Gender-Based Violence in Zimbabwe – Women's Pandemic Experiences and Lessons for the Future

Isaiah Munyiswa, Pauline Mateveke, and Ezra Chitando

This volume brings together researchers from various academic backgrounds to discuss women's experiences during pandemics such as HIV/AIDS[1] and COVID-19, both of which are, to some degree, still active, using Zimbabwe as a case study. Different categories of researchers globally, including the Circle of Concerned African Women Theologians (see, e.g., Manyonganise, 2023), have highlighted that women are particularly vulnerable to various forms of abuse during pandemics owing to societal gender roles that mostly disadvantage women and girls. Carol Smith (2015) reinforces the widely held view that women and adolescent girls are vulnerable during complex emergencies and major disasters as they face many risks, including abuse, sexual exploitation, and violence. In the same vein, Becker (1992) observed that, although most societies insist that women are full citizens, entitled to equal protection, in reality many women lead lives circumscribed by cultural biases and fear of harassment and violence from strangers and non-strangers, and without adequate government protection. Researchers in this volume have used such views as a springboard to investigate and discuss injustices women face during pandemics using concrete facts in the context of Zimbabwe. Knowledge of the risks women are exposed to during pandemics provides insights into possible remedial measures that societies should take during current and future pandemics. To this end, therefore, this volume serves the dual purpose of looking back to document women's experiences of gender-based violence, and looking ahead in terms of pandemic preparedness. Thus, two of the distinctive contributions of the volume are to combine two recent pandemics, namely, HIV/AIDS and COVID-19, with special reference to women's experiences of gender-based violence and to proffer insights into pandemic preparedness.

This volume also takes cognisance of the social injustices women in most societies continue to face on account of their socially assigned gender roles. As Sofjan (2017) argues, gender represents evolving power structures and relations among the sexes in society. Gender in most societies depicts "men" as the first gender dominating over the hapless "women," and many chapters in this volume seem to dovetail with this view. The majority of authors in this volume directly or indirectly

DOI: 10.4324/9781003494546-1

assert that current perceptions and conceptions of the woman are the source of the many injustices women face. While investigating women's experiences during pandemics in Zimbabwe, for example, it is important to have an idea of how the Zimbabwean society defines the ideal woman. Context is important, given that some societies are patrilineal, while others are matrilineal. However, in almost all societies what is deemed the ideal woman is arguably not based on the essential nature of the woman, but a social construction. Following Giddens and Sutton (2017), we firmly believe that social categories like gender, disability, race, and crime are created through historical social processes and social interactions. Giddens and Sutton (2017) argue that gender is a complex social construction and gender roles are learnt through social agencies such as family, school, and mass media. This explains the observed seemingly entrenched gender roles we observe in society. "Socialization processes in the family, peer groups and schools tend to promote gendered forms of self-identity which children internalize, and in this way gender differences are culturally reproduced and men and women socialized into different roles" (Giddens and Sutton, 2017). Gender roles created socially eventually become intertwined into local cultures and subsequently are justified as "our culture." Most cultures in the world thus exhibit some gender orders that are largely patriarchal. At the top of the gender order, according to Giddens and Sutton, is hegemonic masculinity, exercised through culture, which extends into private life and social realms. Giddens and Sutton (2017) define patriarchy as the systematic of domination of women by men in some or all of society's spheres and institutions. For them, the conventional family is a crucial element of patriarchy in which women do the majority of household chores, even when both they and their male partners are in formal employment.

Socially constructed gender roles become more visible during occasions of collective crises such as the HIV/AIDS and COVID-19 pandemics. In Zimbabwe, for instance, women and girls are idealised as caregivers. Care-giving is the essence of womanhood. The Zimbabwean proverb which says "*musha mukadzi*" meaning "the woman makes the home" alludes to this fact. Although it can be deployed to promote women's agency (see, e.g., Chirara and Chisale, 2023), it also increases women's responsibilities in challenging contexts. At the peak of HIV/AIDS-related illnesses, between the mid-1990s and mid-2000s, home-based care was the main method used to manage patients. Women and girls were the main caregivers. Even though most HIV/AIDS-related illnesses were not contagious, the fact that women and girls were the ones to care for patients in their last moments of life was traumatising enough and can be regarded as a form of societal abuse. The care-giving role of women in Zimbabwe extends to the dead (see Mwandayi, 2011: 210–214). It is part of the Zimbabwean culture that the body of a deceased family member has to spend the night at home before burial the following day. The coffin carrying the body is placed in a special room and is cared for by women who sing traditional and religious songs throughout the night. Women are also responsible for washing and dressing the corpse in cases where a funeral parlour is not engaged. Such practices undoubtedly leave women vulnerable, especially where it pertains contagious diseases, and during the COVID-19 pandemic some women unfortunately became super spreaders. A woman coming from a funeral would spread the disease to the rest of her family.

Pandemics affect women's well-being in even more significant ways. For example, some women are forced to leave their jobs and some girls have to stop going to school to take care of patients at home. The peak period of HIV/AIDS in Zimbabwe arguably left serious psychological wounds on some women as they have to leave their jobs to nurse an ailing parent, child, or spouse. More recently, the COVID-19-induced lockdowns brought even more anxious moments for women and girls. With all family members at home, women's role as caregivers became more pronounced. Because women are stereotyped as more caring, tender, understanding, and patient, the care-giving role is seen as natural for them (see Macarov 1995). However, apart from this care-giving role socially assigned to them, women face even more worrying challenges in the home. According to Nanda and Warms (2007), although ideally we might think that families and households are tranquil and benign, this is not always true, as all over the globe violence often occurs within families, significantly because of the extreme vulnerability of some of its residents – especially women and teenage girls. Nanda and Warms blame cultural sanctions of patriarchy (male power) which they think are clearly related to domestic violence. There are many sources of the relative powerlessness of women within families, among them strict cultural rules limiting their options, their physical vulnerability, a cultural support for masculinity defined as control over women, women's isolation from potential sources of support, or the lack of alternative economic opportunities to marriage, among others (Nanda and Warms, 2007). As most chapters in this volume highlight, cases of violence against women increased during the COVID-19 lockdowns.

The previous discussion gives the picture that in most instances pandemics affect men and women differently. This, however, differs from culture to culture. Even though it can be argued that pandemics diminish the agency or the effective freedoms of every person to do what they want to do or to be whom they want to be, women are arguably affected differently in all aspects of their lives, including in employment and health. Contributors to this volume analyse the experiences of women in different spaces (in the home or the larger society) during these pandemics with the hope of fostering positive cultural change, sensitising policymakers on the need for legislation that protects women in moments of disasters, and more importantly, reflect on how to turn current experiences into lessons for the future. Current experiences give insights as to what we need to do, avoid, or change now in preparation for similar or related occurrences in future. In particular, we need to revise some wrong ideologies or world views that we hold in our social groups – ideologies that we use to justify some actions (such as male superiority, leading to gender-based violence) but that cannot be counterpoised to truth.

Gender-based Violence

The concept of gender-based violence (GBV) lacks a straightforward definition. The United Nations defines violence against women as

> any act of gender-based violence that results in, or is likely to result in, physical, sexual, or mental harm or suffering to women, including threats of such acts, coercion or arbitrary deprivation of liberty, whether occurring in public or in private life.
>
> (World Health Organization, 2024)

Researchers in this volume have adopted an equally expanded definition of GBV. A point to note is that GBV is not limited to physical harm but extends to mental or psychological harm and to the deprivation of freedom. Arguably some violence can be meted on women without them knowing it due to factors such as cultural conditioning. Some women adapt to certain oppressive situations to the extent that they may not notice the oppression taking place. As Rutherford et al. (2007) state, gender-based violence is a term that recognises that violence occurs within the context of women's and girl's subordinate status in society, and serves to maintain this unequal balance of power. GBV for them includes some culturally specific forms of abuse and to place women in dangerous situations like making them the sole caregivers for patients suffering from contagious diseases. To this end, cultures, religions, and other social practices can be catalysts for GBV. As the editors, we did not prescribe any one definition of GBV. This enabled the contributors to provide diverse but highly informative interpretations of the phenomenon.

Chapters in this Volume

Chapters in this volume are organised into two thematic sections, even though some overlap of material might still be observed. Researchers in the first section, which is composed of Chapters 1–5, discuss how local cultures, including religion, affect(ed) gender relations during pandemics. An analysis of women's experiences during both the HIV/AIDS and COVID-19 pandemics more likely generates a clearer picture of what they go through during such crises. The authors focus on resilient attitudes and behaviours founded on cultures, including religions, in the face of pandemics.

Contributions in the second segment analyse women's issues during pandemics that have a bearing on policy. Some contributions discuss gender and the media, discussing the extent to which the media cover the experiences of women during pandemics. The question the authors grapple with is, "Do women's experiences during pandemics get equal (to men) and full coverage?" Other chapters discuss how some measures that are introduced to manage pandemics impact women's well-being and rights.

Chapter 1 by Nomatter Sande and Sophia Chirongoma focuses on the observed rise in cases of gender-based violence during the era of COVID-19 across the globe, especially in Zimbabwe. For them, this rise shows the gap between theoretical assumptions, practice, and the failure to learn from previous pandemics such as HIV/AIDS. They argue that society plays a pivotal role in shaping and empowering women to respond to crises, including their response to the outbreak of pandemics. The chapter recommends using Elisabeth Olivius' basic needs, instrumental and developmental approaches to gender as a framework for fresh thinking about infusing behavioural change towards gender-based violence. The chapter concludes by restating the fact that although there has been considerable progress made in terms of activism against gender-based violence, the emergence and negative impact of COVID-19 have challenged this position, showing that people have changed less in their behaviour.

Chapter 2 by Beatrice Taringa argues that among the Indigenous communities, most social phenomena are gendered. She posits that religion and culture are central in defining gender roles. The continuity of these gender roles perpetuates stereotypes and abuses that became rampant in the COVID-19 pandemic era. Through mixed methods of sequential transformative strategy design and variant model that is largely qualitative, she assesses how COVID-19 differentially impacted on men and women in Indigenous societies in Zimbabwe and how this impacted on women's health and well-being. Taringa concludes that while COVID-19 is non-selective and knows no gender in terms of getting infected, its impact is inevitably gendered and its negative effects skew towards the female gender.

Coming from a philosophical background, L. Uchenna Ogbonnaya and Joyline Gwara argue in Chapter 3 that the African duality – a theory that influences the assignment of different roles between men and women – has implications for gender equality during pandemics. For them, the duality theory pervades most sub-Saharan countries, Zimbabwe included. This duality of duties becomes more visible during events such as pandemics. Using different pandemics, such as HIV/AIDS and COVID-19 in the Zimbabwean context, Ogbonnaya and Gwara argue that instead of the African duality theory playing a negative role in gender relations, it can be reconceptualised to play a positive role. The duality theory can be used positively to explain that both the male and the female genders are integral parts of humanity, and they must be treated as equals even during pandemics.

Retaining the philosophical approach, in Chapter 4, Elias G. Konyana discusses the extent of the scourge of violence against women during the COVID-19 pandemic in Zimbabwe. He explores its effects on women's well-being and suggests the possible opportunities available towards its containment and elimination. Using the critical analysis and phenomenological approaches, the chapter seeks to argue that intimate partner violence was exacerbated by the COVID-19 pandemic in Zimbabwe. The final part of the chapter presents possible opportunities that can be pursued towards ending intimate partner violence.

Chapter 5 by Lovejoy Chabata argues that the structural burden of submissiveness and loyalty to culturally determined stereotypes of women's roles has pushed women to the receiving end of most of the mishaps and dangers concomitant with pandemics. The chapter attributes most of the pandemic-related prejudices and suffering of women to naïve interpretations of scripture on the roles of women. The chapter employs Afrocentric Biblical Hermeneutics (ABH) supported by the historical critical method to investigate how the virtues for Christian women in Titus 2:3-5 have influenced the well-being, rights, and demeanour of women during HIV/AIDS and COVID-19 pandemics in Zimbabwe.

In the second thematic section, Chapter 6 by Molly Manyonganise discusses how the COVID-19 pandemic exacerbated already existing gender inequalities globally and Zimbabwe in particular. For her, the genealogy of pandemics shows that a disaggregation of their effects is indicative of the fact that women and men are affected differently with women bearing its brunt. The chapter examines the mandate of selected women's organisations in Zimbabwe with a view to question and critique their silence and selective (re)presentation of women in Zimbabwe. The intention of the chapter is to problematise their naming vis-à-vis the materiality of their operations. Questions to be answered in this chapter are (i) is the term "women's organisations" the same as "organising women"? or (ii) does the term "women's organisations" refer to entities that are led by women who may not pay attention to women's needs? (iii) In a pandemic context, what informs their responses to GBV? (iv) In what way are these responses affected by the prevailing political environment?

In Chapter 7, Tabona Shoko and Tracey Chirara examine the impact of religio-social and cultural beliefs and HIV and AIDS among women in Zimbabwe. They explore the role that cultural and religious beliefs play in influencing the spread and effects of HIV and AIDS among the Shona people. For them traditions, values, and attitudes in Shona culture such as patriarchy, polygamy, inheritance, circumcision rites, genital mutilation negatively affect women more than men. They argue that due to their subordinate status, women have no power to negotiate for safe sex and therefore have no defence mechanism to avoid contracting HIV. It is in that context that Shoko and Chirara propose that due to their vulnerable position, women need empowerment to advocate for their rights in the context of pandemics like HIV and AIDS. Their conclusion is that women bear the brunt of HIV and AIDS infection due to religious and socio-cultural structures, but this can be corrected by education and empowerment to restore their health and dignity.

Coming from a media background, Chipo Musoko in Chapter 8 seeks to establish whether journalists were ethical and professional in reporting cases of GBV during the peak periods of the COVID-19 pandemic in Zimbabwe. She analyses stories from three local dailies in Zimbabwe – *The Herald* (public media), *NewsDay* (private), and *Daily News* (private) through qualitative content analysis of purposively sampled articles on GBV. Feminist theories, Africana womanism, and audience reception theories are employed to help explain gender dynamics as well as how media audiences interact with media messages to give them meaning. Musoko establishes that though GBV cases were rampant during the pandemic, men perpetrated most of the violence against women. For her, the media to some extent fuelled the tensions through consciously or unconsciously negative reportage. Some of the stories lacked detailed research, hence exposed lack of professionalism and ethics among journalists and media houses. This lack of professionalism is evidenced by one-sided court and police reports. Musoko recommends that the number of women in newsrooms be increased to enable them to properly articulate issues affecting women.

In Chapter 9, Thaddeus Igbalumun Agber argues that although the "stay-at-home" policy helped in curbing the spread of COVID-19 in some ways, its effectiveness remains uncertain considering the negative impacts it presented. These impacts include domestic violence, mental health disorders, and financial instability, among other challenges. For him, the stay-at-home policy therefore may be seen as a double-edged policy whose negative impacts seem to supersede its intended purpose, that is, to mitigate COVID-19 pandemic. The challenges posed by the COVID-19 pandemic seem to have affected more women than men. The chapter goes further to argue that the stay-at-home policy should not be seen as a cornerstone for an effective mitigation of the COVID-19 pandemic and other related contagious pandemics if it is not supported by appropriate ways of limiting its negative impacts. The chapter suggests the government should implement different activities such as online jobs, online learning, reliable online shopping, and subsidisation of internet services during the times of any pandemic that would necessitate "stay-at-home" as a solution. For him, the implementation of the aforementioned activities will reduce domestic violence, mental health disorder, and other negative impacts associated with stay-at-home policy for reducing the spread of COVID-19 or other related pandemics.

Chapter 10 by Nyari Kachepa and Nehemiah Chivandikwa adopts Paul Farmer's (2015) concept of structural violence as an analytical lens to interrogate the complexities that aid and hinder the media from unmasking the axes of oppression, whose violence causes the bodily suffering of women particularly in the context of a pandemic. Within the development communication framework, the study analyses the socio-biological factors that lead to the marginalisation of Zimbabwean women, which become visible and embodied as death, sickness, and suffering. The study demonstrates how Kleptocrats/elites have vandalised the economy and health systems – whose severe outcomes were acutely felt during the COVID-19 pandemic in ways that brought untold suffering, bodily sickness, and deaths. The chapter further analyses how the media (television, Facebook, and YouTube) reported and projected the images and narratives of women's sexual reproductive rights in relation to abortion, pregnancy, contraceptives, and general maternity services during the period 2020–2022. While acknowledging the political, economic, technical, and professional factors that aided and complicated the role of media in crisis communication of the COVID-19 pandemic, the authors note that there is room for the media to expand its function by unmasking structural factors that exacerbate the suffering of women in the context of a pandemic. The media, for them, should empower women and other marginalised communities to have a voice in transforming local, regional, national, and global inequalities that deprive them access to effective sexual reproductive health systems and resources.

In Chapter 11, Glory Ruvarashe Chirara and Nehemiah Chivandikwa examine the media effects on vaccine acceptance by Zimbabwean women during the COVID-19 pandemic. The study draws on interview materials with selected female participants on media testimonials, infomercials, sermons, advertisements, infomercials, chain messages, and musical interludes formats that were used to push the vaccine and anti-vaccine drive. Chirara and Chivandikwa note that some of the most common factors that influenced vaccine acceptance are trust in the vaccines and media used, fear of the pandemic through the use of fear appeals as well as information adequacy. They also note that hesitancy amongst participants was influenced by mistrust in vaccines and information source, interaction with social media, and information inadequacy. The chapter concludes that the safety of women in a pandemic will largely depend on how their media literacy, political and health agencies are continuously reinforced before, during, and after a pandemic.

Chapter 12 by Denish Shorayi, Makomborero Bowa, and Nehemiah Chivandikwa describes and interrogates selected Zimbabwean medical doctors' perspectives on the media use of religious influencers in risk communication during the COVID-19 pandemic. Special focus is on the implications of these perspectives to the impact of religion and media on women's behaviour during the pandemic. Churches are acknowledged as a major stakeholder in community engagement and strategic agenda setting in the media. It is against this background that this study interrogates the largely positive views of medical experts on the media use of religious influencers (in selected media sermons and news interviews) in risk communication. Overall, the study concludes that the perspectives of medical experts validate the correlation between religiosity and risk communication, noting that both the media and medical experts seemed to underestimate some potentially negative implications of using religious influencers in COVID-19 risk communication among Zimbabwean women.

Chapter 13 by Tsiidzai Matsika argues against the feminisation of pandemics when women are assigned the role of caring for patients. For her, the duty of caring for patients and doing other unpaid domestic work expose the intersections of gender inequalities and violation of women's human rights. For her, the feminisation of pandemics is widespread and it will only get worse, with women solely bearing the burden if attention is not given to the ultimate victimisation in relation to gender. The chapter aims to support policy and practice actors and scholars to conceptualise sustainability in care as an issue of rights, values, ethics, and justice, as well as of resource distribution. It explores how care arrangements can be made sustainable and deliver better well-being outcomes.

In conclusion, Isaiah Munyiswa, Pauline Mateveke, and Ezra Chitando reiterate the importance of learning from women's experiences in order to prepare more effectively for future pandemics. They draw attention to the sharp increase in GBV and call upon policy-makers to be more sensitive to gender dynamics. They also underscore the need for local policy-makers to be contextually relevant and desist from applying solutions from Global North without the accompanying decolonisation.

Note

1 While we are aware of the guidance to use "HIV and AIDS," we have mostly retained "HIV/AIDS" since in many instances it has been used in combination with "COVID-19" in order to make the phrase less cumbersome.

References

Barker, C. (2008) *Cultural Studies Theory and Practice* (3rd edition). SAGE Publications: London.

Becker, M. (1992) 'Gender and Citizenship', *The Newsletter of PEGS*, 2(2): 16–17.

Chirara, T. and Chisale, S.S. (2023) 'Women in Zimunya and the *musha mukadzi* or *umuzi ngumama* philosophy for sustainable livelihoods', *HTS Teologiese Studies/Theological Studies,* 79(1), a7575. https://doi.org/10.4102/hts.v79i1.7575

Farmer, P. (2015). 'Structural violence and the embodiment of inequality'. In: Collyer, F. (ed.), *The Palgrave Handbook of Social Theory in Health, Illness and Medicine* (pp. 675–690). Palgrave Macmillan: London.

Giddens, A. and Sutton, P.W. (2017) *Essential Concepts in Sociology* (2nd edition). Polity: Cambridge.

Macarov, B. (1995). *Social Welfare: Structure and Practice*. Sage: London.

Manyonganise, M. (ed.) (2023) *Religion and Health in a COVID-19 Context: Experiences from Zimbabwe*. University of Bamberg Press: Bamberg.

Mwandayi, C. (2011) *Death and After-life Rituals in the Eyes of the Shona: Dialogue with Shona Customs in the Quest for Authentic Inculturation*. University of Bamberg Press: Bamberg.

Nanda, S. and Warms, R.L. (2007) *Cultural Anthropology* (9th edition). Thomson Wadsworth: Belmont.

Rutherford, A., Zwi, A.B., Grove, N.J., and Butchart, A. (2007) Violence: a glossary, *Journal of Epidemiology and Community Health*, 61(8): 676–680. doi: 10.1136/jech.2005.043711

Smith, C. (2015) *Women and Girls Vulnerable in Emergencies*. United Nations University: Tokyo.

Sofjan, D. (2017) *Religion, Public Policy and Social Transformation in Southeast Asia Religion*. Identity and Gender, Vol. 2. Globethics.net. Focus no. 4. Geneva 2, Switzerland: www.globethics.net/publications

World Health Organization (WHO) (2024) Violence against women. www.who.int/news-room/fact-sheets/detail/violence-against-women

1 The COVID-19 Pandemic and Gender-Based Violence in Zimbabwe

Nomatter Sande and Sophia Chirongoma

Introduction

Every society, to a greater extent, is responsible for equipping women and girls with essential survival skills, including the capability to deal with pandemics and gender-based violence (Manyonganise, 2022). According to SIDA (2015), gender-based violence is any harm or emotional suffering perpetrated on vulnerable women, girls, men, and boys. Although both women and men experience gender-based violence, statistics show that women and girls are more affected and, in most cases, seriously hurt or killed. Gender-based violence against women and girls is a form of violation of human rights. The challenge of such violence is that it has lasting psychological, physical, sexual, and emotional effects. Although it would be a gross injustice to associate Africa with violence, given the fact that violence is a global phenomenon, it is, unfortunately, also true that Africa experiences multiple forms of violence. This includes violence perpetrated on and in Africa by some global players, epistemic violence, economic violence, violence against the environment, and other forms of violence (see, e.g. Mlambo and Chitando, 2024). In this chapter, we focus specifically on gender-based violence in the context of COVID-19 in Zimbabwe. However, in order to retain a sense of perspective, we shall be periodically drawing attention to global and continental trends.

The emergence of COVID-19 and its drastic spread worldwide was something unexpected and the whole world found itself engulfed by the fear-igniting and life-sapping pandemic. At first, most nations thought that COVID-19 would end quickly, with less impact. Unfortunately, this was not to be. As noted by Chirongoma and Naicker (2023: 1), "as the pandemic unfolded, its impact rippled across various aspects of life, affecting global health, economics, politics, food security, issues relating to religion, gender and socio-cultural structures". The World Health Organization's (WHO) regulations in response to the outbreak of COVID-19 that included social/physical distancing and quarantine forced people to stay indoors, which resulted in new or escalated many existing conflicts. Most governments adopted strict rules regarding social interactions. Performing rituals, such as those associated with funerals and social events, including parties and weddings, was also banned. This put more psychological constraints on the

DOI: 10.4324/9781003494546-2

population. Such a new environment presented a new test and escalated cases of gender-based violence.

In this chapter, our goal is to first reflect on how the COVID-19 pandemic served as yet another factor deepening the already entrenched gender-based disparities in Africa while drawing insights from the Zimbabwean context. The second section discusses how the COVID-19-induced lockdown measures exacerbated women and girls' vulnerability to gender-based violence. The third segment reflects on the issue of behaviour change within the context of gender-based violence in Zimbabwe. It highlights that the COVID-19 pandemic exposed major cracks in the societal efforts to curb incidences of gender-based violence. Also, the third section discusses Olivius' approaches to gender as a framework and recommends the adoption of this trajectory in an endeavour to address the perennial problem of gender-based violence in Zimbabwe. The fourth part of the chapter is the concluding section. It acknowledges that while there has been considerable progress towards addressing the pandemic of gender-based violence, in Zimbabwe, the government and other human rights organisations need to adopt a multifaceted approach to retain the gains lost during the peak of the COVID-19 pandemic. To be sure: the surge in cases of gender-based violence during COVID-19 was a global reality (International Development Law Organization, 2020). Global, regional, and local institutional responses to COVID-19 had serious implications for the health and well-being of women and children (see, e.g. Hosli, 2022).

COVID-19 in the Zimbabwean Context

In order to appreciate the context in which cases of gender-based violence escalated in Zimbabwe (and globally), it is helpful to provide an overview of the official responses to COVID-19. While some critics might contend that this phase has already passed, we remain convinced that it remains critical to describe and critique the responses both for historical purposes and to contribute towards more effective responses to future pandemics.

On 11 March 2020, the WHO declared COVID-19 a global disaster, and many states, including Zimbabwe, gradually accepted this position. The Zimbabwean government stressed that COVID-19 was a national disaster. In tandem with the WHO guidelines, such a declaration resulted in the closure of schools, universities, churches, companies, and most organisations. The restrictions were revised depending on the risk of the general population. According to Dzawanda et al. (2021: 7):

> More recently and during the lockdown period, the Government of Zimbabwe, in a bid to curb the spread of the coronavirus, introduced policies that indirectly promoted informal activities that increased the risk of people in this sector being exposed to the virus, as they desperately tried to provide food for their families. The government also made use of the lockdowns as an opportunity to push through policies aimed at eradicating the informal markets, which

resulted in the demolition of numerous informal trader stalls without notice or consultation.

Zimbabwe implemented restrictions on movement and gatherings at the peak of the pandemic. This included halting worship services and any other social gatherings. The closure of churches impacted heavily on women's well-being, particularly because attending worship services and women's fellowship groups offered them a reprieve from the often repressive domestic sphere, riddled with gender-based violence. Chen et al. (2022: 301) state that:

> The COVID-19 pandemic has brought about massive changes in religious landscapes across the world. Recent research has focused on whether religions create problems or are sources of solution or support in these extraordinary times. Although some studies document religious leaders' and institutions' innovative responses to preserve ritual practices and foster members' sense of belonging, they failed to highlight lay practitioners' bottom-up religious transformations.

According to Pavari (2022: 240), during COVID-19, "the banning of gatherings of faith-based organizations deprived citizens of social and psychological supports at a time they were needed the most". According to Sande et al. (2023), churches were unaware and unprepared to deal with alternative means of worship, and most churches moved to online worship; most people could not attend because of the cost of streaming or networks (Ponde-Mutsvedu and Chirongoma, 2022).

The strict lockdowns were critiqued by some professionals. For instance, the chairman of the Zimbabwe Association of Doctors for Human Rights, Fortune Nyamande, cautioned that:

> Lockdown on its own is not a panacea to solving the COVID-19 pandemic. The lockdown needs to be supplemented by additional measures such as increased case detection, increased community surveillance and as you are aware only less than 200 have been tested for coronavirus in Zimbabwe. These are very low and pathetic figures. So, for us to contain this outbreak, during the lockdown let's test more people.
>
> (Mavhunga, 2020)

COVID-19 evoked new political and economic crises. This resulted in the intensification of abject poverty and hunger among the already struggling poverty-stricken and food-insecure majority population in Zimbabwe (United Nations Zimbabwe Report, 2020). This was explained by the World Bank (2021) report as follows:

> The Zimbabwe Economic Update, Overcoming Economic Challenges, Natural Disasters, and the Pandemic: Social and Economic Impacts cites surveys conducted in 2020 show that nearly 500000 Zimbabwean households have at

> least one member who lost his or her job, causing many households to fall into poverty, and worsening the plight of the existing poor.
>
> (n.p.)

There was a considerable increase in the number of patients admitted in hospital and this posed a huge strain to the health delivery system that had limited human resources and limited medical supplies. Makoni (2020: 147) articulates this situation as follows:

> The negative impact of the COVID 19 pandemic is worsened by the fact that the availability of personal protective equipment (PPE) is insufficient, and most community health workers are not aware of the correct infection prevention and control measures. The Zimbabwe Association of Doctors for Human Rights said on July 28 that 200 health workers in Zimbabwe had tested positive for COVID-19.

Similarly, Chingono et al. (2022: 1) weighed in by noting that healthcare workers experienced "anxiety and psychological distress during the COVID-19 pandemic", and there was not much evidence to show interventions to increase the resilience and the mental health of healthcare workers. Other factors like "financial insecurity, unmet physical health needs and inability to provide quality care within extremely limited resources impede on the mental well-being of healthcare workers" (Chingono et al., 2022: 13).

Many Zimbabweans used herbal concoctions, mixing lemons, garlic, and *Lippia javanica* (*zumbani*), while others also practiced regular steaming with hot water (Sande et al., 2022). The numerous debilitating COVID-19-related ailments revitalised the importance of African indigenous medicine in most communities. As noted by Manyonganise (2023), African indigenous medicine helped many people to navigate the challenges of COVID-19 and the need to safeguard vital plant resources and preserve women's voices in health. To a greater extent, COVID-19 affected the women's sexual and reproductive health. The movement restrictions during the lockdown hindered some women from accessing the contraceptives (Hlatywayo, 2023). This point is affirmed by Dziva et al. (2021: 109) who noted that, "with COVID-19, the fear of the virus has led people to stay away from health facilities for professional care, including reproductive health care". Overall then, COVID-19 affected the social life of most Zimbabweans as they wrestled to stay afloat amidst the devastating impact of the pandemic. While we retain our focus on Zimbabwe, we are acutely aware of the fact that this was true of various other parts of the world, including the Global North. COVID-19 was a truly global pandemic that shook the world in decisive ways, resulting in the slowing down of the global economy. In Africa, like in other parts of the world, COVID-19 brought the reality of gender injustice to the fore (see, e.g. Budoo-Scholtz and Johnson, 2023). In the next section, we discuss the pandemic of gender-based violence during COVID-19 in Zimbabwe.

COVID-19 and Gender-Based Violence in Zimbabwe

Recollection of the accounts of gender-based violence in Zimbabwe is not an easy task. What is available is simply the tip of the iceberg. Most gender-based violence cases are either not reported, or they are not properly documented. As is the case in other parts of the world, there are various reasons why many women do not report cases of gender-based violence. The perpetrators of most gender-based violence incidences in Zimbabwe are usually individuals known to the survivors (Kruttschnitt et al., 2018; United Nations Women (UNW), 2016). What makes gender-based violence even more heart-wrenching is the fact that women are threatened and hunted in their domestic spheres. These are spaces where they should feel safe and secure (Mutepfa, 2009).

The Musasa Project is one organisation which has remained resolute in speaking against gender-based violence for a long time in Zimbabwe. Since its inception, the Musasa Project's mandate has been to prevent and reduce violence against women and girls. As such, they have become synonymous with gender-based violence activists. The Musasa Project reported that during the peak of the COVID-19 lockdown, they received a total of 4,302 gender-based violence distress calls between March and July 2020 (Musasa Project, 2020). Both the Musasa Project and other women's groups concur that there was over a 60% increase in gender-based violence reports during the COVID-19 lockdown. About 94% of the calls were made by women (Goredema and Muwanzi, 2023). These statistics confirm that despite concerted efforts to address gender-based violence, the challenge persists. Further, the statistics themselves need to be analysed in the context of COVID-19. The imposed lockdowns and quarantines were not within the regime of regular routines of people. This turned them into potential factors for increasing tensions and inciting violence on the domestic sphere. The emergence of COVID-19 thwarted the little protection that would previously help women and girls. It follows that even the slightest hope of responses to abuse and violence was shattered during the intermittent COVID-19 lockdown phases. The introduction of extreme COVID-19 restrictions was intended to curb the extraordinary spread of the disease.

Unfortunately, a cocktail of lockdown measures, including social distancing and other restrictions, provided fertile ground for gender-based violence, with women and girls being the majority of those at the receiving end (Gordon et al., 2021).

Pandemics militate against human development, social change, and gender injustices. Dissecting the problem, John et al. (2020: 67) alluded that "the economic, social and cultural implications of COVID-19 have made women the primary victims of this pandemic". Wenham et al. (2020) argue that pandemics affect women more than males. While this assertion by Wenhman et al. is not new in the Zimbabwean context, it only confirms the urgent need to close the gap between information and behaviour change. According to the United Nations Development Programme (UNDP, 2020), pre-existing social norms and gender inequalities sustained by restrictive movements imposed because of COVID-19 led to an increase in gender-based violence. The United Nations Zimbabwe (2020) argued that quarantine measures "can trap women with abusive partners … we have seen a horrifying global surge in domestic violence". In the same vein, the African beliefs of Ubuntu encouraged women to participate more in caring for people during public health crises such as the outbreak of cholera, malaria, HIV, and the most recent COVID-19 pandemic.

As has already been highlighted, women are more vulnerable to gender-based violence due to power imbalance. It is estimated that 18% of women and girls experience physical or sexual violence by their intimate partners (Mlambo-Ngcuka, 2020). Pandemics worsen women's vulnerability to gender-based violence. As it is, the challenge of pandemics is that they can come when society is not ready. This point was reiterated by Dziva et al. (2021: 110) who noted that, "for women who already live with abusive partners, they are now locked in homes with violent persons, separated from people and resources that can provide support. Thus, the victims have few opportunities to distance themselves from their abusers". The United Nations Women (2020), in the context of COVID-19, describes gender-based violence as a shadow pandemic. In the case of women in Zimbabwe, COVID-19 came against the backdrop of most women dealing with pressing issues like economics, politics, and social equality. The Zimbabwe Demographic Health Survey (2020: n.p.) asserts that "1 in 3 women aged 15 to 49 have experienced physical violence, while about 1 in 5 women have experienced sexual violence since the age of 15, usually by their intimate partners". Globally, there are more than 31 million cases of gender-based violence reported within six months of the outbreak of the COVID-19 pandemic (United Nations Population Fund, 2020). COVID-19, which was viewed as a pandemic within a pandemic because of its complexity (Mutongwiza, 2020; United Nations Fund for Population Activities (UNFPA), 2020), intensified women' vulnerability to gender-based violence. The pandemic also affected the world's health knowledge and negatively impacted all social and political sectors, including but not limited to, the economy, education, religion, and social life.

Responding to Gender-Based Violence: Summarising the Challenges

As has already been noted, gender-based violence remains a global challenge. Most African countries, such as Zimbabwe, Namibia, South Africa, Kenya, and Nigeria, had a significant increase in gender-based violence, especially against women and girls (Tsunga et al., 2020). According to Donato (2020), there is a need to blend the voices of governments, private sectors, and youth to continue campaigning against gender-based violence. While blended voices and amalgamation of perception to curb gender-based violence is a brilliant idea, this should be coupled with tackling the challenges that have made it extremely difficult to respond to gender-based violence in an effective way. According to Magezi and Manzanga (2020), the government of Zimbabwe was too slow to observe the dangers of lockdowns to gender-based violence. Other oversights of the government included the contention that "national and local officials have never acknowledged the added damage to some groups like sex workers, refugees, asylum seekers, and migrants …" (John et al., 2020: 66). To protect families and individuals in the context of Argentina,

Polischuck and Fay (2020: 677) suggested that the government could have a "suspension of prison sentences, the creation of online crime registration and payment portals, the creation of virtual services to support sexually abused women, financial support for women, and women's participation in charity". Although Argentina and Zimbabwe are different contexts, these lessons can also be adopted as valuable interventions for dealing with future pandemics.

Success in responding to gender-based violence can also be achieved through disrupting cultures of impunity and patriarchy. Perpetrators of gender-based violence must know that they do not have an open cheque. They must know that there are consequences for being doers of violence. This necessitates the revisions of the judicial systems in a bid to safeguard the vulnerable women and girls, as well as other disadvantaged populations. Abusers must be assisted to resist patriarchal tendencies which either trivialise or condone the emotional and physical abuse of women and girls either at home or other social settings. There are skewed religio-cultural gender norms that exacerbate African women and girls' vulnerability to gender-based violence. It is against this background that our chapter advocates for the government of Zimbabwe's gender policy to make the issue of addressing gender-based violence a top priority. This is consistent with Mlambo-Ngcuka (2020: 3) who proffers that "as we face COVID-19's devastation, there has never been a more important moment to resolve to put our combined resources and commitment behind the biggest issues, and to end violence against women and girls, for good". In the same light, Mageza and Manzanga (2020: 15) highlight that another factor hindering the effective reduction of gender-based violence is the negative impact of culture and patriarchy which have "influenced the employment of women, especially during the COVID -19 pandemic, so women cannot play their political, social and economic roles". As the activist adage goes, "nothing about us, without us". When women and girls are excluded from the key leadership and decision-making boards, where policies and decisions regarding the curbing and treatment methods are made, then their needs and their rights are neglected. It is, therefore, critical that women be actively involved in all the processes that address any future pandemics not only in Zimbabwe but the world over.

Calling for Behaviour Change to Curb Gender-Based Violence

Most behaviours towards gender-based violence are tied to society's perceptions about gender issues. We intentionally use Elizabeth Olivius' (basic needs, instrumental and modernisation) approaches to gender as lenses to think of gender-based violence as an urgent humanitarian need. Olivius uses the basic needs, the instrumental, and the modernisation approaches to gender as her prominent overarching understanding in humanitarian policy and practice (Olivius, 2014). The increase in gender-based violence during COVID-19 requires a gender-sensitive approach to cope with the needed behaviour changes. To address the need for behavioural change towards gender-based violence, there is a need to accept that pandemics are gendered. Pandemics affect women and girls more than men and boys, and one of the common areas is gender-based violence.

Olivius' basic needs approach is motivated by the notion of reducing suffering. According to Olivius (2014), the fundamental needs gender approach responds to the needs of people affected by disasters and displacements after conflicts. The focus is "to ensure that they receive necessities of life" (Inter-Agency Standing Committee [IASC], 2006). Such an assertion in the context of COVID-19 would have meant ensuring that women and girls received adequate assistance and protection. It is, therefore, apparent that the government of Zimbabwe and the humanitarian institutions must make resolute efforts to prioritise the prevention of cases of all forms of gender-based violence as a basic human need. This is critical as Zimbabwe, Africa, and the world take concrete steps to prepare against the next pandemic(s).

According to Olivius, the second gender approach is the instrumentalist approach, which advocates for understanding gender as expressive of differences between males and women. Such a proportion helps to understand that women and men responded to, and were affected by, COVID-19 differently. Such differences should be considered as avenues that need targeted help, especially for women and girls going through gender-based violence. However, it is essential to point out that these differences are not default designs or natures; but social constructions caused by many factors. For instance, women are assumed to possess gender-specific qualities and capabilities. This makes them vulnerable to the threats of COVID-19 and other pandemics. Women were instrumental in caring for children and those infected by COVID-19. The role of women as the chief providers of food heightened during COVID-19. Women faced diverse challenges in acquiring food during COVID-19, resulting in higher workloads (Matanga and Mukurazhizha, 2023). In the context of Zimbabwe, where the economy had been on a downward spiral for several years before the outbreak of COVID-19, women's efforts to provide food for the family were daunting, resultantly triggering mental health issues. In Zimbabwe, as was reported during the pandemic, "the COVID-19 pandemic has brought a lot of challenges and disruptions to our lives. The livelihood of people has been affected and the pandemic has taken a toll on people's mental and psychological health" (Nigeria Health Watch, 2021).

The other gender approach proffered by Olivius is modernisation. According to Olivius, modernisation understands gender as a structural relation of power, deeply rooted in culture as well as the socio-economic and political realms. The concept of modernisation serves to disrupt negative perceptions about women because of underdevelopment. According to Muyangata and Shumba (2023), the COVID-19 pandemic exposed the inequalities within the healthcare and socio-economic spheres in Zimbabwe. In most cases, gender inequality, discrimination, and violence are described as symptoms of underdevelopment. In this approach, the overarching agenda is to transform these societies and communities to become modern, democratic, and liberal. In the context of the aftermath of COVID-19, modernisation has the potential to minimise gender inequalities. This is an important step towards addressing gender-based violence, as well as protecting women and girls in different situations. This includes the provision of security and commitment to programmes that transform into positive behaviour to reduce gender-based violence. Viewing gender as a relational, social, and cultural phenomenon has the advantage of seeing that changing gender roles necessitate overhaul changes in the structures and norms of society. This will make a significant contribution to the attainment of gender equality. Scholars such as Matsungo and Chopera (2020: 210) recommended that "it remains the responsibility of the governments to create a supportive policy environment to enhance the physical and mental health of individuals in the context of COVID-19 pandemic, without also neglecting the potential risk of 'lockdown associated obesity' during lockdowns".

Conclusion

The COVID-19 pandemic provides valuable insights into understanding pandemics and their impact on the health and well-being of women and girls. As the world seeks to become better prepared for future pandemics, the spike in cases of gender-based violence globally and in Zimbabwe must serve as a cautionary tale. The COVID-19-induced restrictions unintentionally forced most family members to remain confined within the same space, oftentimes, in squalid and food-insecure circumstances. This contributed to a sharp increase in cases of gender-based violence. The social construction of the caring nature of women, which includes taking care of children during COVID-19 restrictions as well as caring for family members falling ill during COVID-19, disproportionally affected their health and well-being. Living together fuelled gender-based violence. A separate study is also required to highlight the extent to which women and girls became disadvantaged in accessing sexual and reproductive health services during the pandemic. Overall, the COVID-19 pandemic eroded some of the gains that had been made in terms of addressing the pandemic of gender-based violence in Southern Africa, particularly in Zimbabwe, which was our focus of discussion in this chapter. It is, therefore, pertinent for the government of Zimbabwe, in collaboration with other human rights organisations, particularly, women's rights bodies, to work in collaboration so that they can restore and multiply the lost milestones in flattening the gender gap, and in the process eliminate gender-based violence.

References

Budoo-Scholtz, A. and Johnson, A. (Eds.) (2023). *COVID-19 and women's intersectionalities in Africa*. Pretoria: Pretoria University Law Press.

Chen, N., Chen, J. and Dean, K. (2022). Religion in times of crisis: Innovative lay responses and temporal-spatial reconfigurations of temple rituals in COVID-19 China. *Cultural Geographies*, 29(2), 301–308. https://doi.org/10.1177/14744740211020505.

Chingono, R. M. S., Nzvere, F. P., Marambire, E. T., Makwembere, M., Mhembere, N., Herbert, T., Maunganidze, A. J. V., Pasi, C., Chiwanga, M., Chonzi, P., Ndhlovu, C. E., Mujuru, H., Rusakaniko, S., Olaru, I. D., Ferrand, R. A., Simms, V. and Kranzer, K. (2022). Psychological distress among healthcare workers accessing occupational health services during the COVID-19 pandemic in Zimbabwe. *Comprehensive Psychiatry*, 116, 152321. https://doi.org/10.1016/j.comppsych.2022.152321.

Chirongoma, S. and Naicker, L. W. (2023). African women, religion and pandemics: Collective resilience, responsibility and adaptability. *HTS Teologiese Studies/Theological Studies*, 79(3), a9517. https://doi.org/10.4102/hts.v79i3.9517

Donato, S. (2020). Gender-based violence against women in intimate and couple relationships: The case of Spain and Italy during the COVID-19 pandemic lockdown. *Italian Sociology Review*, 10(3), 869–887.

Dzawanda, B., Matsa, M. and Nicolau, M. (2021). Poverty on the rise: The impact of COVID-19 lockdown on the informal sector of Gweru, Zimbabwe. *International Social Science Journal*, 71(Suppl. 1), 81–96. https://doi.org/10.1111/issj.12285

Dziva, C., Zhou, I. and Zvobgo E.F. (2021). "Covid-19 pandemic and women's vulnerabilities in Zimbabwe". *The Dyke*, 15(1):, 104–115.

Gordon, R., Cheeseman, N., Rockowitz, S., Stevens, L.M., and Flowe, H.D. et al. (2021). Government responses to gender-based violence during COVID-19. *Frontiers in Global Women's Health*, 3. https://doi.org/10.3389/fgwh.2022.857345.

Goredema, D. and Muwanzi, J. (2023). Increased gender-based violence during the COVID-19 pandemic: A Zimbabwean case study. *Research and Analysis Journals*, 60(07), 7–10.

Hlatywayo, A. M. (2023). COVID-19 Lockdown containment measures and women's sexual and reproductive health in Zimbabwe. *HTS Teologiese Studies/Theological Studies*, 79(3).

Hosli, M.O. (2022). Women and children: International institutions and responses to COVID-19. In M.O. Hosli, A. Blessing, and I. Iacovidou (Eds.), *The Global, Regional and Local Politics of Institutional Responses to COVID-19* (pp. 27–45). Sustainable Development Goals Series. Cham: Palgrave Macmillan. https://doi.org/10.1007/978-3-031-09913-7_3

Inter-Agency Standing Committee (IASC) (2006). *Protecting persons affected by natural disasters: IASC operational guidelines on human rights and natural disasters*. Inter-Agency Standing Committee (IASC). Accessed from https://reliefweb.int/organization/iasc

International Development Law Organization (IDLO). (2020). Justice for women amidst COVID-19. Accessed from www.idlo.int/sites/default/files/pdfs/publications/idlo-justice-for-women-amidst-covid19_0.pdf

John, N., Casey, S. E., Carino, G. and McGovern, T. (2020). Lessons never learned: Crisis and gender-based violence. *Developing World Bioethics*, 20(2), 65–68. Doi: 10.1111/dewb.12261

Kruttschnitt, C., Yule, C., Alper, M. and Klassen, A. (2018). Situational variations in, and women's accounts of, avoided acts of serious intimate partner violence. *Violence against Women*, 24(4), 477–501. https://doi.org/10.1177/1077801217708057

Magezi, V. and Manzanga, P. (2020). COVID-19 and intimate partner violence in Zimbabwe: Towards being church in situations of gender-based violence from a public pastoral care perspective. *In Die Skriflig*, 54(1), 1–9.

Makoni, M. (2020). COVID-19 worsens Zimbabwe's health crisis. *Lancet* 396(10249), 457. https://doi.org/10.1016/S0140-6736(20)31751-7

Manyonganise, M. (2022). 'When a pandemic wears the face of a woman': Intersections of religion and gender during the COVID-19 pandemic in Zimbabwe. In Fnda, T. Muyambo, and E. Chitando (Eds.), *Religion and the COVID-19 pandemic in Southern Africa*. London: Routledge.

Manyonganise, M. (2023). COVID-19, gender and health: Recentring women in African indigenous health discourses in Zimbabwe for environmental conservation. *HTS Teologiese Studies/Theological Studies*, 79(3), 1–9.

Matanga, S. Y. and Mukurazhizha, M. R. (2023). The impact of the COVID-19 restrictions on women's responsibility for domestic food provision: The case of Marondera Urban in Zimbabwe. *HTS Teologiese Studies/Theological Studies*, 79(3), 1–8.

Matsungo, T. M. and Chopera, P. (2020). Effect of the COVID-19-induced lockdown on nutrition, health and lifestyle patterns among adults in Zimbabwe. *BMJ Nutrition, Prevention & Health*, 3, 1–8. doi: 10.1136/bmjnph-2020-000124

Mavhunga, C. (2020). *Zimbabwe begins lockdown to fight COVID19*. VOA News. Accessed from www.voanews.com/a/science-health_coronavirus-outbreak_zimbabwe-begins-lockdown-fight-covid19/6186637.html

Mlambo, O. B. and Chitando, E. (Eds.) (2024). *The Palgrave handbook of violence in Africa*. Cham: Palgrave Macmillan.

Mlambo-Ngcuka (2020). Press Release: As impact of COVID-19 intensifies, UN women calls for concrete actions to respond to the concurrent shadow pandemic. Accessed from www.unwomen.org/en/news/stories/2020/11/press-release-16-days-of-activism-against-gender-based-violence

Musasa Project. 2021. Factsheet: Gender Based Violence Cases. Accessed 21 August 2024 from https://zimfact.org/factsheet-gender-based-violence-cases/

Mutepfa, M. M. (2009). *Spousal abuse in Zimbabwe: Nature and extend across socio-economic class, gender and religiosity*. Accessed 19 January 2024, from https://dialnet.unirioja.es/descarga/articulo/5216158.pdf

Mutongwiza, L. (2020). *Gender-based violence, a pandemic within a pandemic*. Accessed 23 June 2020, from https://blogs.lse.ac.uk/africaatlse/2020/04/23/genderbased-violence-in-zimbabwe-a-pandemic-covid19-virus/

Muyangata, J. and Shumba, S. (2023). COVID-19 crisis in relation to religion, health and poverty in Zimbabwe: A case study of the Harare urban communities. *HTS Teologiese Studies/Theological Studies*, 79(3), 7.

Nigeria Health Watch. (2021, June 4). Friendship Bench: Zimbabwe's community-based talk therapy supporting communities during the COVID-19 pandemic. Nigeria Health Watch. Retrieved from https://articles.nigeriahealthwatch.com/friendship-bench-zimbabwes-community-based-talk-therapy-supporting-communities-during-the-covid-19-pandemic/.

Olivius, E. (2014). *Three approaches to gender in humanitarian aid: findings from a study of humanitarian aid to refugees in Thailand and Bangladesh*. Accessed 18 January 2024, from www.diva- portal.org/smash/get/diva2:724367/ FULLT EXT01.pdf

Pavari, N. (2020). Psychosocial impacts of Covid-19 pandemic in Zimbabwe. *Journal of Public Administration and Governance*, 10(3), 1–15.

Polischuk, L. and Fay, D. L. (2020). Administrative response to consequences of COVID-19 emergency responses: Observation and implications from gender-based violence in Argentina. *American Review of Public Administration*, 6(7), 675–684. doi: 10.1177/0275074020942081

Ponde-Mutsvedu, L. and Chirongoma, S. (2022). Tele-evangelism, tele-health and cyberbullying in the wake of the outbreak of COVID-19 in Africa. In F. Sibanda, T. Muyambo, and E. Chitando (Eds.), *Religion and the COVID-19 pandemic in Southern Africa*. London: Routledge.

Sande, N., Ringson, J. and Mabuye, T. (2023). Online worship in the context of Covid-19 within the context of three selected Pentecostal congregations in Johannesburg South Africa. In L.C. Siwila (Ed.), *Church in exile liturgy Covid-19 and lockdown regulations*. Pietermaritzburg: Cluster.

SIDA (2015). *Prevention and responding to gender based violence: Expression and strategies*. Accessed 26 May 2020, from www.sida.se/contentasscrt/67c778a855dc4e92a5a9a/bebc4860a/action-plan-for-sida-work-against-gender-basedviolence-2008-2010-680.pdf

Tsunga, A., Mazarura, T. and Heywood, M. (2020). *Democracy in Lockdown: Authorities clamp down on pro-democrats and civilians under cover of Covid-19 restrictions*. Accessed from www.dailymaverick.co.za/article/2020-05-22-democracy-in-lockdown-authorities-clamp-down-on-pro-democrats-and-civilians-under-cover-of-covid-19-restrictions/

United Nations Development Programme (UNDP) (2020). *Gender-based violence and COVID-19*. Accessed 16 January 2024, from www.undp.org/content/undp/en/home/librarypage/womens-empowerment/gender-based-violence-andcovid-19.html

United Nations Fund for Population Activities (UNFPA) (2020). *Eastern and Southern Africa region COVID-19 situation report no. 1*. Accessed 19 January 2024, from https://reliefweb.int/report/angola/eastern-and-southern-africa-region-covid-19-situation-report-no-1

United Nations Women (UNW) (2016). *Facts and figures: Ending violence against women*. Accessed 20 June 2020, from www.unwomen.org/en/what-we-do/ending-violence-against-women/facts-and-figures#sthash.pxEul6uo.dpuf

United Nations Women (2020). *Press release: As impact of COVID-19 intensifies, UN women calls for concrete actions to respond to the concurrent shadow pandemic*. UN Women. Accessed 18 January 2024, from www.unwomen.org/en/news/stories/2020/11/press-release-16-days-of-activism-againstgender-based violence

United Nations Zimbabwe (2020). *Urgent action on looming violence against women during COVID-19 pandemic*. Accessed 16 January 2024, from http://zw.one.un.org/newsroom/news/urgent-action-looming-violence-against-women-during-covid-19-pandemic

Wenham, C., Smith, J. and Morgan, R. (2020). COVID-19: The gendered impacts of the outbreak. *Lancet*, 395(10227), 846–848.

World Bank (2021). Zimbabwe economic update: COVID-19 further complicates Zimbabwe's economic and social conditions. Accessed 18 January 2024, from www.worldbank.org/en/country/zimbabwe/publication/zimbabwe-economic-update-covid-19-further-complicates-zimbabwe-s-economic-and-social-conditions

Zimbabwe Demographic Health Survey (ZDHS), 2010–2011. (2020). *Key findings*. Accessed 22 June 2020, from https://dhsprogram.com/pubs/pdf/FR254/FR254.pdf

2 The Intersectionality of Culture, Religion, Gender and COVID-19

Implications for Indigenous Women's Health and Wellbeing in Zimbabwe

Beatrice Taringa

Introduction

COVID-19, like other epidemics and pandemics such as HIV and AIDS, impacted on Indigenous women cultural and religious wellbeing in Zimbabwe. The pandemic reconfigured Indigenous people's religio-cultural and gender landscapes (Power et al. 2020). Millions continued to be infected and affected by COVID-19 worldwide. The most sacred Indigenous phenomena of funeral attendance and burial procedures were transformed from the traditional physical attendance into the contemporary virtual attendance. In relation to gender, just like women and children, men inevitably found themselves in restrictive domestic confinement. The move directly flies in face of gender essentialists' perspective and directly challenged masculinity that used to enjoy unrestricted outdoor activities (see e.g. Kufakurinani, 2024). This chapter reviews how COVID-19 prompted reconstruction within Indigenous communities in Zimbabwe, and the implications of this for pandemic preparedness in the near and remote future (see e.g. Marshall, 2022). It calls for expanded understanding of gender-based violence among Indigenous people and cautions against the limited focus on physical violence. In this regard, the chapter adds new knowledge to the understanding of gender-based violence during pandemics.

Background to the Study

In order to locate this chapter properly, this section seeks to clarify the key concepts in relation to COVID-19. Thus, various scholars have come up with different perceptions on the role of religion, culture and gender in communities' health and wellbeing globally. The World Health Organization (WHO) (2019) explored the role of religion in communities' health and wellbeing by designing an assessment tool that provides practical guidance and recommendations to support the special role of religious leaders. The findings reveal that faith-based organisations provide information and support services to protect members and the wider community. Above all, they promote healthy practices and countering misinformation about diseases (see also Sibanda, Muyambo and Chitando 2022; Muyambo, Sibanda and Chitando 2023).

DOI: 10.4324/9781003494546-3

Seifman and Forthomme (2020) note with concern the role of religion in COVID-19 prevention. They warned that while scientists worked flat out on designing a safe and effective vaccine and therapeutic drugs, religion ran the risk of promoting vaccine hesitancy (Seifman and Forthomme, 2020). Thus, religious leaders' pronouncements were likely to be considered more on decision-making by congregants and likely to reduce the likelihood of prevention, as was the case with the use of condoms. Some congregants considered condoms a sin despite the scientists' insistence that they were crucial in preventing HIV transmission (Seifman and Forthomme, 2020). In the same vein, Seifman and Forthomme (2020) noted differences in attitude within and between religions, which does not warrant a one-size-fits-all kind of guide to the religious groups.

One American summer survey on COVID-19 confirmed that the disease strengthened religious faith and tightened family bonds among American citizens (Kowalezyk, Roszkwski, Montane, Pawliszak, Tylkowski and Bajek, 2020). It adds that due to COVID-19, people fell back for family, church, friends and co-workers' support and other social networks and secularism of the people that did not identify with any religion was shrinking. Kowalezyk, Roszkwski, Montane, Pawliszak, Tylkowski and Bajek (2020) revealed that restrictions of gatherings to contain spread of COVID-19 affected the religious complexion. The survey revealed the power of spirituality, especially when the death toll rose in the case of the coronavirus pandemic. Barker, Mart, Brownstein, Whitehead and Yukich (2020) investigated how religious institutions and congregations and individuals were affected by social changes produced by COVID-19. The study revealed that many congregants still longed for face-to-face gathering and religious rituals. Thus, religious leaders can be assessed on how they made their leadership accommodate social distancing and switching to largely remote working environment. Religious gatherings were dubbed as COVID-19 super spreads in Washington and Germany (Barker, Mart, Brownstein, Whitehead and Yukich, 2020). In Zimbabwe, the Johane Marange congregants that normally gathered in Marange were dispersed for fear of the COVID-19 pandemic (Maponga, 2020).

In some instances, there was resistance in relation to adhering to COVID-19 health guidelines. Some congregants resisted social distancing, masking up and were hesitant to be vaccinated. As a result, some critics charged that religion distrusts other authorities from science and medicine (Barker, Mart, Brownstein, Whitehead and Yukich, 2020) and argue that COVID-19 made it very difficult for religions when social gatherings got suspended and banned. This chapter examines the dynamics in the Zimbabwean context with special reference to Indigenous beliefs and practices. In particular, the chapter calls for a more nuanced approach to gender-based violence beyond the preoccupation with physical violence.

Theoretical Framework

Social reconstruction theory is the theoretical framework adopted in assessing the phenomena under study in a bid to reconstruct the implicit theory of change. The theory is a comprehensive description and illustration of how and why a desired change is expected to happen in a particular context. It is a tool for identifying the links between a desired change and the sequence that will make it happen. George F. McLean (1999) noted that social reconstruction is perhaps the most typical challenge of the present age. Couros (2015) supports change through the argument that there comes a time when communities need something new and completely different. The COVID-19 pandemic represented such a reality. Kanu (2007) argues in line with social reconstruction view that tradition is neither monolithic nor is it merely preserved and handed down to subsequent generations. Gunda (2009) reviewed the theology of reconstruction in Africa and identified its motivation and challenges. One may conclude that any shift in the religio-cultural, political and social terrains, no matter how minor, automatically leads to the reconstituting of existing masculine and feminine frameworks. Change is synonymous with survival, especially in the context of pandemics like COVID-19. Throughout history, Indigenous cultures have had to adjust and experience reconstruction as they have navigated diverse challenges. In these different contexts, they have had to struggle with various forms of violence, including gender-based violence.

Culture, Religion and Control/Prevention of Pandemics

Various scholars have examined how culture influences control and prevention of the spread of pandemics. They include Tabane (2004), who conducted an investigation into the influence of cultural practices of Batswana on transmission of HIV/AIDS in Botswana. Empirical findings confirmed that it is acceptable within Batswana culture in Botswana that men can have multiple relationships even after marriage, making polygamy a common practice. Similarly, Arrey, Bilsen, Lacor and Deschepper (2017) concur with Tabane (2004) as they noted the vulnerability of women to HIV/AIDS in male-dominated sub-Saharan communities where men have a culture of multiple and extra-marital relationships. Ngigi and Busolo (2018) reiterate the need for cultural competence training in addressing emergency situations and pandemics in communities. Thus, health and related personnel should not be misled by globalisation into universalising pandemic response programmes. In the same vein, Oluga, Kiragu, Mussa, Muhamed and Walil (2010) draw the attention of intervention mechanisms to note some challenging cultural practices like wife inheritance which caused harm and, in many cases, leading to death. For them, education is a "social vaccine". This would help curtail cultural gatekeepers from frustrating COVID-19 intervention programmes. As highlighted by Ngigi and Busolo (2018), researchers learnt that HIV and AIDS is complex and multifaceted and requires multidimensional strategies. Similarly, Parker (2001) examined the development of an anthropological research in response to HIV/AIDS. The study discovered that most studies focused on correlation between behaviour and HIV/AIDS infection among individuals but failed to examine broader religious, social and cultural factors. This chapter appreciates the insights emerging from earlier studies and applies intersectionality to appreciate complex dynamics in the face of COVID-19. This is designed to strengthen future interventions designed to respond to pandemics and epidemics in Zimbabwe and beyond, paying particular attention to gender-based violence (Ostadtaghizadeh, Zarei, Saniee et al., 2023).

Research Methodology

Utilising two-phased mixed methods sequential transformative strategy design and variant model that is largely qualitative, we seek to uncover how COVID-19 differentially affected women and men among Indigenous communities in Zimbabwe. Cameron (1963, p. 13) says "not everything that is counted counts, and not everything that counts can be counted". Thus, though there is numerically represented data, the final emphasis is not quantity based but the quality of Indigenous gender relations. This is in line with Morgan and Sklar's (2012, p. 73) observation that, "proponents of interpretivism argue that human experience can only be understood from the viewpoint of the people themselves". Thus, reality is relative and socially constructed and even context specific. So, it is based on case study, which is "… an intensive, in-depth study of a specific individual, context or situation" (Murray and Beglar, 2009, p. 48) as well as "… unit of analysis which guides decision on what is to be studied" (Maree and Van Der Westhuizen, 2007, p. 75) while studying the phenomenon in situ. We engaged 12 participants, 6 men and 6 women, from one Indigenous setting in an urban context for in-depth interviews. We also administered a questionnaire-based mini-survey to 20 participants (10 females and 10 males). The survey was meant to tap into the participants' perceptions on how COVID-19 differentially affected them as men and women. All the participants were family persons aged 18 years and above. The study sampled those 20 participants and picked up 12 key informants basing on Punch's (2009, p. 162) warning that "We cannot study everyone, everywhere doing everything", as the scope maybe too wide for an in-depth analysis of the phenomenon. Data collection was done in cycles and continued until theoretical saturation was achieved (Punch, 2009, p. 133). The mini-survey got triangulated with Zoom meetings for the focus group interviews where 12 key informants were selected for an in-depth understanding of how COVID-19 affected differently them as women or men. It interprets their responses within the context of gender-based violence.

Ontologically, the chapter is informed by constructivism which further adds that, "there are varied and multiple truths, leading the researcher to look for complexity of views rather than narrowing few categories or ideas" (Creswell, 2003, p. 8). In organising data and weaving a research story, we employed the thematic web-like data analysis. This also assisted the author to extract themes that formed categories of basic themes (Attride-Stirling, 2001). The study is grounded in Indigenous research methods and interpretations (see, e.g., Chilisa, 2012), paying attention to Indigenous voices and positions in making sense of their experiences of COVID-19. It embraces Indigenous perspectives in reflecting on how future responses to pandemics can become more effective, particularly in having a more nuanced understanding of gender-based violence.

Presentation of Findings

The survey results show that 18 out of 20 responded to the questionnaires. Participants indicated that COVID-19 differentially affected men and women among Indigenous people. However, participants could not project on its far-reaching consequences, but admitted that it had far-reaching effects on masculinity and femininity. The views raised in the survey are related to what came out through in-depth online interviews given further.

The Experiences of Women

The participants drew attention to the dwindling incomes as there was restricted movement due to COVID-19 restrictions and health guidelines. The door-to-door salon service could no longer apply as there were movement restrictions. This restriction had a ripple effect that resulted in sharp decline in many women's income. Thus, when asked on how COVID-19 affected her as a woman, one participant said:

> *Mukadzi (Woman) 1: Ummmm! Amai! Inini semukadzi yakashandura zvakanyanya upenyu hwangu. Ndaisingogadzirira ivava vaienda kubasa nevana vechikoro ndotosara ndogeza ndoenda kunoruka vanhu misoro. Chero ndaibhuroka zvaive nane. Izvozvi hapana achada kuti ndiende kumba kwake. Zvokuuya kumba havachadi vanhu voda kuma*salon *kunotevedzwa mitemo uye kune zvokushandisa zvakatsarukana.* (Woman 1: Ummmm! Mother! (A respectful term for the researcher).As a woman, it transformed my life immensely. I used to prepare for those going to work and children who were going to school and would bath later and go to plait people's hair. Even if I would be broke at times, it was better. Now, no one wants me to get to their homes. Clients no longer want to come home but now prefer to go to salons where COVID-19 guidelines are followed, there is more space and also where there are appropriate implements).

The narration raised two gender issues. The first aspect is about women's financial stability that dwindled. She could not continue with her business of a mobile hair salon ("... *ndoenda kunoruka vanhu misoro*". "go to plait people's hair"; "*Izvozvi, hapana achada kuti ndiende kumba kwake. Zvokuuya kumba havachadi*", "Now, no one wants me to get to their homes. They no longer want to come home ..."). The COVID-19 environment proved to be a changed economic environment that was no longer favourable for hair-grooming business that is mainly dominated by women. The situation greatly disempowered women economically. The second aspect is about the woman's independence which was curtailed by being restricted at home and always be with the husband and children. The woman's narration is testimony of how COVID-19 affected women. This finding clearly confirms the findings by UNCTAD (2021) that women employment fell by 4.2% compared with the 3% of men. The development further disempowers women who already had a far less employment rate compared with men. Here, it is important to appreciate how COVID-19 intensified economic violence against women (see, e.g., Falawole, 2008).

The second widowed woman narrated her ordeal relating to the funeral of her husband during COVID-19. This is what she said:

> *Mukadzi (Woman) 2: Zviri zveCOVID-19 munoti zvinotaurwa here imi! Takarara takagarira coffin remurume wangu tingori vaviri, ini navamwene vangu. Shamwari dzangu dzaindidemba nokundibata maoko pafoni. Rufu urwu rwakaita serwakatora gore ipo pasina svondo. Ndaiti shamwari dzangu pane achauya asi hapana wandakaona. Ndakavenga shamwari dzangu nevanhu vekuchechi ndikademba chandairaramira. Ndakademba kuti dai ndirini ndakafa. Nevana navamwene vangu takaita varanda. Ndakashaya kuti ndozvibatsirawo sei uye kuti ndibatsirewo vana vangu?* (Woman 2: The COVID-19 situation is not a pleasant story to talk about! We spent the night guarding the coffin; being the two of us, just myself and my mother-in-law. My friends consoled and comforted me through the phone. The funeral seemed like it had lasted a year yet in actual fact it took barely a week. I hoped one of my friends would come, but no one came. I hated my friends and church congregants that I regretted why I was alive. I even thought it would have been better had I been the one who had died. With my children and my mother-in-law, we became servants. I had no means to help myself so that I could also help my children).

The utterance confirms signs of emotional pain that the widowed woman and her children underwent as a result of COVID-19. The participant's narration raised another emotional and key gender issue which is to do with women sleeping in the room where the body of the deceased lay in state ("… *takagarira coffin remurume wangu tingori vaviri, ini navamwene vangu*", "We spent the whole night guarding the coffin being the two of us, just myself and my mother-in-law"). COVID-19 health guidelines dispersed crowds and gathering of mourners, thus exposing women to stress. They used to get comfort from friends and relatives that would gather around them singing and joking about the deceased person's personality ("*Rufu urwu rwakaita serwainge rwatora gore ipo pasina kana svondo*", "The funeral seems like it had lasted a year yet in actual fact it took barely a week"). The aspect of virtual mourning also came as a cultural shocker which for this widow has not served the intended purpose of consoling her. The findings from the narration confirm (Oluga et al., 2010) that there are cultural practices that cause harm to women. In this case, having the widow and her mother-in-law sleeping in the room where the coffin of the deceased was was traumatic, especially during COVID-19 era when no one was allowed to be part of mourning crowd. Here, Indigenous rituals that provided support to women were disrupted by COVID-19 restrictions and generated cultural violence.

During some lockdowns, COVID-19 health guidelines to do with the burial of the deceased stipulated that the coffin could not get into the house and neither would it pass through the home of the deceased. This also lived on in the memory of one the widows. WHO guidelines forced a number of people not to get closure in relation to the deaths of their relatives. The emotions of the widow are captured in following narration when she says:

> *Mukadzi (Woman) 3: Eeee! COVID-19 yakauya kuzorwadzisa ini nevana vangu. Murume wangu akashaya COVID-19 ichipisa-pisa muna May 2020 zvokuti coffin rake harina kupinda mumba kana haro kupfuura nekumba. Ini nevana vangu tange tiri muquarantine sezvo taifungidzirwa kunge takaibata paari. Mumwe nomumwe aive muroom make. Ini ndini ndaichiitira vana zvose ndichitsveta kudya nemvura inopisa yekufukira pamusuwo weumwe neumwe nokuzozvibvisa. Ndakadana Mai Chipo*[1] *kuti huya undionere akanditi, "Handiuyi shamwari Tari*[2]*! Murume wako afa neCOVID-19". Ndakademba ndikati, "Vasikana huyai kani mundidongorere nepadurawall". Vakaramba vose. Ndakavaudza kuti ndipeiwo zvokushandisa Tadi*[3] *haasi kunzwa zvakanaka, haasi kumuka. Ndakanzwa kuti nyika yandiramba. Vamwe vaishandisa logic nerationalism ini ndange ndave kuda miracle and divine intervention.* (Woman 3: Eeee! COVID-19 came to cause pain to me and my children. My husband passed on at the height of COVID-19 in May 2020 that his coffin never got into the house and neither did it come home. My children and I were all in quarantine as it was suspected that we had contracted COVID-19 from him. Each one had been in his/her own room. I was the one that had to do everything for the children and give them food and hot water for steaming at their bedroom doors and later on remove them. I called Chipo's mother to come and witness what had happened and she said, "I am not coming friend Tari. Your husband died of COVID-19". I pleaded and said, "Ladies, come and peep at me over the durawall". They all refused. I told them to bring me the accessories since Tadi was unwell and bed ridden. I felt that the world had rejected me. While others were using logic and rationalism, I was in need of a miracle and divine intervention).

In this case, COVID-19 caused untold suffering to people in general and women in particular, as indicated in the utterances in the widowed woman's narration ("*Eeee! COVID-19 yakauya kuzorwadzisa ini nevana vangu*", "Eeee! COVID-19 came to cause pain to me and my children"). The statement is an emotional expression that the widow and her children experienced. The pain was not only through loss of loved one but also, the indecent funeral, burial procedures and rites. The fact that the husband's coffin never got into the house nor pass through the home made the situation difficult and unforgettable for the widow and her children to have closure ("*Murume wangu akashaya COVID-19 ichipisa-pisa ... coffin rake harina kupinda mumba kana haro kupfuura nekumba*", "My husband passed on at the height of COVID-19 … that his coffin never got into the house and neither did it come home"). In Indigenous cultures, women are usually communal in most of their activities that the barring of friends and relatives at funerals is tantamount to having funeral as a one-person event. This would be classified as a religio-cultural anomaly. COVID-19 subjected widowed women to depression, trauma and stress.

Widowed women had hard times in trying to draw the attention of colleagues and friends. The affected and infected felt abandoned. This is further emphasised in the previous widow's plea that "*Ndakademba ndikati, 'Vasikana huyai mundidongorere nepadurawall.' Vakaramba vose. Ndakavaudza kuti ndipeiwo zvokushandisa…*" (I pleaded and said, "Ladies, come and peep at me over the durawall". They all refused. I told them to bring me the accessories). She wanted friends to be present physically. The friends refused and could not even agree to peep at her through the security wall nor bring her the accessories to help her son who was also unwell. In this regard, COVID-19 unleashed psychological violence on women and compromised their mental health (see e.g. Sediri, Zgueb and Ouanes et al., 2020).

In the narration further, the friend to the widowed woman is narrating how she felt helpless when she could not help her friend. While her friend's family was infected and affected by COVID-19, she was affected emotionally. The ordeal she went through is captured in the narration:

> *Mukadzi (Woman) 4: Ummm! Imika imi! Tave kutaura nokuti kukurukura hunge wapotswa. Akandidaidza uyu shamwari yangu Tari*[4] *asi ndakaramba ndikati rufu haruna ushamwari. Ndakamuisira text message kuWhatsApp kuti ndine hurombo asi hapana chandinogona kuita. Pachokwadi ndakashaya kuti ndomubatsira sei shamwari yangu. Mariro ake ndakaaitira kumba kwangu. Kana sadza ndaiita munhikwi ndichida kumedza. Pose pandaiisa text paWhatsApp ndaive ndongobvunza kuti wamuka uri mupenyu? Ndakademba kuti Mwari hamungoiti miracle here* (Woman 4: Ummm! You yourself! We are now discussing this after we survived it. This, my friend Tari, called for help but I refused to entertain her since death has no friendship. I texted her a message on WhatsApp that I am saddened but there is nothing I could do. To be honest, I had no idea on how I could help my friend. I attended the funeral virtually from my house. Even when I tried to eat sadza I would struggle to swallow since I had developed hiccups. Each time I was texting messages I would ask her if she had been able to wake up. I wished God would perform a miracle for her).

The Shona proverb "*kukurukura hunge wapotswa*" (We testify after conquering the challenge) aptly describes the situation after the COVID-19 where a number of people survived death by a whisker. This is evidence that a number of participants testifying in the narrations in this chapter had gotten into difficult, traumatic and stressful situations. Mukadzi/Woman 4 admits that she could not attend to her friend in the very time of need by saying that "*akandidaidza uyu shamwari yangu Tari asi ndakaramba…*" (This, my friend Tari, called me but I refused). In Shona it is said "*husahwira hunokunda hukama*", implying that friendship surpasses blood relationships (see e.g. Chikafu, 2012). The situation where a friend could not come to rescue a friend signals an extremely difficult situation. COVID-19 challenged the Indigenous funeral rites and reconstructed a new narrative that switched to remote funeral attendance. Remote or virtual funeral attendance that had been shun as show-off and devoid of *Unhu/Ubuntu* became new normal. Thus, the abrupt withdrawal of the psychosocial support services from the community made funeral and burial rites stressful and devoid respect of the dead. This precipitated psychological violence and required high levels of creativity on the part of Indigenous cultural leaders. Going forward, the authorities will need to collaborate with Indigenous cultural leaders to alleviate the trauma that Indigenous individuals, families and communities (particularly women) face in the context of pandemics.

While women are regarded as saviours, sometimes saviourhood compromised their health and wellbeing, as well as the health and wellbeing of others. This was the case when women got into a dilemma regarding whether or not to tell the truth about their COVID-19 status. They sometimes chose not to tell their families of their COVID-19 status for fear of victimisation. Women got into difficult situation in a bid to please their husbands and fulfil their womanhood according to Indigenous standards. Some of the womanly and wifely obligations exposed the women and families to COVID-19 infection. This is captured in the ordeal narrated further:

> *Mukadzi (Woman) 5: Ini handina kuudza murume wangu kuti ndakange ndatoita COVID-19 positive nokuti ndaitya anondiramba kana kunditiza. Saka ndakavanza zvakaita kuti murume wangu abatirewo COVID-19. Mwana wangu akanditambira kuairport akarwarawo, mudzimai wake akarwarawo, nemwana wavo mukomana akarwarawo. Ndakazvidemba kuti dai ndakagara kuquarantine zvaive nane ndairambwa pane kuparadza mhuri yemwana wangu* (Woman 5: I could not tell my husband that I had tested positive as I feared that he would divorce me or dump me. So, I concealed information which made my husband contract COVID-19 also. My son who picked me up from the airport also got ill, his wife and their eldest son also contracted it. I regretted that it would have been better if I had stayed in quarantine; it was better to be dumped than to destroy my son's family).

The woman (Mukadzi/Woman 5) in this scenario, by virtue of being a woman, risked herself and her family by not publicly declaring her COVID-19 status. She feared that her husband would reject her, hence she chose to conceal her COVID-19 status. Hence she narrated, "*Ini handina kuudza murume wangu kuti ndakange ndatoita COVID-19 positive nokuti ndaitya kuti murume wangu anondiramba kana kunditiza*" (I could not tell my husband that I had tested positive as I feared that my husband would divorce me or dump me). She failed to disclose her COVID-19 status to the family for fear of being stigmatised. Women fear men who appear as agents of the community's punishing authority. The woman in the previous narration avoids rejection by husband but risked herself and her family members as captured in "*murume wangu abatirewo...Mwana wangu ...akarwarawo, mudzimai wake akarwarawo, nemwana ...mukomana akarwarawo*" (… husband to contract... My son … got ill, his wife got ill and their eldest son too). In a separate study, Arrey, Bilsen, Lacor and Deschepper (2017) note that participants could not disclose their health status for fear of stigmatisation and rejection by relatives and husband in the case of women. The finding brings another psychosocial dilemma that caused stress to women during the COVID-19 era. The COVID-19 era experience made women in some cases to nurse a guilty conscience for the suffering they caused to their families. This psychological burden is another form of violence experienced by women as a result of socially constructed, but nevertheless very effectively enforced, gender roles.

By virtue of being women, women have other sexual and reproductive health rights (SRHR) that may require them to get healthcare services, whether they are sick or not (see e.g. Chirongoma, Manyonganise and Chitando, 2022). These include accessing family planning services. Mukadzi (Woman 6) is narrating an experience related the inaccessibility of healthcare and SRHR during the COVID-19 era. This is what she said:

> *Mukadzi 6: Kuti uwane rubatsiro waitotanga watesitiwa COVID-19 usati wabatsirwa, zvinova zvaidhura. Izvi zvaiunza matambudziko nokuti taida rubatsirwo pane zveFamily Planning. Dzimwe shamwari dzatinotoziva dzakaita vana vavasina kurongerwa. Vamwe ndivo vainobvisa mumaraini.* (Woman 6: For us to get any form of help we were supposed to get tested for COVID-19, which was costly. That had its own challenges as sometimes we would need services about Family Planning. Some of our friends had unplanned babies. Some had unsafe abortions).

This lack of access to family planning services impacted on women's SRHR and caused stress among women. This captured in "*Izvi zvaiunza matambudziko nokuti taida rubatsirwo pane zve Family Planning*" (That had its own challenges as we were in need of Family Planning services). So, apart from violating women's SRHR, COVID-19 also caused stress to women and over-stretched all community services, especially in developing countries and in this case, Zimbabwe. As a result, some women ended up getting care from traditional and untrained health-care-givers which risked their health and wellbeing. The prerequisite condition of getting tested for COVID-19 deterred many would-be health service seekers from going to health centres for healthcare services. "*Kwainzi kuti uwane chero rupi rubatsiro waitotanga watesitiwa COVID-19 usati wabatsirwa, zvinova zvaidhura*" (It was said for us to get any form of help we were supposed to get tested for COVID-19 before getting services, which was costly). The failure to access health facilities findings resonates with Gouaibi's (2021) findings that, healthcare access for women and girls had been disrupted as most health services concentrated on COVID-19 cases. Healthcare systems across the world were said to have been overwhelmed by the COVID-19 pandemic cases and were trying to meet the surging demands. This resulted in collateral damage to women's SRHR and induced a lot of stress among some women of childbearing age. Hence the confession, "*Vamwe ndivo vainobvisa mumaraini*" (some had unsafe abortions). There was an increase in still births, maternal deaths and maternal depression during the COVID-19 pandemic (Ashish, Gurung, Kinney, Sunny, Moinuddin and Basnet, 2020). The United Nations Population Fund reported an average of 3–6 months disruption in women's accessing of family planning services which resulted in unintended pregnancies (Sileo et al., 2023).

The Experiences of Men

From aforementioned narrations, we can infer how COVID-19 impacted women and womanhood. The next section carries narrations of how COVID-19 impacted men and masculinity (see e.g. Mwiine and Katushabe, 2024). According to the men sampled for this study, they were also affected by COVID-19 in a more or less similar fashion to women. While both men and women felt restricted in the domestic confines, the women felt that their business and income sphere was affected, while the men felt their masculinity has been infringed upon. Thus, while women bemoaned their economic and emotional health, men were more concerned about the impact of the pandemic on their standing in the social sphere. Men feel restricted in home environments which they felt are women domains. The participant in the narration feels he is in a territory that is alien, as highlighted by Murume (Man) 1:

> *Murume 1: Munongozivawo kuti kugara mumba kubva richibuda kusvika richivira ihondo. Pamba pagara pane vepo vanotonga ipapo. Saka pamwe taitongokonana nekanhu kadukuduku. Ndinomboti ndanzwa nenzara regai hangu ndipakure nevana. Zvinonzi muchitogona kupakura mange madini kuchitobika murimi. Dzimwe nguva vanoti ndichapakura ndapedza kuwacha. Dzimwe nguva tinotorwa chete pasina kupera kana mazuva matatu chaiwo.* (Man 1: You are well aware that staying at home from morning till evening is a problem. I sometimes say to myself "I am hungry, let me serve myself and the children". She says if you can dish, you could have prepared the food yourself. Sometimes she says she will serve after finishing laundry. We inevitably soon fight, probably within three days).

The man in the last scenario was not used to spending whole day and every day at home. He laments, "*Munongozivawo ...kugara mumba kubva richibuda kusvika richivira… . Pamba pagara pane vene*" (You are well aware that staying at home from morning till evening is a problem. There are owners of homes…). Similarly, men want to prefect women in women's territory, the home, whereas women feel that the area of cooking and food provision is their territory and cannot take directives from men. "*Ndinomboti ndanzwa nenzara regai hangu ndipakure zvangu nevana. Zvinonzi kana muchitogona kupakura zvino mange madini kuchitobika murimi*" (I sometimes say to myself, "I am hungry, let me serve myself and the children". She says if you can dish, you could have prepared the food yourself). The friction led to domestic and gender-based violence as captured in "*… tinotongorwa chete pasina kupera mazuva matatu…*" (… we inevitably fight, probably within three days …). The emergence of COVID-19 marked another turning point in the history of masculinity and femininity in Indigenous cultures. It ensured that women and men had to cohabit in the domestic confines. In the same vein, men had to pay heed to the COVID-19 pandemic clarion call for transformative masculinity into fluidity (Chitando and Chirongoma, 2012) that makes men fit the new COVID-19 setup that demanded that men share the domestic territory with women and children and live in harmony. The finding adds more evidence to Gouaibi (2021) who observes that confinement measures increased gender-based violence, especially in marginalised communities. Crucially, the tension that emerged from partners sharing space generated subtle but significant expressions of conflict. Seemingly minor processes such as the man wishing to serve himself and the children upset the established gender order and could result in physical violence.

Similarly, the man in the following narration also felt his wife overworked, got tired and becomes angry. The COVID-19 restrictions led this man into rediscovering his wife. This is captured in

> *Murume 2: Ndinofunga Mai Tinashe*[5] *vanenge vaneta nebasa. Zuva rose havagari pasi. Ndinomboedzawo kubatsira asi ndinosvika pakuneta, ndosiya nokuti havagari pasi. Ndikavasekerera hanzi ndafunga pfambi dzangu. Hanzi ivo havasi imwe yepfambi dzangu. Ndinovati zororai, tsvina haidzingi vanhu mumba. Vane shavi reNjuzu* (I am sure Mai Tinashe will be tired. She will be standing the whole day. I sometimes try to assist her with the chores but I get to a point where I leave her because she is always busy. If I smile/try to cheer her up, she says I am now missing my mistresses. She says she is not one of my mistresses. I tell her to rest, dirt never drives away people from the house/home. She is possessed by a mermaid spirit).

The previous narration from the man is loaded. While it brings out evidence that men underwent stress due to movement restrictions, it also illustrates how COVID-19 was double-edged sword as it led to women's vulnerability to overworking from morning to evening. Thus, "... *Mai Tinashe vanenge vaneta nebasa. Zuva rose havagari pasi*" (Mai Tinashe will have been tired. She will be standing the whole day). With the advent of COVID-19, men and women were now at home the entire day and were forced to be friends. The excerpt "*Ndinomboedzawo kubatsira asi ndinosvika pakuneta ndosiya*" (I sometimes try to assist her with the chores but I get to a point where I get tired and leave her) indicates that the man was coming face to face with women's unpaid work (see e.g. UN Women, 2023). Actually, this man is admitting that there is more work at home that cannot be exhausted by a single person and that is why he sometimes assisted and asked his wife to have some rest. There was a transformation of masculinity that was taking place as he assisted his wife and asked her to have some rest and even tried to cheer her up as she worked. However, there was some tension as expressed in "*Ndikada kuvasekerera hanzi ndafunga pfambi dzangu. Hanzi ivo havasi imwe yepfambi dzangu*" (If I smile/try to cheer her up, she says I am now missing my mistresses). This might be indicative of the emotional violence that many women experience when some men pursue multiple and concurrent sexual partnerships. Contemporary scholarship tends to place emphasis on the physical confrontations that often emerge out of the issue of extramarital relationships. There is a need to pay equal attention at the emotional violence that accompanies such relationships.

According to the participants' narratives, what troubled men about COVID-19 were the restrictions in the domestic confines together with women. Men came to understand the reality of women within the home environment. Though COVID-19 affected all irrespective of gender, it affected women and men differently. This is captured in the following narration:

> *Murume/Man 3: Ndakaona kuti vakadzi vakaoma vanoswera pamba zuva nezuva. Aaaa! Ndakatanga ndichabatabata asi ndakasvika pakuti zvakwana. Ndaibata mugarden asi ndakasvika pakusimudza maoko ndaneta. Ndakaziva rimwe side romudzimai wangu randaisaziva. Basa rokurera vana chairo vasiri kuchikoro ritori basa guru chairo* (I realised that women who spend all day at home are tough. Aaaa! At first I would be attending to some issues but I get to a point when I realised that it was enough. I was working in the garden but I raised my hands and surrendered as I got tired. I realised something/one side about my wife that I did not know all along. Even caring for children while they are not going to school is a responsibility in itself).

This narration resonates with Man 2 who says that he learnt more about his wife and women in general, hence women are an invaluable source of labour in the family. They continue to work even if they are tired to make the home run. Thus, "*Ndakaziva rimwe side romudzimai wangu randaisaziva*" (I realised something about my wife that I did not know all along). Also, COVID-19 worsened the situation as it increased the women's workload as family members were now spending the whole day at homes and frequency and demand for food increased. In addition, the study participant demonstrated his growing awareness of the pressure associated with child care when he said, "*Basa rokurera vana chairo vasiri kuchikoro ritori basa guru chairo*" (Even caring for children while they are not going to school is a responsibility in itself). The husband meant that he had been underestimating child care. It was only during COVID-19 when he had spent days at home that he noticed that child rearing is a job on its own (see e.g. Valiani, 2022).

The COVID-19 pandemic transformed the funeral rites and reconstructed a new narrative. In some instances, and in contravention of accepted norms, in Zimbabwe, "*mukwasha*" (son-in-law), who according to Indigenous religion and culture has a key role to play in handling father-in-law's funeral processes and procedures, had to do it remotely while in the country. The son-in-law had to send money through electronic transfer to assist with the burial. This is captured in the next narration:

> *Murume/Man 4: Ndakanzwa kuti vatezvara vangu vashaika kumusha kuChivhu ndiri muno muHarare! Ndakafungisisa ndikaona iri nyikamukanza kusingasvikike nelockdown. Ndakangoti variko vanozvionerawo. Ndakangoisawo ecocash kuti vabatsirikane. Ndaigoita seiko nemamiriro ainge akaita zvinhu? Mukadzi wangu akachema asi ndakamusimbisa kuti zvaizogadzikana tozoenda tonobata maoko nekuona pavainge vakaradzikwa. Mukadzi wangu akakumbira shamwari kuti dzitipinze pazoom nekurecorder kuti tipindewo parufu pacho pamasaisai.* (I heard that my father-in-law had passed on there in rural home in Chivhu while I was here in Harare! I thought about it deeply and I realised that it was miles away and out of reach because of lockdown restrictions. I said to myself, those

that are there will do the job. I just sent Ecocash (electronic transfer) to assist those that were in charge. What else could I have done with the state of things during the time? My wife cried but I counselled her by telling her that things would normalise and we would eventually go and pay our last respects and see his resting place. My wife had to liase with her friends to have us attend the funeral on Zoom and record so that we attended online).

COVID-19 reconfigured the Indigenous funeral procedures. Relatives became diasporans while they were in Zimbabwe. Thus, "*Ndakanzwa kuti vatezvara vangu vashaika Kumusha kuChivhu ndiri muno muHarare! ... ndikaona kusingasvikike nelockdown. Ndakangoti variko vanozvionerawo*" (I heard that my father-in-law had passed on there in rural home in Chivhu while I was here in Harare! … I realised that it was miles away and out of reach because of lockdown restrictions. I said that those who were there on the ground would determine how to proceed). In the narration, Chivhu appeared unreachable from Harare because of COVID-19. Further, "*Mukadzi wangu akakumbira shamwari kuti dzitipinze pazoom nekurecorder kuti tipindewo parufu pacho pamasaisai*" (My wife had to liase with/ requested her friends to have us attend the funeral on Zoom and record so that we attended online). Electronic funeral attendance became the only mode of choice unlike in the past when it was viewed as lack of *Unhu/Ubuntu*. Life during COVID-19 became localised. This posed serious challenges to Indigenous people, although they had to reconstruct the practices associated with death and burial. They had to adjust cultural expectations as well. This was a form of violence on its own.

Further, COVID-19 burdened women with care giving to ill family members. This increased women's vulnerability. Such circumstances simultaneously transformed masculinity by making more men to empathise and appreciate women's role in care giving. It enabled many men to pause and celebrate the roles women perform in families during times of crisis. This is captured in the following narration:

Murume/Man 5: Ambuya vangu vakanzwa kuti tarwara vakati mwana wangu haafi ndiripo ndokuuya. Pasina masvondo maviri, isu tichida kunonaya ivo vakabva varwara zvaityisa uye vaive vasina kubaiwa vakabva vashaya. Izvi zvakandirwadza nokuti ndakaziva kuti COVID-19 vakaibata apo vaitibatsira. Ndakarwadziwa ndikashaya kuti ndovaitawo sei kuti ndivabatsire semukwasha. (On hearing that we were not feeling well, my mother-in-law felt her daughter would not die while she was there, and came. Within two weeks, as we were showing signs of recovering, she got ill and she passed on since she not been vaccinated. This pained me since I knew that she contracted COVID-19 when she was nursing us. It was painful and as the son-in-law I could not do anything to help her).

Despite being at risk of contracting COVID-19, women inevitably found themselves on the COVID-19 frontline providing care service to their family members. Sometimes this would be without adequate personal protective clothing and enough information about safety and containment. These challenges have also accompanied women working in the formal health sector (see e.g. Phillips et al., 2023). Some mothers, such as the one in the narration who automatically found herself in the COVID-19 frontline with neither the requisite training nor adequate implements, have paid the ultimate price. They were victims of structural violence. This resonates with the observation by Arrey, Bilson, Lacor and Deschepper (2017) that women are generally at high risk of contracting HIV either due to cultural or behavioural attributes. Overall, women are at the centre of family system. Women find themselves care giving COVID-19 patients and are inevitably in frontline by virtue of being mothers. Arrey, Bilsen, Lacor and Deschepper (2017) found out that, in sub-Saharan Africa public health concerns and awareness campaigns should therefore target women for their distinctive social roles of care giving for sick and ill family members. John and Scott (2007) noted that, there is need for adoption of cultural approach and provide information for empowering communities in the fight against epidemics. Similarly, Mogobe et al. (2016) argue that limited health literacy has been linked to inadequate engagement in care and may serve as contributor to poor health outcomes in health intervention care programmes.

However, just like most women, some men were also subjected to stress when they could not get mourners to console them in times of bereavement due to COVID-19 lockdown restrictions. The man in this scenario was narrating his ordeal when his wife passed on when COVID-19 was at its height:

> *Murume/Man 6: Ndakabuda ndikatenderera pamba pakaita kunge pasina rufu. Paive chete namai vemudzimai wangu nasisi vake nemwana wangu ane* 2 years *achitotamba zvake. Apa ndaiziva kuti ndasiya mudzimai wangu atoiswa mumortuary afa neCOVID*-19. *Ndakange ndamuperekedza kuchipatara neChipiri. Chitatu pandakasvikako ndakawana achiratidza kunge akange ave nane akange atombobva pa*support. *China ndichida kunomuona kudai ndichingogara pa*seat *remota foni ichipinda. Hanzi "Zvazoita nepamwe mudzimai wenyu atisiya". Izvi zvakaramba zvichishanyira ndangariro dzangu pose pandaipinda mu*bedroom. *Ndinongozvinyaradza asi, haaa! Hameno Mwari ndivo vanoziva kwatiri kuenda, chedu kutevera. Sei panguva ino pasina anondichema nokundinyaradza? Ndakademba nechemumoyo kuti, "Ndinozviziva kuti kunofiwaaa! Asi, ndiwo maperero acho hereee?"* (I patrolled the yard and it appeared like there was no funeral at my house. Only my mother-in-law, my wife's sister and our 2-year-old daughter who was playing, completely oblivious to what had just unfolded. I realised I had left my wife in the mortuary, having died of COVID-19. I had accompanied her to hospital on Tuesday. On Wednesday when I got there, she was showing signs of recovery and was no longer on life support. On Thursday when I was about to go for the morning visit, upon getting on the car seat my phone rang. They said, "This have taken an expected turn. We are sorry that your wife passed on". This kept on revisiting my mind each time I got into my bedroom. I consoled myself, but haaa! No one knows, only God knows where we are going, our's is simply following. Why at this point in time is there no one to

console or comfort me? I mourned quietly; "I know that death is inevitable. Is this how life ends?").

While COVID-19 does impact women and men differently, there was common ground when it came to the issue of the dispersed crowd of mourners. In "*Sei panguva ino pasina anondichema nokundinyaradza?*" (Why at this point in time is there no one to console or comfort me?). The husband who had lost his wife, like widowed women in the same situation (described earlier), lamented the loss of the mourning crowd that would console and strengthen him. The crowd had been withdrawn at the time it was needed most. The lamentation captured in interior monologue, "*Ndinozviziva kuti kunofiwaaa. Asi, ndiwo maperero acho hereee?*" (I know that death is inevitable. Is this how life ends?). This is similar to the women participants who wished the mourners had been there in form of friends or church members. The pandemic precipitated psychological violence as it affected the support system where relatives, friends, neighbours and even strangers participated in mourning. The violence associated with mourning without (other) mourners had a profound impact among Indigenous peoples and indicates the need for careful planning in anticipation of future pandemics.

Concluding Analysis

COVID-19, like any other pandemic of its ferocity and magnitude, knew no gender in terms of how it was contracted. Like other pandemics, it added care-giving responsibilities and obligations for family members, especially women. This induced stress among Indigenous communities. As if this was not enough, like its predecessors, it exposed many women who, due cultural expectations, found themselves on the COVID-19 frontline while ill-trained, ill-equipped and ill-informed. As a result, many women experienced diverse forms of violence due to the pandemic. This included economic, psychological, emotional, cultural and structural violence. Unfortunately, the extant literature has overlooked these dimensions and has concentrated on physical violence. This chapter has also highlighted the extent to which men were also affected by the lockdowns and loss of loved ones. Whereas Indigenous cultures do not always grant men the space to grieve, the groans that can be detected from the narratives by the men in the foregoing sections confirm the need for Indigenous societies to rethink the current rigid gender paradigms. Going forward, men and women need to reconsider and rethink the binary and oppositional gender relations so that they recast wo/manhood towards new femininity/masculinity that is fluid and flexible. Future responses to pandemics will need to take Indigenous worldviews and positions more seriously. Responses to COVID-19 tended to prioritise formulations by global institutions (United Nations Department of Economic and Social Affairs, 2020, p. 3; Pickering et al., 2023), with emphasis on strict lockdowns. Such interventions will have a higher level of success and ensure that Indigenous communities can survive and thrive after pandemics. They will also be better prepared to respond to subtle and hidden forms of violence so that all members of society can flourish.

Notes

1 Pseudonym.
2 Pseudonym.
3 Pseudonym.
4 Pseudonym.
5 Pseudonym.

References

Arrey, A. E., Bilsen, J., Lacor, P., and Deschepper, R. 2017. HIV Changed My Life Forever: An Illustrative Case Study of a Sub-Saharan African Migrant Women Living with HIV in Belgium. *Tropical Medicine and Infectious Diseases* 2(2), 1–11.

Ashish, K. C., Gurung, R., Kinney, M. V., Sunny, A. K., Moinuddin, M. D., Basnet, O., et. al. 2020. Effects of the COVID-19 pandemic response on intrapartum care, stillbirth, and neonatal mortality outcomes in Nepal: A prospective observational study. *Lancet Glob Health* 8, 1273–1281. https://doi.org/10.1016/ S2214-109X (20)30345-4

Attride-Stirling, J. 2001. Thematic networks: A analytic tool for qualitative research. *Qualitative Research* 1(3), 385–405. https://doi.org/10.1177/146879410100100307.

Barker, J. O., Mart, G., Brownstein, R., Whitehead, A. L., and Yukich, G. 2020. Religion in the Age of Social Distancing: How COVID-19 Presents New Directions for Research. *Sociology of Religion* 81(4), 357–370.

Cameron, W. B. 1963. *Informal Sociology: A Casual Introduction to Sociological Thinking*. New York: Random House.

Chikafu, P. T. 2012. *Usahwira: A Look at the Old Testament Covenant Traditions from an African Perspective*. Zomba: Kachere.

Chilisa, B. 2012. *Indigenous Research Methodologies*. Los Angeles: SAGE Publications.

Chirongoma, S., Manyonganise, M., and Chitando, E. Eds. 2022. *Religion, Women's Health Rights and Sustainable Development in Zimbabwe* (Vol. 1). Cham: Palgrave Macmillan.

Chitando, E., and Chirongoma, S. Eds. 2012. *Redemptive Masculinities: Men HIV and Religion*. Geneva: World Council of Churches.

Couros, G. 2015. *The Innovator's Mindset: Empowering Learning, Unleash Talent and Lead a Culture of Creativity*. San Diego: Dave Burgess Consulting.

Creswell, J. W. 2003. *Research Design: Qualitative, Quantitative and Mixed Methods Approaches* (2nd ed.). London: SAGE Publications.

Falawole, O. I. 2008. Economic Violence to Women: Is it Receiving the Necessary Attention? *Trauma, Violence, and Abuse* 9(3), 167–177.

Gouaibi, A. 2021. The Pandemic Has Hurt Women's Health. This Is Why That's Bad For Everyone. Community Lead. Accessed from www.gavi.org/vaccineswork/pandemic-has-hurt-womens-health-why-thats-bad-everyone?gclid=CjwKCAjwxr2iBhBJEiw AdXECwwQx0BRJ3B9icYNG5ysUVQUz0GyQX59Drlc0brtBtBfzV-Q9FdGVqRoCkpUQAvD_BwE.

Gunda, M. R. 2009. African Theology of Reconstruction: The Painful Realities and Practical Options! *Exchange* 38(1), 84–102.

John, C., and Scott, M. S. 2007. Concept Paper: Importance of Cultural Competency in Disaster Management, Center for Public Service Communications. Accessed from file:///C:/Users/Ad min/Downloads/6108.pdf.

Kanu, Y. 2007. Tradition and educational reconstruction in Africa in postcolonial and global times: The case for Sierra Leone. *African Studies Quarterly* 9(3), 65–83.

Kowalezyk, O., Roszkwski, K., Montane, X., Pawliszak, W., Tylkowski, B., and Bajek, A. 2020. Religion and Faith Perception in a Pandemic of COVID-19. *Journal of Religion and Health* 59, 2671–2677.

Kufakurinani, U. 2024. Social Media Humour Amongst Zimbabweans: Discoursing Gendered Playful Engagements Around Covid-19. In E. Chitando, O. B. Mlambo, S. Mfecane, and K. Ratele, Eds., *The Palgrave Handbook of African Men and Masculinities* (pp. 975–985). Cham: Palgrave Macmillan.

Maponga, G. 2020. Police disperse 5000 sect members of Johane Marange Apostolic Church. *The Hearald*. 20 July 2020. Masvingo.

Maree, K., and Van Der Westhuizen, C. 2007. Qualitative Research Designs and Data Gathering Techniques, In K. Maree Ed., *First Steps in Research* (pp. 69–97). Pretoria: Van Schaik Publishers.

Marshall, K. 2022. COVID-19 and Religion: Pandemic Lessons and Legacies. *The Review of Faith & International Affairs* 20(4), 80–90.

McLean, G. F. 1999. *Religion and Culture*. Washington, DC: The Council for Research in Values and Philosophy.

Mogobe, K. D., Shaibu, S., Matshediso, E., Sabone, M., Ntsayagae, E., Nicholas, P. K., Portillo, C. J., Corless, I. B., Rose, C. D., and Johnson, M. O. 2016. Language and Culture in Health literacy for People Living with HIV: Perspectives of Health Care Providers and Professional Care Team members. *Hindawi Publishing Corporation AIDS Research and Treatment* 10. Article ID 5015707, http://dx.doi.org/10.1155/2016/5015707.

Morgan, B., and Sklar, R. H. 2012. Sampling and Research Paradigms. In J. G. Maree (Ed.), *Complete Your Thesis or Dissertation Successfully: Practical Guidelines*. Cape Town: Juta and Company Limited.

Murray, N., and Beglar, D. 2009. *Inside Track: Writing Dissertations and Theses*. London: Pearson Longman.

Muyambo, T., Sibanda, F., and Chitando, E. Eds. 2023. *Religion and COVID-19 Vaccination in Zimbabwe*. London: Routledge.

Mwiine, A. A., and J. Katushabe. 2024. Studying Men and Masculinities in Global Crises: Critical Reflections on COVID-19 'Lockdown Masculinities' in Uganda. In E. Chitando, O. B. Mlambo, S. Mfecane, and K. Ratele, Eds., *The Palgrave Handbook of African Men and Masculinities* (pp. 605–633). Cham: Palgrave Macmillan.

Ngigi, S., and Busolo, D. 2018. Behaviour change communication in health promotion: Appropriate practices and promising approaches. *International Journal of Innovative Research and Development* 7(9), 84–93.

Oluga, M., Kiragu, S., Mohamed, M. K., and Wali, S. 2010. Deceptive Cultural Practices that Sabotage HIV/AIDS Education in Tanzania and Kenya. *Journal of Moral Education* 39(3), 365–380. DOI: 101080/03057240.2010. 497617.

Ostadtaghizadeh, A., Zarei, M., Saniee, N., and Mohammad A. R. 2023. Gender-based violence against women during the COVID-19 pandemic: Recommendations for future. *BMC Women's Health* 23, 219. https://doi.org/10.1186/s12905-023-02372-6.

Parker, R. 2001. Sexuality, culture, and power in HIV/AIDS research. *Annual Review of Anthropology* 30, 163–179.

Phillips, G., Kendino, M., Brolan, C. E., Herron, L. M., Körver, S., Motofaga, S., and Cox, M. 2023. Women on the frontline: Exploring the gendered experience for Pacific healthcare workers during the COVID-19 pandemic. *The Lancet Regional Health – Western Pacific* 42(100961), 1–12. DOI:10.1016/j.lanwpc.2023.100961.

Pickering, K., Galappaththi, E. K., Ford, J. D., Singh, C., Zavaleta-Cortijo, C., Hyams, K., Miranda, J. J., Arotoma-Rojas, I., Togarepi, C., Kaur, H., Arvind, J., Scanlon, H.,

Namanya, D. B., Anza-Ramirez, C., COVID – Observatories Team. 2023. Indigenous Peoples and the COVID-19 Pandemic: A Systematic Scoping Review. *Environmental Research Letters* 18(3), 033001. doi: 10.1088/1748-9326/acb804. Epub: 13 February 2023. PMID: 36798651; PMCID: PMC9923364.

Power, T., Wilson, D., Best, O., Brockie, T., Bourque, B. L., Millender, E., and Lowe, J. 2020. COVID-19 and Indigenous Peoples: An Imperative for Action. *Journal of Clinical Nursing* 29(15-16), 2737–2741. doi: 10.1111/jocn.15320. Epub 29 May 2020. PMID: 32412150; PMCID: PMC7272911.

Punch, K. 2009. *Introduction to Research Methods in Education.* London: SAGE. Publications.

Sediri, S., Zgueb, Y., Ouanes, S., Ouali, U., Bourgou, S., Jomli, R., and Nacef, F. 2020. Women's Mental Health: Acute Impact of COVID-19 Pandemic on Domestic Violence. *Arch Womens Ment Health* 23, 749–756.

Seifman, R., and Forthomme, C. 2020. The Role of Religion in COVID-19 Prevention: Where Angels Fear to Tread. *Culture, Health, Politics and Foreign Affairs.* Accessed on http://impact.com/role-religion-covid- prevention-response.

Sibanda, F., Muyambo, T., and Chitando, E. Eds. 2022. *Religion and the COVID-19 Pandemic in Southern Africa.* London: Routledge.

Sileo, K. M., Muhumuza, C., Helal, T., Olfers, A., Lule, H., Sekamatte, S., Kershaw, T, S., Wanyenze, R. K., and Kiene, S. M. 2023. Exploring the Effects of COVID-19 on Family Planning: Results from a Qualitative Study in Rural Uganda following COVID-19 Lockdown. *Reproductive Health,* 20, 31. https://doi.org/10.1186/s12978-023-01566-3.

Tabane, E. M. 2004. The Influence of Cultural Practices of Batswana People in Relation to Transmission of HIV/AIDS in Botswana. D.Phil. in Social Work, University of Pretoria.

UNCTAD. 2021. Prosperity for All. COVID-19 Threatens Four Lost Decades for Gender Equality, 1 October 2021. Available at https://unctad.org/news/covid-19-threatens-four-lost-decades-gender-equality.

UN Women. 2023. Measuring and Valuing Women's Unpaid Care and Domestic Work in Mali. Policy Brief. Available at https://africa.unwomen.org/sites/default/files/2023-06/20230505_UN%20Women_Policy%20brief%20Mali_ENG_web%20pages.pdf, accessed on 7 June 2024.

United Nations Department of Economic and Social Affairs. 2020. The Impact of COVID-19 on Indigenous Peoples. Policy Brief no. 70. Available at https://dgppdh.segob.gob.mx/work/models/Derechos_Humanos/DGPPDH/COVID-19/Anexo10.pdf, accessed on 7 June 2024.

Valiani, S. 2022. The African Care Economy Index. Available at www.undp.org/sites/g/files/zskgke326/files/2022-09/The%20Africa%20Care%20Index%202022_E-version_14%20Sept%202022.pdf, accessed on 7 June 2024.

World Health Organization (WHO). 2019. Practical Considerations and Recommendations for Religious Leaders and Faith Based Communities in the Context of COVID-19. Interim Guide. WHO Headquarters (HQ) WHO World-wide? WHO 2019-n-cov/religious-leaders, 2020. 7 April 2020/COVID-19 Mass Gatherings.

3 Utilising the African Duality Theory for Gender Equality during Pandemics

L. Uchenna Ogbonnaya and Joyline Gwara

Introduction

How can the African duality theory ground gender equality during pandemics? How can it be deployed to prevent and respond to gender-based violence? These questions arise due to the fact that humans in society are faced with the challenge of how their relationships along gender lines are to be defined and explained. Dualism and duality are two ontological systems with which reality is explained in terms of its constituent nature. These two ontological systems define reality in terms of spirit and matter. However, their emphases are distinct and nuanced. On the one hand, dualism absolutizes spirit and terms it good, while matter is relegated to the background since it is considered evil. On the other hand, duality does not see any of the two-constituent nature of reality as absolute. Instead, it holds that both are good and essential aspect of reality that must be treated as such. Hence, in duality, reality is essentially defined as constituting of spirit and matter. The point is that neither spirit nor matter is superior or inferior. An understanding of this duality theory grants equality to spirit and matter. This ontological system has implications for gender relations. It leads to the idea that gender relations could be conceived in terms of gender equality, thereby eliminating the basis and threat of gender-based violence. This is principally due to the fact that gender inequality drives gender-based violence.

However, gender relations in most contexts in human society are defined in terms of inequality. Most scholars have argued that gender inequality is mostly directed towards the female gender (see, among others, Chimakonam 2018; Mosima 2018; Oelofsen 2018; Akiode 2018; Balogun 2010; Ojah 2018). Here, the argument is that in societies, the female gender is regarded as inferior, while the male gender is deemed superior. Only a few scholars contend that gender inequality has the male gender at the receiving end, while the female is the perpetrator (Chinweizu 1990; Benatar 2012). It must be noted that gender inequality is informed by dualism. Some scholars have argued that despite the fact that African worldview seems to promote equality, gender inequality still abounds within African societies (Chimakonam 2018; Oelofsen 2018; Akiode 2018; Balogun 2010; 2018; Ojah 2018).

There are diverse manifestations of gender inequality. These inequalities abound during pandemics. Hence, our argument is twofold. First, we argue that

DOI: 10.4324/9781003494546-4

gender inequalities manifest themselves during various pandemics, instigating or worsening gender-based violence. We employ pandemics such as HIV and AIDS, as well as COVID-19, to substantiate our claim. These inequalities are informed by dualism, which elevates one gender above the other. The second argument is that the African duality theory can function as a philosophical base for promoting gender equality and overcoming gender-based violence. This is because it grants equality to seemingly opposing variables. We approach our task by first articulating this introductory remark. This introduction is then followed by a section on the various manifestations of gender inequality during pandemics. Afterwards, we discuss the African theory of duality. Thereafter, we explore how the African duality theory grounds gender equality during pandemics. This is followed by our concluding remark.

Various Manifestations of Gender Inequality during Pandemics

For a while now the world has been engaged in the drive for gender equality and strides have been made towards this endeavour. However, when pandemics hit, this progress is nullified, and new and existing gender inequalities are brought to light. It is in such contexts that gender-based violence has been known to thrive (Dlamini 2021). The HIV and AIDS pandemic has increased the vulnerability of women and girls in many parts of the world. Gender inequality is prevalent in the wake of HIV and AIDS, since women and girls are perceived as lacking power over their bodies and sexual lives. This is reinforced by social and economic inequalities which make them more vulnerable in contracting the HI virus (UN and WHO 2000: 9). In addition to this, Mazonde and Thurston (2013: 204) argue that low education among women continues to fuel their vulnerability to HIV. This low education hinders women from having access to information, enter the labour force and have self-esteem, which all help one to rise above the poverty datum line. According to Sia et al. (2014), women's lack of financial security and independence may contribute to higher HIV risk through mechanisms such as exchange of sexual favours for physical or financial resources or the inability to negotiate safe-sex behaviours because of financial dependency. These same factors also make women more vulnerable to gender-based violence.

With regards to HIV, women are exposed to risk of infection. This infection is usually through forced sex from their partners, as well as other forms of abuse, hence the greater incidence of HIV among women as compared with men. Moreover, violence or the fear of violence has been identified as interfering with women seeking HIV and AIDS information, voluntary testing or counselling (Goldstein and Manlowe (1997, as cited in Mazonde and Thurston 2013: 204). Moreno (2007, as cited in Mazonde and Thurston 2013: 204) related intimate partner violence (IPV) and HIV to childhood trauma, such as sexual, physical and verbal abuse. This in turn affects women's ways of dealing with relational issues as it affects their trust, lowers their sense of worth and results in self-blame. Intimate partner violence (IPV) also affects men (Nyabena 2024), but the rates differ greatly, with many more women at the receiving end than men. Wagman (2008, as cited in Mazonde and Thurston 2013: 205) suggests that IPV not only undermines women's rights to fundamental freedom but also increases their risk to HIV and other sexually transmitted infections (STIs) and reduces their quality of life. Schleifer (2004, as cited in Mazonde and Thurston 2013: 205) notes the Human Rights Watch as indicating that rape and sexual assault within marriage is not uncommon and husbands may physically force wives to have sex against their will, even where there is a possibility of HIV infection. The threat of violence often results in women deferring decisions about sexual practises to their male partners, such as the use of male or female condoms, which the men often reject (Mazonde and Thurston 2013: 205).

Unlike their male counterparts, women are expected by society to take the care-giver role. However, when diagnosed with HIV, women face more challenges than men. With their roles as care-providers, they must first take care of themselves and provide care and attention to others who need and expect it (Mazonde and Thurston 2013: 204). These expectations by the society take a toll on women, subjecting them to stress, which further weakens their immune systems. This is not peculiar to the HIV and AIDS epidemic, but extends to other pandemics as well. For instance, in cases of Ebola, the burden of care falls to women. IDS (2015: 1) notes that women and men are affected differently by Ebola, with women in the region taking roles and responsibilities as they care for the ill and bury the dead, and as they navigate ever-diminishing livelihood options and increasingly limited health resources available to them. In Liberia, for instance, women made up 75% of Ebola cases because they were more likely to come into contact with the virus when they cared for the infected people in both health centres and at home (IDS 2015: 1). During the COVID-19 pandemic, among the several groups of workers that were deemed essential and required to be physically present at work were healthcare professionals (Ahinkorah et al. 2021: 2). These healthcare workers are considered as frontline staff, against the COVID-19, who are not only at high risk of infection but are also under significant psychological stress due to enormous work schedules (Ahinkorah et al. 2021: 2). COVID-19 institutional actions have inadvertently deepened the vulnerability of workers, especially among women who form the largest proportion of the nursing staff in many health facilities in the region (Ahinkorah et al. 2021: 2). Women in the health sector face patriarchal structural violence as the system is designed to force them to find employment in this sector, having shut them out of employment in other sectors (Mazurana and McKay 2001).

Carlson et al. (2020) as cited in Fisher and Ryan (2021: 238) note that in the wake of COVID-19, household and childcare responsibilities increased and gender inequalities were most apparent among those with children. Ali (2020) as cited in Fisher and Ryan (2021: 238) notes that mothers reported a greater increase in domestic and care work than fathers. They also reported a 5% increase in work hours, while fathers' work hours largely remained stable. Carlson et al. (2020, as cited in Fisher and Ryan 2021) further argue that mothers were more likely to be solely responsible for educating their children. Ahinkorah et al. (2021: 2) argue that although parents were affected by school closures, job losses and primarily working from home to observe social/physical distancing measure, women, especially mothers, had been saddled with multiple responsibilities for work (i.e. formal/informal), domestic work and childcare compared with men and/or fathers. Available records show that while fathers had also seen increased childcare-related tasks during the pandemic, women's childcare-related tasks during lockdown had increased to more than 3 extra hours per day than the reported 2 hours for men averagely (Ahinkorah et al. 2021: 2). This is a hidden form of gender-based violence which emerges from gender injustice.

As healthcare professionals, women's multiple roles conflict with each other. For instance, there was a conflict between women's work schedules in office and family life (i.e. more household and caretaking responsibilities) during the pandemic. This exposed them to heightened risk and enormous pressure compared with men (Ahinkorah et al. 2021: 3). Again, due to workplace expectations, and socio-cultural norms associated with parenting and household responsibilities in sub-Saharan Africa, women were likely to experience additional strain during COVID-19 to manage and/or balance these multiple roles (Ahinkorah et al. 2021: 3).

Furthermore, during the COVID-19 pandemic, women's physical and reproductive health were put in jeopardy as many countries reallocated their resources to the response to the virus. Drawing from the past experiences of Ebola which showed an increase in teenage pregnancies when schools closed, Ahinkorah et al. (2021: 2) argue that COVID-19 had the potential of causing a disproportionate drop out of school by teenage girls and young women for varied socio-economic reasons (e.g. unwanted pregnancies, manual labour). Experiences of previous pandemics and the COVID-19 pandemic showed increases in existing gender health inequalities in reproductive healthcare across many societies, with many compromised health systems (Ahinkorah et al. 2021: 3).

It is clear from the gender inequalities that were experienced in the wake of the HIV and AIDS, Ebola and COVID- 19 challenges that the major cause of these disparities is the long-standing gender role beliefs. Women are believed to be highly communal, with such traits as warmth, concern for others, taking the role of caregivers within the home and lower status roles in society. In contrast, gender roles prescribe that men are highly agentic, with such traits as stoicism, strength and taking the role of provider outside the home and high status in the society (Fisher and Ryan 2021: 239; see also Chitando, Mlambo, Mfecane and Kopano 2024). In other words, differences in sexual decision-making power, domestic and partner violence and societal norms regarding acceptable sexual behaviours for men and women, and caregiving roles all contribute to gender inequalities and the accompanying gender-based violence, in the HIV and AIDS, Ebola and COVID-19 pandemics. All these manifestations of gender inequality discussed so far are the result of understanding reality and the interpretation of it in human relations from the ambience of dualism. The following section provides an overview of the African duality theory.

What Is African Duality Theory?

Reality, as stated in our introductory remark, is conceived from the philosophical cum ontological ambience of dualism and duality. Dualism holds that reality consists of spirit and matter, and that spirit is good while matter is evil. Given the contention that matter is evil, it is regarded as inconsequential, while the spirit that is deemed good is considered as the essential aspect of reality. A good expression of the dualism theory is Plato's conception of the world. According to Plato, the world is divided into the world of forms and the physical world. He argues that the world of forms is the real world and reality is associated with this world. Plato sees the physical world as a carbon copy or a shadow of the world of forms (Copleston 2010 [1946]).

Another example is Aristotle's (1947) philosophy of essence (Asouzu 2011). Aristotle argues that being consists of substance (essence) and accident, and that it is the essential aspect of being that he sees as reality, while accident is inconsequential. Joyline Gwara and L. Uchenna Ogbonnaya (2022) capture this as they assert that Aristotle "famously argued in his *Metaphysics* that substance is what possesses ultimate reality while the accident is dependent on substance. Since accidents are predicable on substance, the latter is what has being". The point is that dualism emphasises an aspect of being or reality and devalues the other.

Contrary to dualism is duality. Duality is an ontological theory that is antithetical to dualism. This ontological theory does not elevate an aspect of being or reality or debase the other. The theory holds that every aspect of reality is important, inseparable and ontologically equal. This ontological theory has been associated with the African conception of reality. It is on this note that this theory is called the African theory of duality or the African duality theory. Hence, some African scholars have described the African duality theory deploying diverse nomenclatures. For instance, Udobata Onunwa (2005) calls it "inseparable duality". Also, Chris Ijiomah describes it as "harmonious monism" (1996, 2006, 2014, 2016). Furthermore, Alexander Animalu and Jonathan Chimakonam (2012) term it "complementary duality".

The central idea in the African duality theory is that reality is dual, that is, two-sided. Emmanuel Edeh (1985: 77) captures this as follows; "...for all beings... existence is a dual and interrelated phenomenon... It has a dual existence, dual in the sense that the reality of its existence is a phenomenon in the visible world and also a reality in the invisible world". As stated earlier on, duality is African and emphasises the harmony of opposites. Augustine Obi reiterates this as he argues that the "African capacity for abstract thought is reflected in their interpretation of duality as harmony of opposites which constitutes the foundation of African traditions and institutions" (2017: 5–6). Two deductions could be made from this assertion. The first is that Africans are capable of abstract thinking. The second is that this abstract thought finds its fullness in their duality theory, which enthrones the harmonising of opposites.

It is germane to note that the African duality theory finds its manifestations in various African worldviews. A good example is in African divination. According to Geoffrey Parrinder (1962: 122), in African divination "some degree of telepathy and extra-sensory perception is at work". The extra-sensory perception is the other side that accompanies sensory divination in the African worldview. John Mbiti (1969: 177) seems to give a vivid expression of this argument as he avers that African "divination adds to the complexity of African concepts and links together in its own way the physical and the metaphysical".

One could think that African divination is only religious. No! It is not only religious. African divination also has to do with African medicine. African medicine that involves divination and diviners also has to do with duality. On this, Robin Horton (1967: 64) contends that although African diviners employ both metaphysical agents in the diagnosing and healing of disease (sickness), they also offer rational accounts of how these metaphysical agents intervene to make this practice of African medicine feasible. Hence, there are metaphysical and rational accounts to African medical practice. Obi (2008: 51–53; 2017: 7) calls this the "principle of dual causality". This, according to Hastings ( ), is "duality of explanation, physical and metaphysical which informs African interpretations of sickness" (cited in Obi 2017: 7).

The African duality theory can be deduced in magic, sorcery, witchcraft, etc., which operate with the principles of causality and remote control, just as in divination (Evans-Pritchard 1939: 21; Obi 2017: 7). Also, the African conception of the world, which is twofold (tripartite and dual) in the final analysis zeroes in as one (duality). The tripartite conception of the world holds that the world is segmented into three compartments, namely, the world above (the sky), the human world and the world beneath (the underworld) (Ijiomah 2014; 2016). These three worlds are reduced to two worlds – the physical and the nonphysical (spiritual) worlds. The human world is the physical world, while the world above and the world beneath are the non-physical worlds. We could also say that the human world is the sensible, tangible and visible world, while the world above and the world beneath are the nonsensible, intangible and invisible worlds.

Likewise, being is conceived within the ambience of duality as that which cannot be restricted to substance to the neglect of accident. Instead, being is seen as that which consists of substance and accident, which are in a mutually complementary relationship (Asouzu 2007; 2011). Innocent Asouzu (2007) explains this further as he contends, using his Igbo parlance, that *ihedi, nwere isi na odu* (whatever is, has head and tail-end). Here, what is *ihedi* is being; head (*isi*) is substance; and tail-end (*odu*) is accident. Being is not and must never be defined as *isi* (head) or *odu* (tail-end). It is always defined as that which has head and tail-end. Some African philosophers and scholars have defined being as that which consists of spirit and matter, spiritual (nonphysical) and physical aspects, material and immaterial parts, etc. (Ijiomah 1996; 2006; 2014; 2016; Iroegbu 2002). Gwara and Ogbonnaya summarise this discussion thus:

> For instance, reality consists of matter and spirit, physical and non-physical aspects, invisible and visible aspects, nonsensible and sensible aspects. Also, being consists of substance and accident. Furthermore, the world consists of

> physical and non-physical, invisible and visible, nonsensible and sensible qualities. Each of the pairs is believed to be inseparable, integrated, and complementary to each other.
>
> (Gwara and Ogbonnaya 2022:43)

Therefore, in the African duality theory, the physical has a metaphysical side. This is because for the African, opposites are reconciled in the interpretation of duality (Booth 1977: 5–6). The opposites are the physical and the metaphysical that always coalesce as one. What this entails is that in the African duality theory, opposites which are perceived as polarities are integrated (Booth 1977: 5; Zahan 1979: 8–9). Here, there is harmonising of opposites as aspects of one and the same reality or thing (Krige 1936: 42–44; Thomas 1959: 41; Zahan 1979: 8–9; Argyle 1966: 177; Chukwukere 1983: 531).

The foregoing discussions demonstrate that reality has two sides, which coexist and are always in an inseparable relationship. As we stated earlier on, Asouzu gives a more insightful philosophical idea of the African duality theory. This is the point he made when he posits that being is that which consists of substance and accident, which are in a mutually complementary relationship (Asouzu 2007, 2011). The central thought is that the two sides of these realities are equal. This is contrary to Aristotle's bifurcating metaphysics, which elevates and equates substance to being even without accident. Therefore, the African duality theory avers that reality is intrinsically dual, with two equal sides that cannot be neglected if reality must be said to exist. In the following section, we discuss how the African duality theory can be deployed to overcome gender-based violence and promote gender equality during pandemics.

How African Duality Theory Can Ground Gender Equality during Pandemics

Our argument is that there are gender inequalities, which have the female gender at the receiving end of these uneven human relationships. These lopsided relationships have always been in human society and contributing to gender-based violence. However, they are heightened during pandemics as the socio-economic gap between the male gender and the female gender becomes more apparent. As discussed earlier, the male gender is less affected by these unequal gender relationships that ensue during pandemics such as HIV and AIDS, Ebola and COVID-19. The female gender during these pandemics is not just relegated to the background, she bears most of the pains that come with them (Mazonde and Thurston 2013; Fisher and Ryan 2021; Ahinkorah et al. 2021). Women suffer the most during pandemics since they are primary caregivers within their respective families and societies. This renders them more vulnerable to infections and gender-based violence due to the power imbalances.

Also, most of the female gender are the first to lose their jobs and become economically dependent on males, who might still have the privilege to work during pandemics. This implies that the males are more economically viable. We can say that the social construct that goes with the male gender gives the man the privilege to be a more outdoor person, while the female gender is seen as indoor gender, who should remain at home at any moment of pandemics. Hence, females are the most affected (the burden of the pandemics falls more on them) because of their gender and social status. As the world prepares for future pandemics, it will be vital to ensure that there is gender equality and gender justice for better outcomes (Sola 2023).

What can be deduced from our discussion so far is that the HIV and AIDS, Ebola and COVID-19 pandemics demonstrate in no small measure the gender inequalities that exist between men and women (Mazonde and Thurston 2013; Fisher and Ryan 2021; Ahinkorah et al. 2021). These gender inequalities have been constructed to position the male gender as superior and the female gender as inferior. These gender inequalities during pandemic, it must be noted, have their roots in dualism – spirit/metaphysical dimension of reality is good, and matter/physical aspect of reality is evil. Thus, spirit/metaphysical dimension of reality is equated to reality even without matter/physical of reality (an inconsequential part of reality). The implication that this dualism has on human gender relations is that it bifurcates and polarises humanity and absolutizes one gender (male), while the other (female) is debased. For instance, the male gender is equated to the spirit/metaphysical dimension of reality (good and essential) and the female equated to the matter/physical aspect of reality (bad or evil and inconsequential). In this case, the male gender is absolutized, while the female gender is debased. With this, we can say that dualism gives the impression that the male gender is synonymous with humanity. Therefore, all the privileges that come with being human are assigned and given to men, while females are denied most of these privileges. This entails gender inequality against women. It is precisely this type of reasoning that leads to the persistence of gender-based violence (Dahal, Joshi, and Swahnberg 2022).

It must be noted that the human society is not fashioned only to follow and manifest the dualism (such as Aristotle's) that leads to gender inequalities. Instead, the human society can follow and manifest the African duality theory – the philosophical/ontological system that holds that spirit and matter are good and equal. Our task at this point is to demonstrate how gender equality can be achieved even during pandemics using African duality theory. We are convinced that such an approach is a panacea to the challenge of the accompanying gender-based violence.

Gender equality is an idea and ideal that holds that the male and female gender are equal and must be treated as such. This equality, it must be noted, is first ontological. Also, it must be noted that this ontological equality ought to translate into socio-economic equality. The question is, how is this possible? What can be said is that male and female ontological equality stems from the belief that they both share a common humanity. Their common humanity is an ontological given that cannot be denied any of the two genders. Also, none can be said to be too human or less human. They are, in all contexts, equally human. Here, humanity is not restrictively associated with either the male or female gender. It is unquestionably associated with both genders. This is rooted in the African duality theory. Here, reality is ontologically defined in terms of its two-sidedness. This is to say that reality must be conceived only within the context of spirit and matter or in terms of the metaphysical and the physical.

In the African duality theory, both spirit and matter or the metaphysical and the physical are two sides of a coin – reality. This ontological system hinges on the view that spirit and matter or the metaphysical and the physical are "missing links" (Asouzu 2004; 2005; 2007; 2011; Edet 2011). This stems from Asouzu's (2007; 2011) assertion that anything that exists serves a missing link of reality. Within the context of human relations, it can be said that male and female are missing links to each other in society. So, as missing links, they are contraries. As contraries, they are complements. Therefore, as complements they are in a binary complementary relationship. This idea of binary complementarity entails that they mutually coexist and are in mutual service to each other. The male and female gender can be said to be binary complement because like spirit/metaphysical and matter/physical they are both good and equal. Neither is more essential nor the other inconsequential. They are both essentially humans and are in a mutual service to each other and the entire humanity. Embracing this interpretation of reality negates gender-based violence and promotes gender equality and gender justice.

If the male and female genders are in mutual service to each other, then, they need to always live in complementarity and solidarity, even during pandemics. In this light, the male and female need to complement each other during pandemics such as HIV and AIDS, Ebola and COVID-19. Hence, males must not see themselves as superior to females. For to do so is to see themselves as absolute and equal to humanity, even without females. Instead, they (males) must realise that they are missing links to females and therefore must assist in providing care to the infected and family members in times of pandemics. Also, females must not be relegated to the background as inferiors in terms addressing the economic needs of the family and society during pandemics. They must be allowed to complement the economic efforts of the males. In this way, the humanity of both the male and female genders are equally maintained, and their dignity mutually affirmed. Thus, like spirit and matter or the metaphysical and the physical, both the male and the female genders can live as equals during pandemics since it is possible for them to coexist in complementarity and solidarity.

One likely question to be raised at this point is: how has the duality theory helped to address the issue of gender inequality? Our argument is that gender inequality (and the accompanying gender-based violence) can be addressed if we see both male and female gender as ontologically equal, just as the African theory of duality holds that both spirit/metaphysical aspect of reality and matter/physical aspect of reality are ontologically equal. In this case, both the male and female genders are sharing in a common humanity, with none being superior or inferior to the other. This is what gender equality connotes.

Conclusion

The central argument that we have put forward in this chapter is that gender inequality is a reality and it finds its manifestation in various forms, particularly through gender-based violence, during pandemics. We also noted that the female gender is disadvantaged, while the male gender is advantaged during pandemics. Without mincing words, we posited that this kind of negative gender relation is informed by dualism. Also, we argue that the African duality theory can lead to gender equality and contribute towards the elimination of gender-based violence. This, for us, is because the African duality theory grants the two sides of reality equal ontological standing. Applying this duality theory, we argue that both male and female genders can live in complementarity and solidarity such that none will be advantaged or disadvantaged. If this is achieved, then gender inequality during pandemics will no longer surface among humanity. It is critical for scholars from diverse disciplines to continue to reflect on the applicability of the African duality theory, particularly in the face of pandemics. This will ensure that the world will be more effectively prepared to negotiate future pandemics.

References

Ahinkorah, B.O., Hagan Jnr, J. E., Ameyaw, E. K., Seidu, A., and Schack, T. (2021). "COVID-19 Pandemic Worsening Gender Inequalities for Women in Sub-Saharan Africa". *Frontiers in Global Women's Health.* 2, 1–6.

Akiode, Olajumoke. (2018). "African Philosophy, Its Questions, the Place and the Role of Women and Its Disconnect with Its World". In Jonathan O. Chimakonam and Louise Du Toit (Eds.), *African Philosophy and the Epistemic Marginalization of Women* (pp. 57–73). Oxon: Routledge.

Animalu, Alexander O. E., and Jonathan O. Chimakonam. (2012). "4×4 Magic Square Representation of Complementary Duality of African Thought Logic". *African Journal of Physics.* 5m, 141–168.

Argyle, W. J. (1966). *The Fon of Dahomey.* Oxford: The Clarendon Press.

Aristotle. (1947). "Metaphysics". In W. D. Ross (Ed.), *The Basic Works of Aristotle.* Oxford: Clarendon.

Asouzu, Innocent I. (2004). *The Method and Principles of Complementary Reflection in and Beyond African Philosophy.* Calabar: University of Calabar.

Asouzu, Innocent I. (2005). *The Method and Principles of Complementary Reflection in and Beyond African Philosophy.* Zurich: Lit Verlag GmbH and Co. KG Wien.

Asouzu, Innocent I. (2007). *Ibuanyidanda: New Complementary Ontology, Beyond World Immanentism, Ethnocentric Reduction and Imposition.* London: Transaction.

Asouzu, Innocent I. (2011). *Ibuanyidanda and the Philosophy of Essence (Philosophy, the Science of Missing Links of Reality). 50th Inaugural Lecture.* Calabar: University of Calabar.

Balogun, Oladele Abiodun. (2018). "Conceptual decolonization in African philosophy: Views on women". In Jonathan O. Chimakonam and Louise Du Toit (Eds.), *African Philosophy and the Epistemic Marginalization of Women* (pp. 142–154). Oxon: Routledge.

Balogun, Oladele Abiodun. (2010). "Proverbial Oppression of Women in Yoruba African Culture: A Philosophical Overview". *Thought and Practice: A Journal of the Philosophical Association of Kenya (PAK).* 2(1), 21–36.

Benatar, David. (2012). *The Second Sexism: Discrimination against Men and Boys.* Malden: John Wiley and Sons.

Booth, N. S. (1977). *African Religions: A Symposium.* New York: Nok Publishers.

Chimakonam, Jonathan O. (2018). "Addressing the Epistemic Marginalization of Women in African Philosophy and Building a Culture of Conversations". In Jonathan O. Chimakonam and Louise Du Toit (Eds.), *African Philosophy and the Epistemic Marginalization of Women* (pp. 8–21). London: Routledge.

Chinweizu, I. (1990). *Anatomy of Female Power: A Masculinist Dissection of Matriarchy*. Lagos: Pero Press.

Chitando, Ezra, Obert B. Mlambo, Sakhumzi Mfecane, and Kopano Ratele (Eds.). (2024). *The Palgrave Handbook of African Men and Masculinities*. Cham: Palgrave Macmillan.

Chukwukere, B. I. (1983). "Chi in Igbo Religion and Thought: The God in Every Man". *Anthropos*. 78(3 & 4), 30–45.

Copleston, Frederick. (2010 [1946]). *A History of Philosophy: Greece and Rome*. London: Continuum.

Dahal, P., Joshi, S. K., and Swahnberg, K. (2022). "A Qualitative Study on Gender Inequality and Gender-Based Violence in Nepal". *BMC Public Health*. 22, 2005. https://doi.org/10.1186/s12889-022-14389-x.

Dlamini, N. J. (2021). "Gender-Based Violence, Twin Pandemic to COVID-19". *Critical Sociology*. 47(4–5), 583–590.

Edeh, Emmanuel. (1985). *Towards an Igbo Metaphysics*. Chicago, IL: Chicago University Press.

Edet, Mesembe. (2011). "Being as Missing Links". *Journal of Complementary Reflections: Studies in Asouzu*. 1(1), 28–32.

Evans-Pritchard, E. E. (1939). "Nuer Time Reckoning". *Africa*. 2(12), 11–20.

Fisher, A. N., and Ryan, M. K. (2021). "Gender Inequalities during COVID-19". *Group Processes and Intergroup Relations*. 24(2), 237–245.

Gwara, J., and Ogbonnaya, L. U. (2022). "Rethinking God's Omnibenevolence and Omnipotence in the Light of the COVID-19 Pandemic: An African Perspective". *Filosofia Theoretica: Journal of African Philosophy, Culture and Religions*. 11(4), 31–53.

Horton, Robin. (1967). "African Traditional Thought and Western Science. Part 2". *Africa*. 37(2), 155–187.

IDS Practice Paper in Brief. (2015). *The Pathology of Inequality: Gender and Ebola in West Africa*. www.ids.ac.uk/publications/the-pathology-of-inequality-gender-and-ebola-in-west-africa/

Ijiomah, Chris O. (1996). *Contemporary Views about Philosophy of Education*. Calabar: Uptrico Press.

Ijiomah, Chris O. (2006). "An Excavation of Logic in African Worldview". *African Journal of Religion, Culture and Society*. 1(1), 29–35.

Ijiomah, Chris O. (2014). *Harmonious Monism: A Philosophical Logic of Explanation for Ontological Issues in Supernaturalism in African Thought*. Calabar: Jochrisam.

Ijiomah, Chris O. (2016). *Harmonious Monism: A Philosophical Logic of Explanation for Ontological Issues in Supernaturalism in African Thought*. Bloomington, IN: Xlibris.

Iroegbu, Pantaleon. (2002). *Beyond Materialism and Spiritualism*. Ibadan: Hope Publications.

Krige, E. J. (1936). *The Social System of the Zulu People*. London: Shutter and Shooter.

Mazonde, J., and Thurston, W. (2013). "HIV Is My "Best" Problem: Living with Racism, HIV and Interpersonal Violence". In P. Liamputtong (Ed.), *Women, Motherhood and Living with HIV/AIDS: A Cross-Cultural Perspective* (pp. 201–213). New York: Springer.

Mazurana, D., and McKay, S. (2001). "Women, girls, and Structural Violence: A Global Analysis". In D. J. Christie, R. V. Wagner, and D. D. N. Winter (Eds.), *Peace, Conflict,*

and Violence: Peace Psychology for the 21st Century (pp. 130–138). Upper Saddle River, NJ: Prentice Hall/Pearson Education.
Mbiti, John S. (1969). *African Religions and Philosophy.* New York: Fredrick A. Praeger.
Mosima, Pius M. (2018). "Henry Odera Oruka and the Female Sage: Re-evaluating the Nature of Sagacity". In Jonathan O. Chimakonam and Louise Du Toit. *African Philosophy and the Epistemic Marginalization of Women* (pp. 22–41). London: Routledge.
Nyabena, Susan M. (2024). "Breaking the Silence: Exploring the Challenges and Support Mechanisms for Male Survivors of Gender-Based Violence in Sub-Saharan Africa". In Obert B. Mlambo and Ezra Chitando (Eds.), *The Palgrave Handbook of Violence in Africa* (pp. 849–864). Cham: Palgrave.
Obi, Augustine C. (2008). "Philosophy of Divination". *Uche: Journal of the Department of Philosophy University of Nigeria, Nsukka.* 14(2), 48–57.
Obi, Augustine C. (2017). *Being as Duality and African Hermeneutics of Foundation.* Enugu: Snapp.
Oelofsen, Rianna. (2018). "Women and Ubuntu: Does Ubuntu Condone the Subordination of Women?" In Jonathan O. Chimakonam and Louise Du Toit (Eds.), *African Philosophy and the Epistemic Marginalization of Women* (pp. 42–56). London: Routledge.
Ojah, Egbai Uti. (2018). "Women in the Kitchen of Philosophy: Re-asking the Questions of African Philosophy". In Jonathan O. Chimakonam and Louise Du Toit (Eds.), *African Philosophy and the Epistemic Marginalization of Women* (pp. 207–218). London: Routledge.
Onunwa, Udobata R. (2005). *Tradition, Culture and Underdevelopment of Africa.* Suffolk: Arima.
Parrinder, G. (1962). *African Traditional Religion*. London. SCPK Publishing.
Sia, D., Onadja, Y., Nandi, A., Foro, A., and Brewer, T. (2014). "What Lies Behind Gender Inequalities in HIV/AIDS in Sub-Saharan African Countries: Evidence from Kenya, Lesotho and Tanzania". *Health Policy and Planning.* 29, 938–949.
Sola, A. (2023). *Ethics and Pandemics: Interdisciplinary Perspectives on COVID-19 and Future Pandemics*. Cham: Springer Nature.
Thomas, E. M. (1959). *The Harmless People.* New York: Knopf Press.
UN and WHO. (2000). "The HIV/AIDS Pandemic and its Gender Implications". *Report of the Expert Group Meeting*, Namibia, 13–17 November. www.un.org/womenwatch/daw.
Zahan, D. (1979). *The Religion, Spirituality and Thought of Traditional Africa.* Chicago, IL: Chicago University Press.

4 Philosophical Reflections on Intimate Partner Violence (IPV) during the COVID-19 Pandemic in Zimbabwe

Elias G. Konyana

Introduction

Globally, domestic violence has been a big social problem with devastating effects on individuals, families and society. Efforts to curb domestic violence or mitigate against its impact have been of great proportions but yielding not much success. In fact, domestic violence has been prevalent in many societies, with far-reaching socio-economic consequences ranging from physical injuries to socio-economic deprivation, especially for women. The United Nations (2019) global report claims that one in three women worldwide experience physical or sexual violence mostly by an intimate partner. It is quick to point out that violence against women and girls is a human rights violation which cannot continue to be treated as just a country or community problem. During the outbreak of COVID-19, emerging data and reports from those in the front line showed that all types of violence against women and girls, particularly domestic violence, intensified. However, even before the COVID-19 pandemic began, domestic violence, particularly intimate partner violence (IPV), existed as an overlooked and underestimated relational problem.

Theoretical Framework

Confidentiality is the theory under which this chapter is constructed. Most domestic violence cases have often been treated as private and confidential matter, with victims[1] wishing to keep the matter within the family. This makes IPV a delicate type of domestic violence because of the contexts that give rise to it. As such, IPV is often treated as a private matter or personal issue requiring a personal response and solution. In this chapter, the principle of confidentiality is used as a theoretical framework to explore how IPV has not been treated as a public health, social, economic and political matter for long. The principle of confidentiality respects privacy and individual private space. It means that professionals should not share personal details about someone with others, unless that person has said they can or it is absolutely necessary to share. Confidentiality is a principle that speaks to the respect of rights to privacy. According to Rheeder (2018: 9):

DOI: 10.4324/9781003494546-5

> A right to privacy guarantees a control over personal information in many ways. It restricts access to personal and medical information and it provides a claim of non-interference in various private spheres of the individual. Privacy extends beyond data protection, as certain private spheres of the individual that are not manifested in data processing can also be protected by the right to privacy.

From this submission, IPV falls under the purview of the framework of confidentiality since most, if not all, of the causes of such violence are private or personal in nature. This approach to the subject helps in understanding why IPV is always a challenge in many societies, principally because it is shrouded with confidentiality.

The Context and Extent of Intimate Partner Violence

IPV is understood as behaviour, within an intimate relationship, that causes physical, sexual or psychological harm, including acts of physical aggression, sexual coercion and psychological abuse as well as controlling behaviours (World Health Organization, 2019). Intimate partners include but are not limited to spouses, former spouses, boyfriends/girlfriends and dating partners (Breiding et al., 2010). Cognizant of the aforementioned forms of intimate partners, men and women in same-sex relationships are also included in the definition of intimate partner relationships that can result in IPV (Breiding et al., 2010). For the purposes of this chapter, however, focus is on IPV among married partners in heterosexual relationships in Zimbabwe. Knowledge about the extent of IPV in Zimbabwe is still limited as most studies mainly focus on the causes and effects of domestic violence in general. Very few, if any, go into detail to analyse the specific form of domestic violence that is prevalent in most marital relationships. An understanding of the distinctions that exist among different forms of domestic violence prevents researchers from generalising domestic violence as a unitary phenomenon and is helpful when creating holistic intervention approaches. Kelly and Johnson (2008) argue that domestic violence can be witnessed in several forms that mainly include, but not exclusively, intimate violence, violent resistance, mutual violent control and situational couple violence. Such types of IPV are also evident in Zimbabwe where each violent act occurs due to different causes and circumstances.

IPV occurs when one partner in a relationship uses power or coercive control against the other spouse (Kelly and Johnson, 2008: 7). The situation refers to violence where one partner exercises control over the other, thereby instilling fear and inferiority in the other partner. IPV is the most prevalent form of domestic violence among married women in Zimbabwe. In some cases, threats, intimidation and isolation are often used by the male partner to control every other aspect of the female partner's life in areas such as finance, emotional stability and sexual liberation among others (Ansara and Hindin, 2010). Such forms of abuse persist unnoticed and unreported over long periods, and IPV often results in drastic chronic mental health effects such as depression on the victim. Other consequences of prolonged exposure to IPV include chronic pain, gastrointestinal and gynaecological problems and post-traumatic stress disorders, just to mention a few. IPV further affects the mental health of the victim as it creates more problems such as anxiety, substance abuse and regrettably low self-esteem (Kelly and Johnson, 2008).

Why Intimate Partner Violence Remains Difficult to Eradicate

There are multiple reasons to account for the obscuring of IPV by pandemics or other social ills. The most common explanation comes from the Foucauldian theory of power which claims that power and control foreground the context of intimate partner fighting. With respect to intimate relations, Kelly (2014) argues that power is the central reason for controlling exposure because it has the ability of making one entity to influence the action of another entity. Furthermore, Kelly (2014) explains that a Foucauldian model of power provides us with an understanding of the ways in which identities are produced within and by various discourses. This chapter argues that in Zimbabwe, customary law is one such reason that has been used to create an identity of subservience and docility for women by legitimating IPV. Since most of the perpetrators of IPV are men, who also happen to be breadwinners, perpetrator-dependence is another reason for persistence of IPV in communities.[2] Perpetrators of IPV use subtle controlling tactics to reduce the level of independence of the victim (Sullivan, 2017). For example, a perpetrator may use financial dependence to increase the likelihood that a survivor would never escape an abusive relationship as they keep relying on financial support from the perpetrator. Therefore, perpetrators could use such a tactic to limit the victim's possible engagement in employment and access to financial resources on their own. Consequently, the victim remains tied to and dependent on the perpetrator's control.

In rural communities, the compliance with dictates of customary law is another basis upon which IPV has never been easy to eradicate. By definition, customary law comprises "customs that are accepted as legal requirements or obligatory rules of conduct; practices and beliefs that are so vital and intrinsic a part of a social and economic system that they are treated as if they were laws" (World Intellectual Property Organization, 2013: 11). Customary laws are also understood as consisting of established patterns of behaviour that can be objectively verified within a particular social setting (Kuruk, 2002). In effect, Ndulo (2011) argues that customary law has a great impact on the lives of the majority of Africans in the area of interpersonal relationships in regard to matters such as marriage, inheritance and traditional authority. For this reason, all marital relationships, family matters and any issues pertaining to gender relations are always governed by customary law in rural communities in Zimbabwe. The major debate among scholars concerns the compatibility of customary law and respect for human rights as they all advocate for completely different things. For instance, while the Roman-Dutch law, the civil law that the courts in Zimbabwe use, promotes human rights and equality, customary law generally views women as subordinate to men. To mitigate the effects of this inconsistency between the two legal systems, the government of Zimbabwe has placed the written law to operate alongside with the unwritten customary laws. This is in order to make sure that communities are not run on the basis of the written laws only at the expense of the people's traditions and customary practices which existed well before colonisation. To this end, Ndulo (2011: 95) argued that

> From the inception of colonial rule, customary law was applicable on two conditions: (1) that it was not repugnant to justice, equity, or good morality and (2), that it was neither in its terms nor by necessary implication in conflict with any written law.

Yet, up to the present, many traditions and customs observed by communities regarding marriage and inheritance continue to conflict with the Constitution of Zimbabwe and the Domestic Violence Act, particularly in all issues that involve interpersonal relationships. Some customary practices continue to encourage the different treatment of men and women in relationships.

Bride Wealth (*roora/lobola*) Payment as a Catalyst for IPV

One fundamental practice of customary law that seemingly encourages IPV is the payment of bride wealth (*roora/lobola*) by men at marriage (see, e.g. Togarasei and Chitando, 2021). This practice of *roora/lobola* inadvertently creates attitudes of ownership among some men when it comes to how they relate to their female spouses. Nkomo (2017) refers to (*roora/lobola*) as the transfer of property, usually livestock, by the husband (or his guardian) to the wife's family as part of the process constituting a marriage. Although the practice is a way for the husband to appreciate his soon-to-be-wife's family, it might be said to commodify women and allows some men to carry a form of ownership over their spouses. Some husbands feel that they are allowed to abuse their wives in any way simply because they paid the bride price for them. Hence, payment of bride price results in male spouses having a form of ownership over their wives. Kelly (2014) maintains that power is tolerable only on condition that it masks a substantial part of itself.

Recognising Intimate Partner Violence as a Global Scourge

A growing number of population-based surveys have measured the prevalence of IPV and realised that IPV has been pervasive in many countries over the years. Most notably, the World Health Organization's (WHO 2012) multi-country study on women's health and domestic violence against women report collected and presented data on IPV from more than 24,000 women in 10 countries, representing diverse cultural, geographical and urban/rural settings. The study confirmed that IPV is widespread in all countries studied and that this trend has always been the case for many years. It also revealed that efforts to end IPV in many communities have been numerous but not yielded the desired results.

IPV occurs in all settings and among all socio-economic, religious and cultural groups. Admittedly, the overwhelming global burden of IPV is borne by women (Mburia-Mwalili et al., 2010). In Zimbabwe, the Domestic Violence Act (Chapter 5:16) (Act 14/2006) criminalises all forms of domestic violence that include but are not limited to physical, sexual, emotional, verbal, economic and psychological abuse as well as intimidation (Chapter 5:16). The enactment of the Domestic Violence Act was an apt recognition of the scourge of domestic violence and a response to the prevailing IPV across the diverse communities. The law was introduced to protect both men and women from all forms of domestic-violence-related abuses. The aim of the law was to provide relief and ensure the protection of domestic violence victims as well as establish long-term measures for the prevention of the same.

Prior to the enactment of this law, there was no statute which recognised domestic violence *per se*, let alone protecting victims of any form of domestic violence, including IPV. Most women and men in intimate relationships suffered in a dark corner, as the traditionally pivoted society did not take into account such crucial matters. Differences and violence between intimate partners were unfortunately treated as private and confidential information and activities.

The Escalation of Intimate Partner Violence during the COVID-19 Pandemic

The outbreak of the COVID-19 pandemic worldwide in March 2020 drew the world's attention from efforts to curb other existing pandemics in order to focus on containing spread of the coronavirus disease. Other pandemics such as HIV and Ebola were eclipsed by the COVID-19 pandemic. In the course of fighting the COVID-19 pandemic in Zimbabwe through Statutory Instrument 83 of 2020, also known as the Public Health (COVID-19 Prevention, Containment and Treatment) National Lockdown Order, 2020, IPV cases increased. According to Peterman et al. (2020), there was a sharp increase of IPV perpetration during the coronavirus outbreak. The COVID-19 pandemic containment measures such as the lockdown, which prohibited movement and gatherings, increased rates of unemployment to unprecedented levels and pushed many households into poverty. With the lockdown in force for prolonged periods through extensions, many men and women were forced to stay indoors, which increased the time intimate partners were together.

In the prevailing economic situation in Zimbabwe where most people were self-employed, the lockdown restrictions led to financial hardship which resulted in reduced earnings. In effect, financial hardship increased stress and put more strain on intimate partner relationships. So, the lockdown measures gave rise to IPV (Mukanagana et al., 2014). In addition, social distancing and isolation measures related to the COVID-19 pandemic left many victims, mostly women, without social contacts and confined to the home with the perpetrator during lockdown. In many instances, social isolation has been associated with increased risk of IPV in some contexts such urban settlements, and usually prevents the victim from seeking help from others (Peterman et al., 2020). Indeed, isolating victims from their social support network is a common strategy employed by perpetrators to control their victims and the COVID-19 pandemic escalated IPV (Minna and Gayle, 2022). Increased contact with the perpetrator in the home, coupled with reduced social movement and contacts with others further put many already vulnerable victims into even more precarious situations. The COVID-19 pandemic further exacerbated IPV situation when abusers made use of the social isolation measures as an excuse for further controlling and isolating the victims.

Some Philosophical Reflections on Intimate Partner Violence

Some philosophical reflections on IPV shed light on the underlying causes, ethical considerations and potential solutions to address IPV. One of the philosophical reflections involves gender inequality and power dynamics. The role of gender inequality and power imbalances in IPV cannot be underestimated (Chingarande and Chingarande, 2020). From a philosophical perspective, there is a need to challenge patriarchal norms and systems that perpetuate violence against women. This involves questioning deeply ingrained cultural beliefs, traditions and social structures that contribute to the subjugation of women and the normalisation of violence. Furthermore, philosophical perspectives underscore the importance of recognising IPV as a violation of human rights. Every human has a right to decent treatment in a relationship (Fuller, 2015). There is a need to protect the rights and dignity of survivors, promote equality and ensure access to justice. Such reflections advocate for a society that upholds social justice, where every individual is treated with respect and afforded equal rights and opportunities. These philosophical reflections explore the ethical implications of the pandemic response on IPV. They raise questions about the impact of lockdowns and movement restrictions, as well as the economic impacts on IPV survivors' safety and well-being (Fuller, 2015). These reflections emphasise the importance of considering the unintended consequences of public health measures on containing the corona virus and ensuring that policies and interventions did not inadvertently exacerbate IPV or hinder access to support.

Another philosophical reflection focuses on the ethics of care and empathy of survivors of IPV during the COVID-19 pandemic. This reflection often emphasises the ethics of care and empathy in addressing IPV (Mpofu and Nkomo, 2020). It stresses the importance of creating a compassionate and supportive environment for survivors, understanding their experiences, and providing holistic care and assistance. Additionally, the ethics of care and empathy calls for a shift in societal values towards responsiveness, compassion and solidarity with survivors. Since IPV often happens in closed doors and in privacy, it is important to help victims once they seek support and protection. This philosophical reflection encourages individuals and communities to cultivate empathy towards survivors, challenge victim-blaming attitudes and foster a culture of support and understanding. It calls for individuals to engage in critical self-reflection, examining one's own biases and assumptions, and actively participating in efforts to shift societal norms and attitudes that perpetuate IPV.

It is important to acknowledge that some victims of IPV suffer multiple oppressions that are best approached from the angle of intersectionality. In such cases, philosophical considerations are meant to highlight the intersectional nature of IPV, whereby individuals may face multiple forms of oppression based on their gender, race, class or other social identities (Hegarty et al., 1998). Reflections emphasise the need to adopt an intersectional lens to understand the complex dynamics and experiences of IPV, and to develop inclusive and culturally sensitive interventions. These philosophical reflections recognise that IPV is not solely the result of individual actions but is influenced by broader social and structural factors. Such reflections highlight the social determinants of IPV such as poverty, inequality, limited access to resources and discriminatory norms. They call for policy-makers to address these structural issues to create a society that is more conducive to non-violence and well-being.

It is important that perpetrators of IPV are held responsible and accountable for their actions (Camp, 2018). A philosophical reflection on the role of IPV perpetrators explores notions of responsibility and accountability in addressing IPV. It calls for collective responsibility, urging individuals, communities, institutions and governments to take proactive measures to prevent violence, support survivors and hold perpetrators accountable (Ncube and Ndlovu, 2020). This reflection emphasises the importance of creating a culture of accountability and rejecting the culture of silence and impunity surrounding IPV. It builds into the transformative justice and healing agenda. Thus, such philosophical perspectives often advocate for transformative justice approaches to address IPV by making sure that all reported cases are prosecuted. Furthermore, these approaches focus on healing, restoration and addressing the root causes of IPV rather than solely providing punitive measures. They emphasise the need for comprehensive support services, trauma-informed care and programmes that promote healing, rehabilitation and behaviour change (Rakovec-Felser, 2014).

Human dignity and well-being are critical aspects of human flourishing (Konyana, 2023). Philosophical reflections on the dignity of victims of IPV emphasise the inherent dignity and worth of every individual, underscoring the importance of promoting the well-being of survivors of IPV. These reflections call for comprehensive support systems that prioritise the physical, emotional and psychological well-being of survivors, ensuring their rights, safety and autonomy (WHO, 2012). Such philosophical reflections can inform the development of ethical frameworks, policy decisions and interventions to address IPV in Zimbabwe during and after the COVID-19 pandemic. They provide a broader perspective that goes beyond immediate responses, encouraging deeper reflection on the underlying values, beliefs and societal structures that contribute to IPV and the pathways towards long-term changes in intimate relationships.

Philosophical perspectives underscore the role of education and critical thinking in preventing IPV. They advocate for comprehensive and age-appropriate education that promotes healthy relationships, consent, gender equality and non-violence. These reflections call for equipping individuals with the knowledge, skills and critical-thinking abilities necessary to challenge societal norms and actively contribute to creating a violence-free society.

By delving into these philosophical reflections, policy-makers, activists and communities can gain deeper insights into the complex nature of IPV and develop more nuanced and effective strategies to address it. These reflections encourage critical thinking, ethical considerations and a holistic approach to creating a society free from violence.

Can Intimate Partner Violence Be Contained?

In response to this question, this section can answer in the positive way. Global efforts to prevent IPV and all other forms of domestic violence against women are intensifying following the acknowledgement that IPV is a scourge which disproportionately affects women and girls. To this end, the United Nations Women's 16 days of Activism against Gender-Based Violence (25 November–10 December), which started in 1991, has been an annual programme. It is important to note that the activism to end violence against women is no longer confined to the 16 days. It has become an everyday activity to increase awareness of the pandemic, galvanise advocacy and share information and innovations. The 2022 theme was "UNITE! Activism to end violence against women and girls by 2030." Although sexual harassment and other forms of violence against women continue to occur on streets, in public spaces and online, emerging research findings show an increase in calls to ending all forms of domestic violence in many countries, particularly after the outbreak of the COVID-19 pandemic which magnified IPV and other forms of domestic violence (Davies et al., 2022). However, it has been noted that IPV survivors have limited information and awareness about available support services. In some countries, huge resources and efforts have been diverted from other programmes to respond to violence against women and the COVID-19 pandemic but the uptake of these programmes has been small due to lack of information. At the global level, the UN Women is working on prevention of violence and access to essential services such as health, justice and policing, social services, helplines and coordination of these services, to provide support to those who have experienced and/or witnessed IPV. Faith-based organisations (FBOs) have also sought to address the challenge of IPV (Le Roux and Pertek, 2022).

Interventions to Prevent Intimate Partner Violence during the COVID-19 Pandemic

During the COVID-19 pandemic, the risk of IPV increased globally, including in Zimbabwe. The pandemic brought about additional stressors, economic challenges and restrictions on movement, creating an environment where IPV could escalate. To address this issue, specific intervention strategies could be implemented to deal with the rise of IPV against women during the COVID-19 pandemic. The challenges faced globally and the need for immediate action became imminent. To this effect, the National Institute for Health and Care Excellence [NICE] (2017) provided guidelines aimed to improve the response to domestic violence and abuse in general, ensuring that victims receive comprehensive support and that perpetrators are held accountable. The early detection of IPV was the first step to intervention. Early detection is often instituted by healthcare professionals during routine check-ups, as research has shown that victims often complain of various symptoms (chronic pain, back pain, headaches, among others) requiring medical attention (Di Franco et al., 2021). However, early detection of IPV is not obvious. It involves everyone, including health, social and mental healthcare professionals, people working in the criminal justice system and abuse services, police officers, victims of violence and the general public among others. Awareness of the signs of IPV and reporting such an awareness to the appropriate agency is important for both professionals and the general public.

Evidence suggests that multi-disciplinary interventions can minimise the shadow of IPV. To this end, Su et al. (2021) suggested some intervention strategies which include the reform and development of regulations and laws plus educational programmes that are meant to curb IPV. The development and increase of shelters or homes for victims of IPV is another strategy that can reduce the impact of IPV. Furthermore, the provision of mental health support and the development of face-to-face solutions are the other intervention strategies including the creation of new escape plans. It is important that the strategies are implemented in a culturally sensitive manner, taking into account the unique context of Zimbabwe and the diverse needs of survivors. Collaborative efforts involving government agencies, civil society organisations, community leaders and individuals are essential to successfully curb IPV during the COVID-19 pandemic.

Governments can reform and develop regulations and laws to improve the prevention of IPV against women. One possible way is to develop a national registration system for abusers that would allow people to investigate whether their partner has a history of abusive behaviour (Express Web Desk, 2021). This can go a long way in reducing the potential dangers faced by victims. The database could also provide valuable insight for future cases and could potentially improve the prevention of IPV. In some instances, after victims reported IPV, due to threats and fear for their lives, they drop the charges. It would be best if new legislation would accelerate the court action process and at the same time ensure the continuation of investigations, regardless of whether the victim has withdrawn the charges. This would further prevent the recurrence of IPV (European Parliament, 2020). It is important, once a report is filed by victims, for police and social services to demand immediate court action according to the assessed risk.

Educating individuals about domestic violence, the different types of violence, how to seek help and gather support is important in acknowledging this social phenomenon and preventing it (Taub, 2020; The Guardian, 2020). Many non-governmental associations and government organisations are developing psycho-educational programmes to inform the public about domestic violence. These psycho-educational programmes are available for different communities, such as schools, businesses, companies, universities, among others. Psycho-educational campaigns could inform more women that might be experiencing abuse on how to acknowledge abuse and seek help from the appropriate services. Raising awareness about IPV can help both victims and perpetrators seek support and minimise their engagement within the abusive environment. Educating different communities could also help to prevent women from experiencing IPV in the future. Changing norms, values and prejudices towards IPV is a goal that should be relentlessly pursued.

Conclusion

The chapter has argued that IPV has been a huge but overshadowed plague of all times. This argument is premised on the scope and magnitude of IPV across the world. It has been highlighted in this chapter that the outbreak of the COVID-19 pandemic in 2019 globally did not overshadow IPV. Instead, the outbreak escalated IPV when the lockdown stringent measures to contain the spread of the coronavirus restricted movements and kept people in their homes (Ndlovu and Ncube, 2020). And, for three years, the COVID-19 pandemic witnessed a significant increase in social risk factors of IPV and subsequent escalations in the frequency and severity of IPV. The world is geared towards ending IPV and all forms of gender-based violence by recognising violence against women and girls as a worldwide pandemic and through the continued activism to end violence against women by 2030. As noted earlier, FBOs and Churches, as well as non-governmental organisations (NGOs), have all joined hands in this mammoth fight in ending violence against women.

By delving into the philosophical reflections submitted in this chapter, policy-makers, activists and communities can gain deeper insights into the complex nature of IPV and develop more nuanced and effective strategies to address it. These reflections encourage critical thinking, ethical considerations and a holistic approach to creating a society free from violence. The COVID-19 pandemic had a significant impact on societies worldwide, and Zimbabwe was no exception. According to Okoro and Mubako (2021), the pandemic exacerbated existing gender inequalities and social norms, leading to increased rates of domestic violence, intimate partner violence and sexual exploitation.

When examining the philosophical reflections on IPV during this period, several key points emerge. First, the pandemic exacerbated existing social inequalities, economic hardships and stressors, which can contribute to an increase in IPV. The philosophy of social justice highlights the importance of addressing these underlying factors to create a more equitable society and reduce violence in intimate relationships.

Second, the ethical principle of non-violence and respect for human dignity underscores the necessity of preventing and addressing IPV. It is essential to recognise the rights of every individual to live free from violence and to foster a culture that promotes healthy relationships based on equality, consent and mutual respect.

Third, philosophical perspectives on empathy and compassion emphasise the need for support systems and services for survivors of IPV. The pandemic has presented challenges in accessing such resources, making it crucial to prioritise their availability and ensure that survivors have the necessary assistance, counselling and legal protection.

Furthermore, philosophical reflections on power dynamics and gender inequality shed light on the underlying causes of IPV. Addressing these issues requires not only immediate interventions but also broader societal changes, including education, awareness campaigns and challenging harmful gender norms and stereotypes.

In conclusion, the philosophical reflections on IPV during COVID-19 in Zimbabwe underscore the need for a comprehensive approach that encompasses social justice, non-violence, empathy and gender equality. By addressing the root causes of violence and providing support to survivors, Zimbabwe can strive towards building a society that values and promotes healthy relationships while working towards a more just and equitable future.

Notes

1 The chapter recognises the value of the activists' preference for the term, "survivors." However, there are also strong philosophical reasons for retaining the term, "victims," as this chapter does in some instances. The chapter uses the two concepts interchangeably.

2 Although the male perpetrator and a female victim is the most common pattern in IPV cases, female perpetrators and male victims are not uncommon.

References

Ansara, D. and Hindin, M. (2010). Formal and informal help-seeking associated with women's and men's experiences of intimate partner violence in Canada. *Journal of Social Science Medicine*, 70(34), 1011–1018. Doi.10.1016/j.socscimed.2009.12.009.

Breiding, M. J., Chen J. and Black, M. C. (2010). *Intimate Partner Violence in the United State*. Atlanta, GA: CDC, National Center for Injury Prevention and Control.

Camp, A. R. (2018). Pursuing accountability for perpetrators of intimate partner violence: The peril (and utility?) of shame. *Georgetown Law Faculty Publications and Other Works*. Available at: https://scholarship.law.georgetown.edu/facpub/2122

Chingarande, A. and Chingarande, G. (2020). Philosophical reflections on the impact of COVID-19 on intimate partner violence in Zimbabwe. *Journal of African Studies and Development*, 12(2), 40–53.

Davies, R. L., Rice, K. and Rock, A. J. (2022). The effects of COVID-19 social restrictions and subsequent informal support limitations on intimate partner violence: An opinion piece. *Frontiers in Global Women's Health*, 3, 829559. Doi: 10.3389/fgwh.2022.829559.

Di Franco, M., Martines, G. F., Carpinteri, G., Trovato, G. and Catalano, D. (2021). Domestic violence detection amid the COVID-19 pandemic: The value of the WHO Questionnaire in Emergency Medicine. *QJM International Journal of Medicine*, 114, 637–641.

European Parliament (2020). *Tackling Violence against Women and Domestic Violence in Europe—The Added Value of the Istanbul Convention and Remaining Challenges*. Brussels, Belgium: Think Tank, European Parliament. Available at: www.europarl.europa.eu.supporting-analysesExpress Web Desk. Chinese City.

Express Web Desk.(2021). Chinese City launches database for couples considering marriage to check if partner has domestic abuse history. Available at: www.indianexpress.com/article/world/chinese-city-launches-database-for-couples-considering-marriage-to-check-if-partner-has-domestic-abuse-history-6474157/

Fuller, R. (2015). *Domestic Violence: Characteristics of Abusers and Victims*. New York, NY: New York Behavioral Health.

Hegarty, K. and Roberts, G. (1998). How common is domestic violence against women? The definition of partner abuse in prevalence studies. *Australian and New Zealand Journal of Public Health*, 22(12), 49–54.

Kelly, J. B. and Johnson, M.P. (2008). Differentiation among types of intimate partner violence: Research update and implications for interventions. Available at: www.terapiafamiliar.cl/intranet/archivos/kELLY%20%20jOHNSON%202008.pdf

Kelly, M. G. E. (2014). *Foucault and Politics: A Critical Introduction*. Edinburgh: Edinburgh University Press.

Konyana, E. G. (2023). "Indigenous Conceptions of Human Dignity." In: Brett G. Scharffs, M. Christian Green, and Simeon O. Ilesanmi (Eds.), *African Conceptions of Human Dignity* (pp. 29–46). Stellenbosch, South Africa: African Sun Media. Available at: https://doi.org/10.52779/9781991260253.

Kuruk, P. (2002). Customary law: A sociological perspective. In P. Kuruk (Ed.), *Customary Law and the New Generation*. New Delhi: Serials Publications.

Le Roux, E. and Pertek, S. (2022). *On the Significance of Religion in Violence Against Women and Girls*. London: Routledge.

Mburia-Mwalili, A., Clements-Nolle, K., Lee, W., Shadley, M. and Wei, Y. (2010). Intimate partner violence and depression in a population-based sample of women: Can social support help? *Journal of Interpersonal Violence*, 25, 2258–2278. Doi: 10.1177/0886260509354879.

Minna, L. and Gayle, B. (2022). Experiences of intimate partner violence during lockdown and the COVID-19 pandemic. *Journal of Family Violence*, 37(6), 969–977. Doi: 10.1007/s10896-021-00260-x.

Mpofu, E. and Nkomo, L. (2020). Intimate partner violence in Zimbabwe during COVID-19: A philosophical reflection on the ethical implications. *Journal of Ethics in Social Sciences* 8 (2), 257–272.

Mukanagana, F., Moyo, S., Zvoushe, A. and Rusinga, O. (2014). Gender based violence and its effects on women's reproductive health: The case of Hatcliffe, Harare, Zimbabwe. *African Journal of Reproductive Health Women's Health and Action Research Centre*, 18(1), 110–122.

National Institute for Health and Care Excellence [NICE] (2017). Domestic violence and abuse: Multi-agency working. Available at: www.nice.org.uk/guidance/ph50 (Accessed on 3 December 2022).

Ncube, G. and Ndlovu, N. (2020). Intimate partner violence in Zimbabwe during COVID-19: A philosophical perspective on transformative justice approaches. *Journal of Social and Development Sciences*, 11(2), 12–28.

Ndlovu, N. and Ncube, G. (2020). Perspectives on gender-based violence during COVID-19 lockdown in Zimbabwe: A philosophical inquiry. *Journal of Research in Gender Studies*, 10 (2), 387–403.

Ndulo, M. (2011). African customary law, customs, and women's rights. *Indiana Journal of Global Legal Studies*, 18(1), 12–25. Available at: www.repository.law.indiana.edu/ijgls/vol18/iss1/5.

Nkomo, M. (2017). Roora/lobola as a transfer of property: A critical analysis of the concept in Zimbabwean law. *Journal of African Law,* 61(2), 147–162.

Okoro, E. A. and Mubako, S. (2021). Gender-based violence and the COVID-19 pandemic in Zimbabwe: A philosophical analysis. *Journal of Gender and Social Issues*, 20(2), 44–61.

Peterman, A., Potts, A., Thompson, K., Shah, N., Oertelt-Prigione, S. and van Gelder, N. (2020). *Pandemics and Violence against Women and Children. CGD Working Chapter 528.* Washington, DC: Centre for Global Development. Available at: www.cgdev.org/publication/pandemics-and-violence-agaisnt-women-and-chidlren.

Rakovec-Felser, Z. (2014). Domestic violence and abuse in intimate relationship from public health perspective. *Health Psychology Research*, 2(5), 182.

Rheeder, A. L. (2018). Respect for privacy and confidentiality as a global bioethical principle: Own reasons from a Protestant perspective. *Scientific Electronic Library Online.* 52(3). Available at: www.dx.doi.org/10.4102/ids.v52i3.2316

Su, Z., McDonnell, D., Roth, S., Li, Q., Šegalo, S., Shi, F. and Wagers, S. (2021). Mental health solutions for domestic violence victims amid COVID-19: A review of the literature. *Global Health*, 17(2), 59–67.

Sullivan, C. (2017). Understanding how domestic violence support services promote survivor well-being: A conceptual model. *Journal of Family Violence*, 33, 123–131. Doi: 10.1007/s10896-017-9931-6.

Taub, A. (2020). A new COVID-19 crisis: Domestic abuse rises worldwide. *The New York Times*, 6 April 2020.

The Guardian (2020, 12 April). Revealed: Surge in domestic violence during Covid-19 crisis | Domestic violence | The Guardian.

Togarasei, L. and E. Chitando (Eds.) (2021). *Lobola (Bridewealth) in Southern Africa: Implications for Gender Equality*. Cham: Palgrave Macmillan.

United Nations. (2019). *Advice for the public: Getting vaccinated.* Available at: www.who.int/emergencies/diseases/novel-coronavirus-2019/covid-19-vaccines/advice.

Walby, S. and Towers, J. S. (2017). Measuring violence to end violence: Mainstreaming gender. *Journal of Gender Based Violence*, 1, 11–31. Doi: 10.1332/239868017X14913081639155.

World Health Organization (WHO). (2012). *Global and regional estimates of violence against women: Prevalence and health effects of intimate partner violence and non-partner sexual violence.* Geneva: WHO. Doi: 10.2471/ BLT.12.111798.

World Health Organization (WHO). (2019). *COVID-19 Dashboard.* Available at: https://covid19.who.int.

World Health Organization (WHO). (2020). *The rise and rise of interpersonal violence-an unintended impact of the COVID-19 response on families*. Available at: www.euro.who.int/en/health-topics/Life-stages/pages/news/news/2020/6/the-rise-and-rise-of-interpersonal-violence-an-unintended-impact-of-the-covid-19-response-on-families.

World Intellectual Property Organization. (2013). *Customary law, traditional knowledge and intellectual property: An outline of the issues.* Microsoft Word - overview Customary_Law.doc (wipo.int).

5 The Feminine Quadrant of Girlhood, Motherhood, Wifehood, and Widowhood in Titus 2:3–5

A Hermeneutical Discussion in the Context of Christian Women, HIV and AIDS, and COVID-19 in Zimbabwe

Lovejoy Chabata

Introduction

HIV and AIDS and COVID-19, like sadistic siblings, have combined to inflict gendered suffering of womenfolk as girls, mothers, wives, and widows. This researcher postulates a quadrant of girls, mothers, wives, and widows as peculiar victims and survivors of HIV and AIDS, and COVID-19. While the two pandemics have scathed menfolk as well, but, due to gender stereotypes relating to prescribed roles of the girl child, mothers, wives, and widows, women have been hit harder by the repercussions of HIV and AIDS and COVID-19 than men (Manyonganise 2022: 233). Plan International (2020) stated that the world was home to one and a half billion girls, of whom 600 million are adolescents whose future was bleak due to COVID-19-related disruptions in education, diminishing social support structures, early marriages, unplanned pregnancies, and child-headed families. Vanderhout et al. (2020) argued that COVID-19 had uniquely affected the girl child and the family by disrupting routines, changing relationships and roles, and altering usual childcare.

An exegesis of Titus 2:3–5 reveals that the patriarchal community of Crete had prescriptive onerous roles for elderly women, mothers, young women, and for widows. This study seeks to unpack how the Cretan Church's Christian values governing women's behaviour have been affected by the exigencies and vicissitudes of HIV and AIDS and COVID-19 with a particular reference to the Zimbabwean context. Thus, we investigate how HIV and AIDS and COVID-19 have impacted on women as they fulfil their gendered roles in Zimbabwe's male-dominated society. The chapter examines distinct impacts of the pandemics on the girl child, mothers (both the single and the married), the elderly women, and widows. It brings focus to areas of fundamental women's rights, economic development, health, education, and childcare. The goal of the chapter is to expose the ways in which HIV, AIDS, and COVID-19 have affected Christian women as they are sandwiched between patriarchal and religious gender stereotypes. In essence, the chapter is undergirded

DOI: 10.4324/9781003494546-6

by the United Nations' Sustainable Development Goal (SDG) (5) which focuses on gender equality and SDG (10) aimed at reduced inequalities. In this pursuit, the chapter interrogates contemporary approaches to gender-based violence and draws attention to the need for new strategies to counter gender-based violence in preparation for future pandemics.

Methodology

This exegetical analysis of Titus 2:3–5 assumes an Afrocentric Biblical Hermeneutical (ABH) paradigm called "textual appropriation". "Textual appropriation" denotes the practice of allowing two different cultural contexts to dialogue and relate through interpolation, critique, genre comparison, juxtaposition of one text against another, reading two contexts alongside each other for purposes of drawing comparisons (Sanders 2016: 35). Rugwiji (2020: 1) defines hermeneutics of appropriation as a scientific interpretation of a theme that is applied in a context different from its original one. Textual appropriation in this study refers to the adoption and application of Titus 2:3–5 to an African, Zimbabwean context. This approach is largely informed by the ABH paradigm that makes the African social cultural context the subject of interpretation (Adamo 2001). This chapter follows Adamo's (2015) view that ABH is interpreting the *Bible* for transformation in Africa. Guided by Adamo's view of interpreting scriptures for social change, communal engagement, and development, ABH is employed in this chapter to discuss how cultural and religious gender stereotyping sentenced the girl child, mothers, elderly women, and widows to the worst scenarios of pain and suffering exacerbated by the effects of HIV and AIDS and COVID-19 in Zimbabwe. Considering that the chapter is dealing with women, our methodology deliberately adopts Mercy Amba Oduyoye (2001: 38), Musa Dube (2001), Isabel A. Phiri (2004: 16), and Fiedler and Hofmeyr (2011), among others' contention that the subject of women's liberation is a key aspect in ABH. The chapter is informed by the agenda of the Circle of Concerned African Women Theologians to liberate women from violence in the church and society. Feminist theological hermeneutics is, therefore, within the eagle's eye lens of ABH in this chapter.

The ABH approach is supported by the historical critical method (HCM) as a window for unpacking the context in which Cretan Church women were laden with heavy burdens that have found their way into the contemporary Christian world, the Zimbabwean Christian community being no exception. Soulen and Soulen (2001: 79) argue that the HCM investigates the origins of ancient texts to understand the world behind the text. The primary goal of HCM is to discover the text's primitive or original meaning in its original historical context and *sensus literalis historicus* (literal meaning). The method further seeks to reconstruct the historical situation of the author and recipients of the text. The HCM is used to examine the text's historical origins such as the time, the place in which the text was written, people and customs that are mentioned or implied in the text. The HCM umbrellas source criticism, textual criticism, form criticism, redaction criticism, and tradition criticism. Soulen and Soulen (2001: 79) further state that the method operates under two assumptions. First, that the social, political, and cultural contexts affect the creation of any literary work. Second, that the meaning of literature can change over time as the same contexts do change. In this chapter, the HCM provides insights into the social, political, and cultural worldviews of Titus 2:3–5 in terms of their impingement on the rights and welfare of women. After gaining an understanding and appreciation of that world behind the pericope, the researcher then applied textual appropriation in a dialogue between the Cretan Christian Church and the Zimbabwean Christianity and women contexts.

Data Collection

The chapter mainly relied on secondary sources, which include books, journals, newspapers, magazines, websites, government and United Nations publications, and civic organization publications. The purposive sampling technique was used as a supportive tool in the information-gathering process. The author held open discussions with prominent theologians in Zimbabwe, whose identities have been withheld for ethical reasons. The discussants were selected because of their experience working with women organizations, their extensive research on gender issues in Zimbabwe, and their broad interactions with church and parachurch organizations that are involved in advancing the rights of the girl child. The following section approaches Titus 2:3–5 from an Afrocentric perspective.

Exegesis of Titus 2:3–5: An Afrocentric Textual Appropriation

The Context of Titus 2:3–5

Cohick (1989) states that in the Greco-Roman world, women's roles mainly revolved around the household. Cohick (1989) further mentions that mothers took care of their children, lands, and households, while their husbands served in the military or travelled on business. Mahaney (2004) argues that the Greco-Roman household was for a girl child, a waiting room for marriage as life's goal. Mowczko (2014) finds that in the Christian community of Crete the dominant view was that the woman's primary domain was the home for purposes of caring for her husband and children. Mowczko (2014) further argues that the Cretan Christian community relegated the girl child to a destiny of marriage and having children. In Titus 2:3–5, Paul instructs older women to train (σωφρονίζωσιν) young women to love their husbands (φιλάνδρους), love their children (φιλοτέκνους), to be self-controlled and to be pure (ἁγνάς), to be busy at home (οἰκουρούς), to be kind or good and to be submissive (ὑποτασσομένας) to their husbands so that the Gospel would not be besmirched. The charge given to older women (πρεσβύτιδας) in the text was consistent with the roles of mature Christian women in New Testament times generally (Huizenga 2013). Their roles included teaching and admonishing young women in the work of God, visiting the sick, prisoners, provided hospitality to Christian travellers, as well as caring for abandoned infants and orphans. The older women ministered to each other as well as to women in the church of any age, single, married, or widowed.

The social and religious milieu in Crete at the time the pericope was written should be understood. From chapter one, we glean that some ascetic beliefs were catching up with young Christian women who no longer valued marriage and having children. Some women were choosing to remain single, to be single mothers, to stay independent of husbands and family ties. Mowczko (2013) argues that the prevailing Jewish myths and epicurean philosophies circulating in Crete were luring Christian women into asceticism. Titus is given the curriculum of the training for young women, married and single mothers, some of whom could be parenting widows. The facilitators of the training are older women. Krell (2007) states that the content of the training was addressing behavioural gaps in women that include negligence of conjugal obligations, laxity in and dereliction of child-care duties, abandonment of household chores such as preparing meals, washing, cleaning, and maintaining a proper home ambience.

Questions that arise as we read Titus 2:3–5 are (1) Does the text sentence the girl child to homemaking?; (2) Are older women, young women, mothers, and young girls to be confined to the home and be restricted to domestic duties?; (3) Does the text prescribe and define womanhood for all situations and contexts, including pandemic circumstances?; (4) What are the implications of this pericope for contemporary settings in terms of women empowerment? To answer these questions, we isolate a few keywords in the text for study. The purpose for doing so is to explore the author's intended meaning which will be used later to mirror the Cretan Christian women's social setting into the modern Zimbabwe Christian women's *sitz-im-leben* (setting in life).

Ambiguous Use of οἰκουρούς (Titus 2:5): Women Working at Home

Thayers' Greek-English Lexicon (1889: 442) states that the original word used to denote persons who work in a home is οἰκουργος. Thayer contends that the term only appears in Titus 2:5 and not anywhere else in the New Testament. Thayer (1889: 442) propounds that οἰκουρος is used in reference to keeping a home or taking care of household or domestic affairs. Liddell and Scott (1940) translate οἰκουρούς in the fifth verse of Titus 2:3–5 to mean that young women should consider working at home. However, an etymological analysis of the contextual usage of "workers at home" in BDAG (2000: 700) suggests that the appropriate term should have been οἰκουργούς, not οἰκουρούς. The term οἰκουργούς is a compound term made up of οἰκος (house) and ἐργούς (workers). The combination of the two terms, therefore, produces the sense of workers at home, which is not implied in οἰκουρούς, whose sense is that of a person who keeps a house or simply staying in a house. The sense that is cascaded by οἰκουρούς is that of gardeners and housemaids who could be described as home-watchers or -keepers. I, thus, categorically argue that if the intended meaning was that young women should be circumscribed to homemaking and domestic chores, οἰκουργούς should have been used.

From the previous discussion, a two-tier possible meaning of Titus 2:5 is deducible: (1) Either the text suggests that the older women, young women (girls or just married), and mothers (single or married or widowed) were required to be confined to the domestic and household vicinity as full-time homeworkers in the sense of οἰκουργούς (workers), whereby they would not be allowed to engage in outdoor formal occupations. Or, (2) women would be expected to take care of household chores as moral obligations but not as an occupation in the sense of οἰκουρούς (keepers, carers). Mowczko (2014) contends that the sense of οἰκουρούς in Titus 2:5 should not be taken above or beyond the idea of young women having to comply with the usual moral standards of the typical Roman matron. The usual moral standards expected of a Greco-Roman woman included sexual purity, looking after the house, rearing children, one who gladdens in health, one who tends in sickness, one who partners in good fortune, and one who consoles in misfortune.

φιλάνδρους: Lovers of Husbands

Thayer (1889: 653) states that φιλάνδρους denotes the special love that only a wife can give to her husband. BDAG (2000: 1055) says that the term φιλάνδρους is used in Titus 2:4 to describe the affection, fondness, and craving that a woman has for her husband. The word captures the idea of a commitment to fulfilling conjugal rights, soothing, keeping company, and befriending within the confines of marriage. Mowczko (2014) finds that the moral standards expected of young married women in a Greco-Roman society included the ability to whet the sexual desires of their young husbands. Older women were also expected to temper the unseasonable harshness of old age in their husbands by ensuring adequate emotional stability through sexual gratification. Paul encouraged that young women comply with social norms governing moral conduct so that the Word of God would not be maligned. Young wives and young widows who Paul refers to in Titus 2:5 and elsewhere in 1 Timothy 5:14 were expected to manage their conjugal rights in a manner that did not put the Gospel into disrepute.

φιλοτέκνους: Lovers of Children

Thayer (1889: 655) translates φιλοτέκνους as referring to the protective and caring love that a mother has for her offspring or children. The sense depicted is that of love that fights and strives for the good of the offspring. BDAG (2000: 1059) interprets the term to not only connote the mother's love for her children but also the children's love for the mother. There is thus a sense of mutuality in the love that Paul is encouraging between mothers and their children in Titus 2:4. BDAG further emphasizes the need for parental indulgence in the welfare and well-being of the children. The mothers are admonished to demonstrate self-control (σώφρονας) and lead a pure life (ἁγνάς). These virtues constitute a behaviour (καταστήματι) pattern that the mothers are expected to pass on to their children. The mothers are, therefore, supposed to be teachers of good morals (καλοδιδασκάλους) to their children. Mothers were expected to inculcate virtues of chastity, purity, and self-control, especially in the girl child given that Greco-Roman wives were arrogated the duty of training girls, while the husband trained the male child (Cohick 1989). Vine et al. (1985: 583) explain that the virtue of self-control (σώφρονας) in Titus 2:5 entailed abstinence, continence, temperance, sobriety, and temperateness. Mothers were, thus, expected to teach their children to avoid sexual indulgence outside of marriage. The following section reflects on the appropriation of the passage in the Zimbabwean context.

The Appropriation of Titus 2:3–5 in the Zimbabwean Context

The question of the roles prescribed for Christian women discussed in Titus 2:3–5 is very much relevant to the Zimbabwean context as the country strives to introduce gender equality in terms of United Nations SDG (5) on gender equality and SDG (10) on reduced inequalities. The Cretan Christian Church is a gendered space, just as the Christian Church generally, but most eminently African Independent Churches in Zimbabwe hold socially constructed views on what behaviours and roles are designated as male or female (Mapuranga 2013). In both the Cretan Christian Church and the Zimbabwean contexts, women are expected to be submissive to their husbands (ὑποτασσομέναςτοῖςἰδίοιςἀνδράσιν) and not to compete or upstage men in church roles of leadership. It is also notable that some African independent churches in Zimbabwe cite Greco-Roman settings of gendered pericopae such as 1 Timothy 2:11–15 and 1 Corinthians 14:34 to prescribe roles for women (Mapuranga 2013). The subordination of women to men is apparently a ubiquitous phenomenon in Christian churches in Zimbabwe whereby women mostly exercise leadership responsibilities in their own ladies' fellowships but still need to consult with and report to their male counterparts (Machingura and Nyakuhwa 2015: 112). Women in such spaces experience theological and cultural forms of violence, with the *Bible* and culture being weaponized to keep them away from taking up leadership positions in church and society.

Taringa and Mushishi (2016) argue that while there are attempts to liberate women from oppressive biblical traditions in mainline Christian churches in Zimbabwe, Christian women are still bound at home by an oppressive traditional Shona patriarchal culture and customs. Chabata (2021) contends that Christian women in Zimbabwe are still caught up in the labyrinth of patriarchal shackles given that most of the leaders at the helms of churches in the country were born and raised in gendered roles, norms, and values. Fiorenza's (1989) idea of the "discipleship of equals" in which she called for the recognition of women as equals with men in salvation has remained elusive due to die-hard gender stereotypes that continue to relegate women to an inferior status in the churches. In this chapter, we argue that a patriarchally corrupted interpretation of Titus 2:3–5 finds a congenial base in Zimbabwe's Christian *sitz-im-leben* where women's place continues to be subordinate to that of men both in the church and at home (Magezi and Manzanga 2021).

We argue that an appropriate and contextual interpretation of Titus 2:3–5 which is diachronically consistent with contemporary drives for gender equality and women empowerment in Zimbabwe eschews and repudiates the traditional

Greco-Roman-based exegesis which enslaves women to gender stereotyped domestic duties. Consistent with the United Nations SDG (5) on gender equality and SDG (10) on reduced inequalities, this chapter adopts an interpretation that intends to advocate for the sharing of domestic duties between men and women. Such a trajectory is consistent with the admonition in the sixth verse for Titus to exhort young men to be sound minded in their dealings with their women counterparts. Paul says to Titus, τοὺςνεωτέρουςὡσαύτωςπαρακάλειςωφρονεῖν (the younger men, likewise, exhort to be sound minded). From the exegesis of Titus 2:3–5, we established the following phenomena which are analogous to the Zimbabwean ecclesial environment:

1 In the wifehood role, women are expected to maintain subservience (ὑποτασσομένας) to their husbands, to love their husbands (φιλάνδρους), and to train young women to also love their husbands.
2 In the motherhood role, women are expected to love their offspring (φιλοτέκνους), to ensure that the girl child remains sexually pure and not engage in promiscuity prior to marriage.
3 In the widowhood role, women are expected to raise children according to sound Christian standards as well as get married and love their husbands if they are still below the age of 60 years.
4 In the girlhood role, women are expected to exercise self-control (σώφρονας), remain chaste until marriage, and not engage in behaviour that tarnishes the image of the church.

Having appropriated the text to the Zimbabwe Christian context, we now discuss how HIV, AIDS, and COVID-19 impacted on women in their girlhood, motherhood, wifehood, and widowhood roles.

Reflections on How HIV, AIDS, and COVID-19 Impacted on Perceptions of Wifehood in Zimbabwe

The general social position of women in Zimbabwe makes it obligatory, mandatory, and unconditional for wives to render what are considered conjugal obligations to their husbands. As Bassett and Mhloyi (1991) contend, cultural norms which require women to comfort, love, and nurse their husbands, especially in times of the latter's health breakdown, expose wives to the challenging repercussions of HIV and AIDS. Basset and Mhloyi (1991) observe that there is an intersection of traditional cultural norms and Western Christian ethics that make married women helpless victims of the effects of pandemics. Generally, wives are not expected by cultural norms to refuse their husbands for sex on the grounds that the husband might transmit HIV to them. Nyamayemombe et al. (2010: 5) argue that wives have been exposed to spousal violence or intimate partner violence due to socially and religiously constructed gender stereotypes. Wives are censured if they insist on using protection, as African patriarchal values often anathematize condoms in marriage (Musandirire 2016: 66; Rwafa et al. 2019). Nyamayemombe et al.

(2010: 15) find that due to both cultural and religious reasons, wives often lack the ability to negotiate safer sex. Christianity, on the other side, also teaches wives to love their husbands in sickness, for better or worse until death, do they part. The misinterpretation of texts such 1 Corinthians 7:3–5 which state that married spouses should not restrict one another concerning sexual intercourse exacerbate the challenges that Christian wives face if the husband tests HIV positive. Many wives have been infected by HIV due to the cultural and religious requirement for them to love, care, nurse, soothe, and support their husbands for better or for worse till death (Sandasi and Cherewo 2006).

Titus 2:3–5 belongs to the category of biblical texts that have been used to augment and sustain power dynamics, gender roles, and those cultural practices that have deprived married women of their sexual autonomy and reproductive rights in Zimbabwe. Such texts are deployed as a form of spiritual and scriptural violence and have been dubbed "texts of terror" (Trible 1984). We have noted that unequal gender power between men and women sentences women to increased risk, vulnerability, and suffering. As Rwafa et al. (2019) argue, young women faced with the obligation of submission to their husbands lack the power to protect themselves against gender stipulations that arrogate to men control over women's sexuality and decision-making.

Women as wives were also on the receiving end of COVID-19-related complications. Primarily, the duty to sexually satisfy their husbands became a double burden due to the COVID-19 lockdowns. Some wives were almost reduced to sexual slaves as husbands who usually spent days at work now stayed in homes, with intensified sexual activity (Chigevenga et al. 2020). In some cases, the number of pregnancies astronomically increased due to hypersexual engagement of spouses during the COVID-19 lockdowns. This, however, is not to deny the agency that some wives exercised during the same period.

In the event of some husbands testing positive to COVID-19, the wife's role of comforting, loving, nursing, and soothing the husband was expected to continue according to cultural and religious customs. In cases where the wife was infected by COVID-19, she was still expected to ensure that the family had eaten a meal and that the home was well kept. The regulation of social distancing to curb the spread of COVID-19 could not be applied to husbands and wives even if one of them had contracted the virus. The wife was expected by the community and the church to stick with her husband in all situations, for better or for worse according to marriage vows. The exposure and risk of wives to COVID-19 infection through positive husbands was just as bad as it has been in the case of HIV spousal transmission. Gender injustice often reared its ugly head when the wife tested positive for COVID-19. In such a case, the husband usually did not take the responsibility of nursing the wife, choosing rather to refer her to her relatives or to medical centres. Thus, as Nhapi (2021) argues, there was a need for understanding COVID-19-induced social injustices for women and girls in Zimbabwe. Nhapi (2021) rightly observes that one of the key drivers reinforcing COVID-19-related social injustices against women was their socially constructed role as caregivers of the family and community. Wives are particularly expected to provide for family meals, nurse the sick, and to provide a safe and clean home environment. Among Shona communities, there is an adage that says, "*musha mukadzi*" (the wife makes the home) meaning that the married woman is pivotal to order and serenity in a home setting. HIV and AIDS and COVID-19 have made the responsibilities of wives heavier and more cumbersome than ever before. They precipitate gender injustice and intensify the psychological violence that many married women have had to contend with.

HIV and AIDS and COVID-19 Impacts on Motherhood

Women as mothers are expected to be paragons of love for their children (φιλοτέκνους) particularly and for the family generally. It is important for us to reflect on how the HIV and AIDS and COVID-19 pandemics have radicalized the role of mothers in family settings in Zimbabwe. As Tshuma et al. (2022) have observed, gender shifts have taken place in the home during COVID-19-related lockdowns and social distancing. The mother–child bond was no longer as intact as it used to be. The girl child had now found a new confidante in social media. As mothers strove to find means of putting food on the table for the children, they hardly found time to train the girl child in the ways prescribed by the community and the Christian church. On the other hand, Dziva et al. (2021) argue that pregnant and breastfeeding mothers are vulnerable to malnutrition and those who must take medication after meals end up succumbing to chronic infections such as HIV and AIDS due to insufficient food. During lockdowns and social-distancing restrictions, the churches were closed, schools were closed, and communal life was at a standstill. The influence of mothers on the girl child dwindled as COVID-19 combined with HIV and AIDS to exacerbate gendered inequalities between males and females in pandemic situations. There was a marked increase in the number of teenage pregnancies during the COVID-19 lockdowns in Zimbabwe (Ndlovu et al. 2020) and other parts of the world, including the Global North.

Nevill (2020) points out that single mothers in Zimbabwe found themselves having to work doubly hard to make ends meet as COVID-19 combined with the country's ever worsening economic instability to tighten screws of penury. Nevill (2020) observed that as mothers embarked on self-help projects, the traditional and religiously determined role of training the girl child in sound morals suffered lack of attention. Nevill (2020) further observes that rural mothers and the girl child were more on the receiving end of coronavirus than men and the boy child because as women they are responsible for household chores such as fetching water, firewood, gardening, washing, and cleaning at home. Social distancing to mitigate the spread of the coronavirus was difficult for mothers and the girl child in the rural setting since they inevitably met at village waterholes and washing rendezvous along rivers (Dziva et al. 2021). Plan International (2020) established that the outbreak of the coronavirus and HIV- and AIDS-related diseases increased young women's duties as they cared for ill family members as well as for children who were out of school.

Mususa et al. (2021) note that COVID-19 forced many mothers in Zimbabwe to revise their traditional hospitality and philanthropic roles as family incomes drastically dwindled. Loss of incomes, loss of savings, cost of home-based educational services, and food deficiencies forced the usually caring mothers to reduce their levels of support to members of extended families. It became normal to tell those who usually depended on the caring mothers that requests for help had to be minimized.

HIV and AIDS and COVID-19 Impacts on Girlhood

Both secular society and the church expect the girl child to exercise self-control, remain chaste, and maintain sexual purity until marriage. Tshuma et al. (2022) contend that one of the main challenges of COVID-19 was child marriages and teenage pregnancies. Due to COVID-19-related restrictions and lockdowns many teenage girls got engaged for marriage, while others were literally coerced to marry by their poor parents due to escalating poverty and food shortages. The influence of social media on the girl child during COVID-19 was also noteworthy. As some girl children spent the whole day on social media due to COVID-19-related restrictions, some ended up visiting dating sites, pornographic sites, same-sex marketing blogs, and revelling orgies sites (Dziva et al. 2021). There was a temptation galore for the girl child as some teenage girls fell prey to marauding sugar-daddies who preyed on vulnerable and desperate teenage girls. United Nations AIDS (2021) states that in Zimbabwe for people between 15 and 24 years, young women are twice living with HIV than men in the same age group. It has been further found that of the new infections during COVID-19, the majority were girls and women, with girls making up 63% of all infections (United Nations AIDS 2021).

The COVID-19 and HIV and AIDS pandemics have created conditions where structural poverty has more than doubled in Zimbabwe, resulting in many teenage girls dropping from schools, colleges, and universities. As the girls dropped from educational institutions, some found themselves in sex work, while others were married off by their poor parents. Yet others found themselves with unwanted pregnancies, while others found themselves infected with sexually transmitted infections, including HIV. Plan International (2020) notes that in Zimbabwe COVID-19 triggered new risks for girls which included early and forced marriage, violence, early pregnancy, and sexual exploitation, limited or no access to education, the increased risk of not ever returning to school when schools re-opened after coronavirus induced closures. Plan International (2020) also established that in the event of food shortages because of the pandemic, mothers sacrificially ate less, ate last, or may not eat at all as they sought to ensure that the family would have been fed. These factors confirm the structural violence that women and girls have faced in the context of pandemics.

It has been established so far that patriarchy, culture, religion, and poverty amalgamated with COVID-19-induced conditions which include loss of incomes, school closures, company closures, heightened gender-based violence, loss of employment, diminishing safety nets, deteriorating sexual and reproductive health to create disproportionately tough conditions for women and the girl child (Dziva et al. 2021). Gender-based violence is thus largely an outcome of social structures that are heavily skewed in favour of male chauvinism and dominance. Beliefs that relegate girls and women to the margins of authority, decision-making, and power are in the main causes of gender-based violence.

HIV and AIDS and COVID-19 Impacts on Widowhood

Dube (2022) argues that in Zimbabwe widowhood sentences women to extraordinary isolation in addition to stripping them of socio-economic decisions. Like other women who have husbands and children, widows are expected to keep a home and raise children according to moral standards approved by both the cultural and Christian communities. Dube (2022) explains that widows in Zimbabwe usually suffer social isolation whereby the widow is left disengaged in social interactions due to stigmas associated with losing a husband. The widow is also dealt another blow when in some instances her in-laws deprive her of the wealth and assets such as properties and land she acquired with her late husband (Field 2019). Such a state leaves widows vulnerable to exploitation by men who ride on patriarchal cultural norms to pounce on the hapless widows. The United Nations Zimbabwe (2020) notes that before the advent of COVID-19, widows were already struggling to sustain their livelihoods due to insufficient infrastructure and services in rural areas. COVID-19 then came as a double-edged sword to inflict more suffering on widows as it pushed widows further below the poverty datum line. Social distancing and other coronavirus-related restrictions worsened the social isolation of widows. Widows who depended on informal trading such as vegetable vending, clothing flea markets, and cross-border trading were not spared from the COVID-19 restrictions (Chikazhe et al. 2021). Burke et al. (2021: 18) found that in Zimbabwe most families headed by widows experienced a full day without eating. As COVID-19 escalated from March 2020 to February 2021, it emerged that conditions in female-headed families further deteriorated to a level where meal sizes had to be decreased as a coping mechanism. In field research carried out in the southern part of Zimbabwe, Burke et al. (2021: 18) found out that the biting conditions of the pandemic caused a reduction in donor assistance, resulting in some widows getting too overwhelmed by family welfare responsibilities. In most cases, the widows ended up falling prey to sexual exploitation and gender-based violence at the hands of callous men.

Most of the evidence from secondary data and from oral discussions held with selected discussants buttressed the view that circumstances of the COVID-19 period made mothering responsibilities twice as difficult for widows than for women who were in marital unions with their husbands. As Field (2019) contends, stigmas and traditional superstitions have profound social, psychological, and moral impacts on women whose husbands have died. Communities and churches do not fairly consider the plight of widows when they judge them. In Paul's teaching on widows in the pastoral letters, including Titus 2:3–5 and 1 Timothy 5:9–11, he instructs young widows below the age of 60 years to get married and be joined to a husband so that they are not prone to sexual impropriety and temptation.

Overall Findings

The research has established that the social setting of Titus 2:3–5 where women perform communally determined roles is similar to the Zimbabwe situation where we find socially ascribed roles for women, girls, men, and boys (Masomera and Chigwanda 2020: 8). Like the situation in the life of the Church of Crete, women and girls in Zimbabwe are responsible for domestic chores, caregiving, and nursing the sick and elderly members of the family, cooking, cleaning, washing, fetching water and firewood. Over and above the basic domestic duties, women in both the Cretan and Zimbabwean contexts could do income-generating work outside the home, although their male counterparts dominated the outdoor world. As Masomera and Chigwanda (2020: 8) contend, COVID-19 upended and increased the burdens of women in their quadrant as girls, mothers, wives, and widows.

It has emerged that society's high moral expectations of the girl child often fail to take cognizance of structural vulnerabilities, violence, poverty, deep-rooted cultural and religious norms, and stereotypes that militate against her compared with the boy child. As Bird and Prowse (2009: 8) argue, the girl child belongs to the category of "fragile groups" of people together with widows, the elderly, and the landless. The girl child is more exposed to risk due to factors beyond their control such as peer pressure, a broken social background, loss of parents, beliefs that favour the male child in matters of property acquisition and inheritance laws. The research also revealed that the vulnerability of the girl child worsens during pandemic situations with the concomitant decline in support services and safety nets.

The research has also shown that pandemics create very tough conditions for motherhood. The combination of HIV and AIDS and COVID-19 increased the caring, nursing, cleaning, washing, cooking, and philanthropic obligations of mothers. Motherhood tasks became more cumbersome and overwhelming for mothering women whether single or married. However, the tasks became insurmountable for single mothers and widows whose susceptibility to gender-based violence increased as they fell prey to men who exploit women's desperation. The coronavirus global crisis disproportionately affected mothers and girls (Henriques 2020; UN Women 2020). The lockdowns that were introduced to prevent the spread of COVID-19 gave impetus to an increase of gender-based violence, especially intimate partner violence (United Women 2020).

The research has unearthed that women, who as wives were expected to love their husbands, found themselves having to "carry the cross" of not only loving the husbands but also to nurse the sick day and night due to the COVID-19-imposed lockdowns. Prior to the COVID-19 lockdowns many men would go to work, giving wives some breathing space. Both employed and unemployed women had to spend unusually long periods in the company of their husbands. The 24-hour presence of husbands in the home exposed some wives to gender-based violence in its physical, emotional, psychological, sexual, and verbal forms. Some wives got entangled in divorce cases due to intimate spouse frictions and violence.

This chapter has shown that COVID-19 exposed widows to debilitating and confounding socio-economic challenges against the unfavourable background of cultural and religious dynamics, norms and values that tend to stigmatize widowhood. The chapter has also revealed that pandemic situations in Zimbabwe tended to increase the number of widows as more men succumbed to the virus than women. COVID-19's combination with HIV and AIDS further entrenched gender inequalities between men and women as demonstrated by the fact that some women whose husbands had died continued to look for men who could help them look after them and their children in return for sexual favours. Pandemic restrictions also closed cross-border trading opportunities for widows who ended up resorting to illicit means of putting food on the table for their children.

Recommendations

If Zimbabwe is to win the war against gender injustices in terms of the United Nations SDG (5) on gender equality and SDG (10) on reduced inequalities, the following actions are recommended:

1 Community and church leaders need to do much more than hollow women empowerment rhetoric by allowing the voice of women in public policy formulation and implementation at all levels of society.
2 Discriminatory social, cultural, and religious norms that close opportunity doors in the face of women should be rid of through enforceable legislative instruments.
3 Deconstructionist, liberational, transformational, and gender-equality-driven biblical hermeneutics should be encouraged in theological institutions and faculties of theology and religious studies at universities.
4 Gender-equality advocacy should be scaled down to lower echelons of society as opposed to current practices whereby advocacy initiatives are circumscribed mostly to halls of fame such as academic conferences, United Nations symposia, African Union conferences, and ecumenical bodies and human rights associations' holiday resorts workshops where huge sums of money are gobbled up.

Conclusion

This chapter has shown that more research is needed on how pandemics affect women in their quadrant of girlhood, wifehood, motherhood, and widowhood. An area that needs special attention of scholarly research is how single mothers and widows have borne the burden of childcare in the wake of the diminution of social safety nets for the vulnerable during pandemics. There is also a glaring need for field-based research on how girl-child-headed families in rural settings have survived in pandemic situations in Zimbabwe. Previous research has focused on women and girls, often generalizing on how women are affected by patriarchal and cultural stereotypes. Future research on gender parity must create a methodological praxis that accommodates the views of the victims of social disparities as opposed to an elitist research paradigm in which academics and civic organizations speak or surmise on behalf of the marginalized girls, mothers, wives, and widows. This study has demonstrated that biblical scriptures can be deployed in the field of social transformation, elimination of violence, and the quest for gender equality and reduced inequalities.

References

Adamo, D. T. (2001). *Reading and Interpreting the Bible in African Indigenous Churches*. Eugene, Oregon: WIPF and Stock Publishers.

Adamo, D. T. (2015). "The task and distinctiveness of African Biblical Hermeneutics", *Old Testament Essays*, 28(1), 31–52.

Bassett, M. T. & Mhloyi, M. (1991). "Women and AIDS in Zimbabwe: The making of an epidemic", *International Journal of Health Services*, 21(1), 143–156.

BDAG (2000). *A Greek-English Lexicon of the New Testament and Other Early Christian Literature*, 3rd Edition, Revised and edited by Danker, F. W. Chicago: University of Chicago Press.

Bird, K. & Prowse, M. (2009). "Vulnerability, poverty and coping in Zimbabwe", *Chronic Poverty Research Centre Working Paper*, 136, 1–39. www.files.ethz.ch/isn/127317/WP136%20Bird-Prowse.pdf

Burke, N., Homan-Kee Tui, S., Madajewicz, M., Hambloch, C. Mlambo, S., Dube, T., Valdivia, R., Mare, L. & Mutter, C. et al. (2021)"Impacts of COVID-19 pandemic on the livelihoods in southern Zimbabwe", Report to the International Development Research Centre. https://agmip.org/wp-content/uploads/2021/08/Covid-19-impacts-in-Zimbabwe-FINAL-070221.pdf

Chabata, L. (2021). "Matthew 1:1-17: cultural subjugation of women in Shona communities in Zimbabwe: A hermeneutical study", *Studia Historiae Ecclesiasticae*, 47(2). http://dx.doi.org/10.25159/2412-4265/8174

Chigevenga, R., Mukorera, O., Masawi, P. & Mambure, R. D. (2020). "COVID-19: Double tragedy for women in high density suburbs of Zimbabwe", *Journal of Emergency Medicine Trauma and Surgical Care*, S1, 004.

Chikazhe, L., Mashapure, R., Chavhunduka, D. & Hamunakwadi, P. (2021). "Socio-economic implications of Covid-19 pandemic to women entrepreneurs: A case of the informal sector in Zimbabwe", *Business Management and Strategy, Macrothink Institute*, 12(1), 1–15.

Cohick, L. H. (1989). "Women, children and families in the Greco-Roman world", In Green, J. and McDonald, L. M. (eds.) *The World of the New Testament: Cultural, Social and Historical Contexts*. Michigan: Baker Academic.

Dube, M. W. (2001). *Other Ways of Reading: African Women and the Bible*. Atlanta: SBL.

Dube, M. (2022). "Isolation and its impact on widows: Insights from low-resourced communities in Binga District, Zimbabwe", *Social Sciences*, 11, 298. https://doi.org/10.3390/socsci11070298

Dziva, C., Zhou, I. & Zvobgo, E. F. (2021). "Covid-19 pandemic and women's vulnerabilities in Zimbabwe", *The Dyke*, 15(1), https://hdl.handle.net/10520/ejc-dyke_v15_n1_a8

Fiedler, R. N. & Hofmeyr, J. W. (2011). "The conception of the Circle of Concerned African Women Theologians: Is it African or Western?", *Acta Theologica*, 31(1), 39–57. DOI: https://doi.org/10.4314/actat.v31i1.3

Field, M. (2019). "Fighting the global burden of widows in poverty", *The Borgen Project*. https://borgenproject.org.

Fiorenza, E. (1989). *In Memory of Her: A Feminist Theological Reconstruction Origins.* New York: Crossroads.

Henriques, M. (April 2020). "Why Covid-19 is different for men and women", *BBC*. www.bbc.com/future/article/20200409

Huizenga, A. B. (2013). *Moral Education for Women in the Pastoral and Pythagorean Letters: Philosophers of the Household*. Leiden: Brill.

Krell, K. R. (2007). "Motherly mentoring" (Titus 2:3-5). *Timeless Word Ministries Publication*. http://media1.razorplanet.com/share/511079-7965/siteDocs/Titus2.3-5MothersDay2007ep.pdf

Liddel, H. G. and Scott, R. (1940). *A Greek-English Lexicon*. Revised and augmented by Sir Henry Stuart Jones. Oxford: Clarendon Press.

Machingura, F. & Nyakuhwa, B. (2015). "Sexism: A hermeneutical interrogation of Galatians 3:28 and women in the Church of Christ in Zimbabwe", *Journal of Pan African Studies* 8(2), 92–114.

Magezi, V. & Manzanga, P. (2021). "A public pastoral assessment of the interplay between 'she was created inferior' and cultural perceptions of women by Christian men in Zimbabwe as accessory to gender-based violence", *Verbum et Ecclesia*, 42(1), a2139. https://doi.org/10.4102/ve.v42i1.2139

Mahaney, C. (2004) *Feminine Appeal*. Wheaton: Crossway.

Manyonganise, M. (2022). "When a pandemic wears the face of a woman: Intersections of religion and gender during the COVID-19 pandemic in Zimbabwe". In Sibanda, F., Muyambo, T. & Chitando, E. (eds.), *Religion and the Covid-19 pandemic in Southern Africa* (pp. 232–243). London and New York: Routledge.

Mapuranga, T. P. (2013). "AICs as a gendered space in Harare, Zimbabwe: revisiting the role and place of women", *Studia Historiae Ecclesiasticae*, 39(2), 303–317.

Masomera, A. & Chigwanda, E. (2020). "Care rapid gender analysis for Covid-19", *Care International in Zimbabwe*. https://careevaluations.org

Mowczko, M. (2014). "Did Paul mean 'workers at home' or 'keepers at home' in Titus 2:5?". https://margmowczko.com/workers-at-home-or-keepers-at-home-in-titus-25/via@MargMowczko (accessed 23 September 2014).

Musandirire, B. (2016). "Is marriage a haven or a risk for women in Zimbabwe in the era of HIV and AIDS: Interrogating women's reproductive rights in marriage", University of Zimbabwe, Master's Degree in Women Law, Harare, Zimbabwe.

Mususa, D., Jowah, E., Satuku, S. & Mutungamiri, H. (2021). *Field Based Evidence on the Impact of COVID-19 on Citizens in Zimbabwe.* Vol. 2. SIVIO Institute. www.sivioinstitute.org

Ndlovu, C. C. C., Makoni, P. & Gundani, H. V. (2020). "COVID-19 lockdown related teenage pregnancies: Concept analysis", *International Journal of Advance Research in Nursing*, 4(1), 101–108.

Nevill, C. (2020). "Zimbabwe: Coronavirus will affect women and girls more than anyone", *World Food Programme Newsletter*, 9 April 2020.

Nhapi, T. (2021). "COVID induced social injustices for women and girls: Perspectives from Zimbabwe", *Social Dialogue Magazine*, University of Johannesburg, Department of Social Work and Community Development, South Africa.

Nyamayemombe, C., Mishra, V., Rusakaniko, S., Benedict, C., Gwazane, M., & Mukweza, P. et al. (2010). The association between violence against women and HIV: Evidence from a National Population-Based Survey in Zimbabwe. *Zimbabwe Working Papers*, Number 4. United States Agency for International Development (USAID Funded Project).

Oduyoye, M. A. (2001). *Introducing African Women's Theology*. Sheffield: Sheffield Academic Press.

Phiri, I. A. (2004). "African women's theologies in the new millennium", *Religion and Spirituality*, 18(61), 16–24. DOI: https://doi.org/10.1080/10130950.2004.9676034

Plan International (2020). "Covid-19: The impact on girls", *Plan International Publications*, 23 April 2020. https://plan-international.org

Rugwiji, T. (2020). "The quest for hermeneutics of appropriation as a thematic approach for critical biblical interpretation", *HTS Teologiese Studies/Theological Studies*, 76(1), a5392. https://doi.org/10.4102/hts.v76i1.5392

Rwafa, T., Shamu, S. & Christofides, N. (2019). "Relationship power and HIV sero-status: an analysis of their relationship among low-income urban Zimbabwean postpartum women", *BMC Public Health*, 19, 792. https://doi.org/10.1186/s12889-019-7137-y

Sandasi, M. & Cherewo, N. (2006). "The impact of HIV and AIDS on women in Zimbabwe", *Third World Network*, 186. www.twn.my/title2/women/2006/TWR186p38.doc

Sanders, J. (2016). *Adaptation and Appropriation: The New Critical Idiom*. London and New York: Routledge.

Soulen, R. N. & Soulen, K. R. (2001). *Handbook of Biblical Criticism*. Louisville, Kentucky: Westminster John Knox Press.

Taringa, N. T. & Mushishi, C. (2016). "Mainline Christianity and gender in Zimbabwe", *Fieldwork in Religion*, 10(2), 173–189. DOI: https://doi.org/10.1558/firn.v10i2.20267

Thayer, H. J. (1889). *Greek-English Lexicon of the New Testament*. New York: Harper & Brothers.

Trible, P. (1984). *Texts of Terror: Literary-feminist Readings of Biblical Narratives*. Philadelphia: Fortress Press.

Tshuma, B. B., Tshuma, L. A. & Ndlovu, N. (2022). "Media discourses on gender in the time of COVID-19 pandemic in Zimbabwe". In Dralega, C. A. and Napakol, A. (eds.), *Health Crises and Media Discourses in Sub-Saharan Africa* (pp. 267–283). Cham: Springer.

United Nations AIDS (2021). *Global HIV and AIDS Statistics*. www.unaids.org/en/resources/fact-sheet

United Nations Women (April 2020). "Violence against women and girls: The shadow pandemic". www.unwomen.org/en/news/stories/2020/4/statement-ed-phumzile-violence-against-women-during-pandemic

United Nations Zimbabwe (2020). *Building Back Resilience of Rural Women after Covid-19*. zimbabwe.un.org

Vanderhout, S. M., Birken, C. S., Wong, P., Kelleher, S., Weir, S., & Maguire, J. L. et al. (2020). "Family perspectives of COVID-19 research", *Research Involvement and Engagement*, 6(69). DOI: https://doi.org/10.1186/s40900-020-00242-1

Vine, W. E., Unger, M. F. & White, W. Jr. (1985). *Vine's Complete Expository Dictionary of the Old and New Testament Words*. Nashville: Thomas Nelson.

6 Women's Organizations versus Organizing Women?

Questioning Silences and Selective (Re)presentation of Women in a COVID-19 Context in Zimbabwe

Molly Manyonganise

Introduction

COVID-19 led to a surge in cases of gender-based violence (GBV) cases in Zimbabwe, with statistics showing that women were mostly the unfortunate victims (see Manase and Bhatasara, 2022). It is interesting to observe how the women's movement reacted/responded to cases of GBV on women in different standings in life. The women's movement is a global phenomenon, but distinctive in each particular context, both in terms of structures and agendas (Margolis, 1993: 379). Molyneux (2002) views women's movements as fundamentally modern phenomena. She argues that "although there have been forms of female collective action in pre-modern societies, these have tended to be either small-scale, or spasmodic eruptions of social protest." Rupp (2011, n.p.) provides a detailed analysis of the emergence and historical development of the transnational women's movement. She explains that the first wave of a transnational women's movement emerged in the late nineteenth century out of a variety of connections forged across national borders. For example, a variety of movements comprising abolitionism, socialism, peace, temperance, and moral reform called women's attention to the cross-national character of their causes and brought together women from different nations in mixed-gender meetings (Rupp, 2011, n.p.). In her analysis, the transnational development of feminist ideologies led to formalized contacts among women committed to women's rights. While Rupp's work is insightful in understanding transnational women's movements, it is limited in that it concentrated on developments in North America and some parts of Europe. It left out developments in the so-called Third World countries. Ray and Korteweg (1999) provide a glimpse into the context in which women's movements emerged in Third World countries. They argue that many of the women's movements in these countries have been tied to nationalist and anti-colonial projects. Hence, they call for the need to examine the complex relationships between women's movements in the first and third worlds, on the one hand, and between women's movements in the Third World and the nationalist movements in which they are linked (Ray and Korteweg, 1999: 55). While

DOI: 10.4324/9781003494546-7

this may be true, Ray and Korteweg generalized their analysis and failed to consider how women who were disillusioned by the way they were excluded by post-colonial governments went into civil society and founded women's organizations. As Kumar (2000: v) notes, some women became disillusioned with the leaders of political parties who initially professed commitment to gender equality, but later reneged on this commitment. I will return to this discussion later on in this chapter.

Within each context, the women's movement comprises various women's organizations. Women's organizations refer to all voluntary organizations, led and managed by women that promote women's welfare and gender equality (Kumar, 2000: vi). Harcourt (2006) classifies women's organizations into three categories, namely: (i) radical women's organizations that operate as much as they can as women-only groups outside 'patriarchal' institutions and do not accept outside funding; (ii) professional women's organizations; and (iii) religious and charity organizations. These categories speak directly to the Zimbabwean context. Hence, this chapter seeks to analyze the operations of women's organizations in Zimbabwe. Its intention is to examine the mandate of selected women's organizations in Zimbabwe with a view to question and critique their silence and selective (re) presentation of women in Zimbabwe. The focus of the chapter is to problematize their naming vis-à-vis the materiality of their operations. Questions to be answered in this chapter are (i) Is the term 'women's organizations' the same as 'organizing women'? Or (ii) Does the term 'women's organizations' refer to entities that are led by women who may not pay attention to women's needs? (iii) In a pandemic context, what informs their responses to GBV? (iv) In what way are these responses affected by the prevailing political environment? Data for the chapter were gathered through online media response analysis as well as newspaper articles. Secondary sources were used to support primary data. Theoretically, the chapter is informed by the African Womanist-centered community organizing framework.

Theoretical Framework

The study is informed by the African Womanist-centered community organizing framework. It, therefore, utilizes the woman-centered model in community organizing. Pyles (2009: 6) notes the complexities of trying to define 'community' as a concept in a diverse, globalized, and technological world. The notion of community is perceived as harkening a wide range of ideas, including trust, mutuality, commitment, and solidarity as well as the ideas of contestation, conflict, and exclusion (Smith, 2001, cited in Pyles, 2009: 6). For Pyles (2009), a community may be united by shared racial, ethnic, cultural, or other identities, though not necessarily sharing of geographic location. As such, 'community' can be defined as a group of people with a common affiliation, identity, or grievance that may be geographically or non-geographically based (Pyles, 2009: 7). Shields (2021) views community as an ever-expanding space of inclusion, and that the aspirational vision of inclusive community presupposes power within relations. In this case, by community, the study's focus is beyond geographical boundaries as it conceptualizes the category 'women' as a community bound together by their gender identity as well as a desire to be free from patriarchal oppression in all its forms within Zimbabwe's socio-economic and religio-political arenas.

Community organizing is difficult to define. Pyles (2009: 6) notes that most organizations and organizers do not necessarily fall under a strict definition of community organizing. For example, in her opinion, grassroots and non-governmental organizations (NGOs) or non-profit organizations are variously engaged in social services, advocacy, and any attempt to include some activities and exclude others is difficult and ultimately a false construction. Stall and Stoecker (1998: 730) opine that "community organizing can refer to the entire process of organizing relationships, identifying issues, mobilizing around those issues, and building an enduring organization." This study specifically focuses on women's organizations in Zimbabwe through the lens of a woman-centered organizing model. Staples (2012: 287) situates community organizing within the social justice discourse. Thus, he defines community organizing as "collective action by community members drawing on the strength of numbers, participatory processes, and indigenous leadership to decrease power disparities and achieve shared goals for social change" (Staples, 2004: 1–2). Such organizing for Staples is linked to distributive justice, equal rights, self-advocacy, and collective empowerment. He further argues that organizing for social justice "is rooted in collective processes for political education, critical analysis, consciousness raising, reflecting, envisioning, goal-setting, planning, acting, evaluating/assessing and reflecting again" (Staples 2012: 294). Within the discourse of community organizing, scholarship on gender has highlighted the need to look at the concept through a gender lens (Crenshaw, 1991; Naples, 2009; Mizrahi and Greenwalt, 2017). These scholars urge us to be cognizant of the multiple ways in which gender is produced and reproduced in the arena of social organizing. Stall and Stoecker (1998: 730) are of the view that gender structure as social products of interactional work are produced and reproduced through social movements' action. In their analysis, community organizing is part of social movements' work that takes place closest to the grassroots and is more often done by women. They further aver that the women-centered model begins with 'organizing' community through building expanded private sphere relationships and empowering individuals through those relationships. In this case, women-centered organizers view justice not as a compromise between self-interested individuals but as a practical reciprocity in a network of relationships that make up a community (Shields, 2021). For the women-centered model, while organizing efforts are rooted in the private sphere, issues, or relationships, the organizing process problematizes the split between public and private spaces, since it includes 'activities' which do not fall smoothly into either category (Stall and Stoecker, 1998: 733). As a model, it also focuses on narrowing the divide between private and public spaces. For example, Stall and Stoecker (1998: 749) note that issues formerly perceived to be private like violence against women have been made public issues. In this case, they view a women-centered model's strength as in building relationships that can sustain the struggle. However, in their analysis, its weakness lies in the fact that the model cannot transform the public sphere. To this, they argue, "after moving issues into the public sphere, their resolution is subject to the competitive, masculine, zero-sum processes of that sphere" (1998: 750). Stall and Stoecker's analysis is crucial for this study as it informs it on whether women's organizations in Zimbabwe have managed to organize women in such a way that the struggle for women's liberation from all forms of patriarchal oppression is sustained. Before turning to this discussion, the study provides a brief history of women's organizations in Zimbabwe.

Women's Organizations in Zimbabwe: An Overview

Women's organizations in Zimbabwe make up the women's movement in the country and are part of the African as well as the global women's movement. In a way, the emergence of the Zimbabwe women's movement can be located within the broader feminist movement of the 1960s and the 1970s, though formal organizations representing women became visible after the 1980 independence. Women had successfully protested the 1961 Rhodesian constitution, which allocated less parliamentary seats to blacks while favoring whites (Charumbira, 2020). Such protest acted as a catalyst for the struggle for independence against the Rhodesian government to get to its militant phase (Bhebe, 1989). During the armed struggle, women played significant roles both as combatants as well as supporters. The Marxist ideology upon which the armed struggle was anchored enabled women to analyze their marginalized status under colonial rule as well as African patriarchy. They came to the conclusion that while they were fighting racism, this struggle needed to go hand in hand with their own struggle against patriarchy. Hence, they began to question oppressive cultural practices such as *lobola* (bride price). In their analysis, *lobola* was the major cause for their marginalization as it promoted women's objectification. They, therefore, demanded full recognition and the dismantling of oppressive cultural practices. Nudged by the desire to overthrow colonial rule, political parties in the struggle for independence promised women that they would recognize the equality of men and women after the struggle. A speech given by Robert Mugabe at the Xai Xai ZANU Women's League conference in 1979 attested to the party's desire to recognize that men and women were equal since they had fought in the struggle side by side (Lyons, 2004). Scholarship focusing on gender and history has shown the hypocrisy in all these promises as men in political leadership in post-colonial Zimbabwe reneged on all of them (Nhongo-Simbanegavi, 2000; Chogugudza, 2006; Chung, 2006; Manyame-Tazarurwa, 2011). The post-colonial state pushed women to the margins and expected them to go back and fulfil the culturally constructed women's roles, while men did the governing of the state. Most women who had held high hopes for gender equality felt that the state was not accommodative to women becoming equal partners in building the new state. Law (2014) explains this clearly when she says

> During Zimbabwe's protracted liberation struggle of the 1960s and 1970s, the leaders of the Zimbabwe African National Union (ZANU) consistently argued that women's liberation would be prioritized in the post-colonial dispensation.

> However, shortly after independence in April 1980, it became clear that other factions of ZANU felt that women's emancipation had been satisfied through the achievement of national liberation itself.

Women, therefore, moved away to civil society. Geisler (2004) notes that women's organizations emerged as a result of women being disillusioned by the patriarchal nature of the new nation state. Van Eerdewijk and Mugadza (2014) provide a historical perspective of the women's movement in Zimbabwe. They argue that the women's movement in the country grew tremendously after independence as pressure mounted from women who were part of the liberation movement as well as what Essof (2013: 33) calls university-educated professional women. Throughout Zimbabwe's history, just before and after independence, a number of women's organizations were formed, namely, Zimbabwe Women's Bureau (ZWB) (1978), Women's Action Group (WAG) (1983), the Zimbabwe Women's Resource Centre and Network (ZWRCN) (1990), Musasa Project (1991), the Women and Land Lobby Group (WLLG) (1998), and Women's Coalition of Zimbabwe (WCoZ) (1999). It is beyond the scope of this chapter to provide the clients' charter for each of these women's organizations suffice to say generally they focus on (re)presenting women on issues to do with their rights as well as organizing women to protest inequality (see Ranchod-Nilsson, 2006; Manyonganise, 2023). After 2000, more women's groups emerged which were even more militant such as Women of Zimbabwe Arise (WOZA) (2003), Women in Politics Support Network (WIPSU) (2003) among others. Therefore, Win (2004a: 19) argues that the women's movement in Zimbabwe grew both quantitatively and qualitatively. The movement also became associated with regional women's organizations such as Women in Law and Development in Africa (WILDAF) (1990). Since government focused on improving the lives of citizens, more effort was put on development. As such, most women's organizations collaborated with the state and donors in this endeavor. Win (2004a) notes that coalescing around common goals enabled the women's movement to grow, as there was no conflict between the women's organizations and the state. However, some scholars have noted the confrontation that happened between the state and WAG in 1983 when some women were rounded up and arrested in Harare and Bulawayo for cases of suspected prostitution. For Win (2004a: 21), this 'clean up' campaign was aimed at getting rid of 'undesirable' elements, that is, single and unmarried women in the urban areas. This was viewed by WAG as a blatant abuse of these women's rights particularly to freedom of movement and association. McFadden (2005: 9) is of the view that in Zimbabwe, the women's movement was the first expression of women's demands for an autonomous identity, when women rejected the persistence of colonial laws that restricted their mobility, particularly in the cities and marked them as prostitutes. Unfortunately, the rest of the other groups in the first decade after independence premised their survival on depoliticized messaging. The introduction of the Economic Adjustment Structural Programme (ESAP) led civil society to start having questions about human rights, democratization of the state, and governance. Women's organizations began to question women's exclusion from governance processes. Hence, when the process of coming up with a new constitution arose, women's groups in Zimbabwe formed a Women's Coalition in 1999 and produced a Women's Charter which raised their demands on women's rights. When the final draft of the proposed constitution was tabled in 2000, it had left out women's demands, hence, the Women's Coalition joined opposition forces against the draft.

Lobbying and Advocacy: Counting the Women's Movement's Successes

There have been gains realized through the women's movement's engagement in lobbying and advocacy. The women's movement worked closely with the Ministry of Community Development and Women's Affairs as well as the Ministry of Justice to push for gender-sensitive legislation. This resulted in the enactment of the Legal Age of Majority Act (LAMA) (1982), which recognized that both men and women become adults at the age of 18; Sex Disqualification Removal Act (1985) which dealt with issues of equal pay for equal work regardless of one's gender; Matrimonial Causes Act (1985) and the Labour Relations Act (1985) which govern divorce procedures and guarantees paid maternity leave for women, respectively. The LAMA was a historic win for women who had been treated as minors until then.

While Win (2004) notes the non-confrontational nature of the majority of women's organizations in Zimbabwe in their engagement with the state, McFadden provides a different view. She particularly notes the influences of the United Nations conferences in Nairobi (1985) and the Beijing Platform for Action (1995) as platforms that changed the way the women's movement engaged with the state. In her analysis, such conferences enabled women in the movement to acquire more radical perspectives and new strategies of engagement (2005: 10). When the movement realized that the legal statutes were anti-women, it started training women in the use of gender analysis and feminist approaches to women's rights. It also played a key role in the formulation of the African Women's Charter. The use of the law against women led to the movement confronting the state. McFadden (2005: 12) explains that:

> Several key confrontations with the state occurred in the 1990s related directly to women's aspiration to ownership of the bodily integrity and family property, which served as turning points in terms of black women's consciousness as individuals within a resistant patriarchal neocolonial state. Beside the poor response on the part of the state to actively respond to rising rates of femicide and brutal sexual violation of women across the class spectrum, Zimbabwean women faced off with the state on the use of inheritance of family property. The culturally approved plunder of family resources at the death of a male spouse brought women to the point where they demanded state protection of their property rights.

Hence, some of the positive changes being witnessed in inheritance laws today need to be credited to the women's movement. Organizations such as Musasa Project have been very consistent in challenging GBV against women and girls as well as providing shelter/safe havens to victims of GBV.

In 2000, the ZANU PF-led government lost the constitutional referendum to the coalition led by the National Constitutional Assembly (NCA) to which the Women's Coalition belonged. The women's movement was emboldened to see that victory against the government was possible. However, the government became more hostile to civil society organizations. I will return to this discussion later. When Zimbabwe became a signatory of some international and regional conventions and protocols on gender, the women's movement pushed for the realignment of national laws and policies to convey this reality. For example, the women's movement demanded that government should recognize the United Nations Declaration of Human Rights (UNDHR), the Convention for the Elimination of All Discrimination against Women (CEDAW), the African Charter on Human Rights (ACHR), the Maputo Gender Protocol, as well as the Southern African Development Community (SADC) Gender Protocol. In the 2013 constitution, the women's movement lobbied for Zimbabwe to take note of these conventions and protocols in order for it to be part of the global community. Through the UNDHR and CEDAW, the women's movement pushed government to adopt the Affirmative Action Policy in 1995. From a gender perspective, the policy was aimed at gender-mainstreaming in all sectors of society through the recognition of the historical marginalization of women. The widely discussed quota system today is a result of the policy.

The Women's Movement in Turmoil: Challenges of Negotiating the Political Terrain of a Patriarchal State

Despite the successes, failures of the movement are also notable. The women's movement in Zimbabwe has historically suffered from disunity and a failure to focus on a common goal. Political events obtaining in Zimbabwe from 1995 to the present have had a profound effect on the women's movement in Zimbabwe. McFadden blames the influence of what she calls 'moderate' elements within the movement in the first decade after independence, which for her reflected the continuing influences of nationalist ideology and an uncritical relationship with the state implying that the movement remained largely mainstream and unthreatening to the state. By 2004, Win had noted that political events in the country had affected the existing unity of the women's movement (at times due to infiltration) and necessitated the need to go beyond female identity as the sole unifying factor between individuals and organizations. To start with, Win notes that when WAG confronted the state in 1983, most women's organizations remained silent and actually sidelined it. She argues that "it became apparent that the reluctance of many to be associated with WAG came from the perceptions of its political positions and its confrontational approach to both the state and to patriarchy." This was indicative of disharmony in the movement of how far and using which methods the movement could go in challenging the excesses of the state. Hence, when the Women's Coalition was formed in 1999 out of women's organizations in the country during the constitutional process, the state formed its own Constitutional Commission and appointed some members of the coalition into this commission. Win (2004) and McFadden (2005) allude to the fact that this was a litmus test for the coalition which it failed to pass. It was worse that some directors of women's organizations accepted the government appointments to the commission. A good example was Selina Mumbengegwi, who was then the director of WAG. McFadden (2005) goes further to also accuse the National Constitutional Assembly (NCA) which the Women's Coalition had chosen to work with in coming up with a new constitution on abusing the Women's Coalition to further patriarchal interests. She argues that the Women's Coalition failed to participate alongside other players as an equal partner in the constitution-making process. Hence, a reflection shared by Essof (2013) shows a movement that was tired and unconvinced of what it had managed to achieve. As a result, in 2004, Win (2004: 25) saw a movement in disarray, while McFadden in 2005 concluded that the women's movement was in doldrums both ideologically and in activist terms (2005: 15).

While the government advanced the rhetoric of women's empowerment, its actions showed the contrary. For example, while the Ministry of Community Development and Women's Affairs was mandated to advance gender equality, the government felt threatened by it. Hence, as years went by, it was relegated to a department within the Ministry of Political Affairs which was then housed at the ZANU PF headquarters. Ranchod-Nilsson (2006) views this action as a way of trying to monitor and control women's activities. Due to its close proximity with a political party (ZANU PF), the Women's Affairs Department lost legitimacy and the women's movement dissociated itself from it. Hence, if this was meant to coopt the women's movement in Zimbabwe, it dismally failed. Essof (2013: 35) argues that the Ministry of Community Development and Women's Affairs was never powerful within government. However, the disempowerment of the women in government enabled the patriarchal state to undo the gains women had up to that point. The men in government began to attack women's demands for the abolition of *lobola*. When the women's movement demanded that women be protected from being victimized by their husbands' relatives when their husbands die, Mugabe cautioned them not to make unnecessary demands. He refused women the right to inherit their husbands' property and advised women to allow their husbands' relatives to inherit and then take care of the widowed women. The 1999 Venia Magaya case (Magaya vs. Magaya) in which the Supreme Court ruled that women can never be treated as equal with men under customary law, and therefore, could not inherit their father's estate even if they were recorded in his will, did not only challenge LAMA but was also the last nail in the coffin for the movement. It is at this point that the women's movement saw the insincerity of government. Hence, women's organizations had to lobby for international support for their cause to be heard.

The hostility of the state towards civil society is also to blame for the ineffectiveness of the women's movement beyond 2000. McFadden pinpoints the 1995 Private Voluntary Organizations Act (PVOA) as a tool used by the Zimbabwe government to mute and/or crush civil society organizations that had become powerful contestants with the state. Van Eerdewijk and Mugadza (2014: 16) view the enactment of the Public Order and Security Act (POSA) and the Access to Information and Public Privacy Act (AIPPA) in 2002 as negative developments that greatly constrained the work of the women's movement. This legislation forced women's organizations to narrow the scope of their activities and advocacy strategies. Some organizations were stopped from implementing activities in parts of the country, while others faced suspensions. Out of fatigue and threats of government, some women leaders fled the country. A good example is Betty Makoni of Girl Child Network. Women's organizing was, therefore, greatly affected by the sudden departure of a sizeable number of women activists. Van Eerdewijk and Mugadza (2014) correctly note that WAG, Musasa Project, and the Association of Women's clubs found themselves unable to operate in areas where they had functioned since the early 1990s. The NGO bill, which was passed into law in 2004 and was meant to repeal the 1995 PVOA, was castigated by human rights activists as authoritarian. It increased government surveillance of NGO activities as well as restricted demonstrations which were mostly used by women's organizations. This greatly impacted on the women's movement's ability to meaningfully organize women. For Van Eerdewijk and Mugadza (2014: 17), "the slump in the women's movement's mobilization needs to be understood in the context of shrinking space for civil society actors due to the political upheaval at the national level and the general socio-economic decline." For them, these factors placed focus on economic survival at the expense of organizing. From then until now, women's organizations have been closely monitored by the state. Hence, COVID-19 happened in a context of a women's movement under suspicion and a highly volatile political environment.

Women's Organizations in a COVID-19 Context in Zimbabwe

The COVID-19 pandemic aggravated already existing gender inequalities globally and Zimbabwe in particular (Manyonganise, 2022). The genealogy of pandemics shows that a disaggregation of their effects is indicative of the fact that women and men are affected differently with women bearing much of their impact. Women have seen their lives being affected in almost all areas that define their existence, that is, socially, economically, politically, and religiously. The world in general and Zimbabwe in particular experienced an increase in GBV in all its forms during the pandemic. Hence, GBV has been named 'a shadow pandemic' alongside the COVID-19 pandemic. At its onset, a number of women's organizations in Zimbabwe collated statistics of domestic violence particularly emanating from intimate partners. They also responded through a demonstration when a victim of child marriage died while giving birth at a Johanne Marange African Apostolic Church shrine. However, they were accused of silence when Marry Mubaiwa was being persecuted by her husband, Vice President Constantino Chiwenga. The silence of the organizations was also noted when the MDC-Trio (now CCC) was abducted, tortured, sexually abused, and later arrested for allegedly faking their abduction. When Thokozani Khupe was recalled from parliament by Douglas Mwonzora, their silence was also noted. The following were some of the headlines in the media in Zimbabwe:

- Women's pressure groups abandon Mary Chiwenga in her time of need (*New Zimbabwe*, 12 September 2021).

Despite the MDC-Trio having faced their ordeal in May 2020, women's organizations only reacted in April 2021 and the media carried reports like

- Women's groups statement on the harassment of Hon Joana Mamombe (WALPE).

For Marry Chiwenga, the groups finally broke their silence at the end of September 2021 and the media reported that

- Women rights organizations finally rally behind Marry Chiwenga (Bustop TV, 25 September 2021).

It needs to be noted that the women's organizations only responded after an outcry from the public noting their silence. A cursory analysis of Twitter postings by Zimbabweans show their displeasure with the way the women's movement remained silent when women in politics were being victimized by the state. It is possible that the repressive nature of the Zimbabwean state and the COVID-19 WHO protocols restricted the organizations' activities during the pandemic. Like in all sectors, the pandemic led the women's movement to adopt technology as a tool for its activism (Toyana, 2020), but this has not been very effective. In the face of accusations of the movement for its silence and selective (re)presentation of women in Zimbabwe, it is imperative to decipher the possible causes of such attitudes.

Women's Organizations versus Organizing Women

Van Eerdewijk and Mugadza (2014) view the women's movement in Zimbabwe as having been engaged in women's organizing since its inception in Zimbabwe after independence. However, they note that the movement has gone through highs and lows in its long history of mobilizing at different levels and on various issues. I have already indicated the harsh political terrain that the movement has had to negotiate. Despite all this, questions arise as to why we continue to see the mushrooming of women's organizations with little meaningful women's organizing on the ground. I argue in this chapter that the nomenclature 'women's organizations' does not always translate to the practical organization of women for purposes of confronting oppressive patriarchal systems. After all, what is in a name? If anything, the naming can remain but with no effect at all. Within the Zimbabwean context, the organizations have become toothless bulldogs and the state does not care about them at all. As the COVID-19 was raging, the state was in the process of amending the PVOA without fear of the resistance from civil society. Legal experts have raised questions about the amendments which are generally viewed as regressive. Fears were raised that if passed into law, the amendments directly affect gender development in Zimbabwe. The amendment bill seeks to restrict the operations of civil society organizations and silence them from demanding accountability from government on perceived political and human rights abuses. Women are the major victims of political violence. Such restrictions would result in government going scot-free when it fails to guarantee security to its citizens or when it is violating the rights of citizens. Ray and Korteweg (1999: 62) note that more often the state directly intervenes in women's organizing and that many newly independent states have forbidden any form of autonomous political organizing including women's organizations. In this case, their observation that women's movements are fundamentally shaped by political processes, specifically the crises of the state, is true of Zimbabwe.

One of the things that is clear in Zimbabwe is that working in the NGO sector has its own benefits. As the NGO sector largely depends on donor funding, getting a position in women's organizations is lucrative for the salaries paid in foreign currency, the imposing vehicles driven, as well as the many opportunities for foreign travel which bring with them travel allowances. Women's organizations have become sources of livelihood for most middle-class women who lead them. Hence, at times they take pictures of people at gatherings that have nothing to do with their line of operations in order to prove that they are effective on the ground, when nothing concrete is being done in the area of organizing women for effectively challenging oppressive patriarchal systems working against women's liberation. I, therefore, view the mushrooming of women's organizations like Katswe Sisterhood and Nhanga among others, being led by young women as a reaction to the gatekeeping by old women in this sector for purposes of safeguarding their livelihoods. What still needs to be established is whether there is anything new being brought by the new organizations particularly in effectively organizing women to demand their full rights and dignity. The greatest challenge for the women's movement has been its failure to construct context-relevant programs due to its strong reliance on foreign funding. As donors dictate agendas, the movement has developed 'follow the money' attitude. Hence, when people expect it to respond to certain issues, the movement has remained silent for fear of aggrieving its funders. To a certain extent, this has led the movement to remain elitist. An article written by Stewart and Taylor (1995) titled 'Women Organising Women – Doing It Backwards and in High Heels' attests to this elitism.

Geisler (1995, 2004) has shown how the women's movement is suspicious of women politicians even if it would have seconded them to the positions. The bone of contention is in how women politicians quickly elevate their offices above sisterhood at times supporting oppressive patriarchal structures instead of working towards their demolition. This suspicion and disgruntlement could have informed their response to the cases of the MDC-Trio as well as Marry Mubaiwa-Chiwenga. Win (2004) has dismissed gender as a common denominator that can unify women in the movement. This can extend to women who seek the movement's support in times of need. In response to Joice Mujuru's elevation in 2004, Win cautioned women against celebrating a woman who, all her life, had sided with the 'boys' to the extent that Christiansen (2007) calls her 'father of the nation'. She argued:

> Those of us in civil society who are called upon to support women in leadership, need to know why we are supporting them. I do not want to work with radarless women who seem to think that politics is a value-free science, or those who abuse office. What we need are women who will use their leadership positions to liberate themselves and other women. Trading on their biology alone is not enough. I am angry with the kind of women who at every other time in their lives forget they are one of us, and remember their vaginas when it suits them.
>
> (Win, 2005)

I am of the view that this is a widely held view in women's organizations in Zimbabwe and it could have informed the general silence on Marry Mubaiwa-Chiwenga's predicament. My interaction with a director of one of the women's organizations in Zimbabwe got me the understanding of why they were also silent when Thokozani Khupe was recalled from parliament. For her, it was karma. Khupe had recalled other women from parliament, yet the movement had been working flat out to increase the number of women in politics. She never consulted them prior to her taking that action, yet when she was recalled, she remembered that they were an important constituency. Hence, their response is generally informed by the need for justice as well as interests. Molyneux (2002) has shown that the women's movement does not have homogeneous interests. Hence, while some focus on practical interests, others are concerned with strategic ones, which eventually determine how they respond to issues. As Margolis (1993: 393) notes, "specific issues often hold very different connotations for women from different national and class backgrounds." What this entails is that identity matters in women's movements.

Earlier on, I alluded to the effects of AIPPA and POSA on the women's movement. The 'new' government enacted the Maintenance of Peace and Order Act (MOPA) to replace POSA. However, the law has been viewed as more brutal than POSA. What this entails is that women's organizations continue to be restricted by oppressive laws in their operations. For example, since they have been perceived as regime change agents, it means that delving into political issues can be detrimental for their existence. The Marry Mubaiwa-Chiwenga case is both political and civil, while that of the MDC-Trio and Thokozani Khupe are political. The volatility of the political environment in Zimbabwe effectively silences women's organizations. They, therefore, become selective in their responses. Non-political cases receive more attention as the organizations play it safe.

Conclusion

The intention of this chapter was to analyze what informs the women's organizations' selective response to women's issues in Zimbabwe. It attempted to interrogate the politics of naming, for example, whether the nomenclature 'women's organization' automatically translates to practically organizing women. The overall discussion brings us to make a number of conclusions. For example, women's organization can retain the name, while no meaningful organizing of women happens. In this case, naming merely becomes a label that has got nothing to do with what the organizations claim to be doing. Second, the political environment coupled with restrictive legal instruments have greatly hampered women's organizations' effort at mobilizing women for a common cause. Third, advancing the agendas of donors result in the organizations focusing on non-relevant issues. Fourth, the organizations are also informed in their responses by concepts of justice particularly when high-ranking political women figures are victimized. The movement questions their previous record on standing for women. Fifth, the movement has remained largely elitist, hence, grassroots mobilization is done when it directly benefits the organizations. More research is required to ascertain how the response of women's organizations in Zimbabwe to women's issues can be more inclusive and effective.

References

Bhebe, N. (1989) 'The Nationalist Struggle, 1957–1962', in Banana, C. (ed.), *Turmoil and Tenacity, 1890–1990*. Harare: College Press, pp. 50–116.

Charumbira, R. (2020) 'Historians and Nehanda of Zimbabwe in History and Memory', in Boyd, C. Judge, J. & Shobet, A. (eds.), *History and Memory: Women Warriors and National Heroes – Global Histories*. London: Bloomsbury Publishing, pp. 39–54.

Chogugudza, P. (2006) *Gender and War: Zimbabwean Women and the Liberation Struggle*. London: CPI Group.

Christiansen, L.B. (2007) 'Mai Mujuru: Father of the Nation?', in Muponde, R. and Muchemwa, K. (eds.), *Manning the Nation: Father Figures in Zimbabwean Literature*. Harare: Weaver Press, pp. 88–101.

Chung, F. (2006) *Re-living the Second Chimurenga: Memories from the Liberation Struggle in Zimbabwe*. Uppsala: Nordiska Afrikainstitutet.

Crenshaw, K.W. (1991) 'Mapping the Margins: Intersectionality, Identity Politics and Violence against Women of Color'. *Stanford Law Review*, 43, 1241–1299.

Essof, S. (2013) *SheMurenga: The Zimbabwe Women's Movement, 1995–2000*. Harare: Weaver Press.

Geilser, G. (1995) 'Troubled Sisterhood: Women and Politics in Southern Africa: Case Studies from Zambia, Zimbabwe and Botswana'. *African Affairs*, 94(377), 545–578.

Geisler, G. (2004) *Women and the Remaking of Politics in Southern Africa: Negotiating Autonomy, Incorporation and Representation*. Uppsala: Nordiska Afrikainstitutet.

Harcourt, W. (2006) *The Global Women's Rights Movement: Power Politics around the United Nations and the World Social Forum*. UNRISD Working Paper 25. Geneva: United Nations Research Institute for Social Development.

Kumar, K. (2000) *Women and Women's Organizations in Post-conflict Societies: The Role of International Assistance*. Washington, DC: Centre for Development Information and Evaluation United States Agency for International Development.

Law, K. (2014) *Review: Shereen Essof. Shemurenga: The Zimbabwe Women's Movement 1995–2000*. Harare: Weaver Press.

Lyons, T. (2004) *Guns and Guerrilla Girls: Women in the Zimbabwean National Liberation Struggle*. Trenton: Africa World Press.

Manase, K.C. and Bhatasara, S. (2022) Intervention — "Sexual and Gender Based Violence and COVID-19 in Urban Zimbabwe". Antipode Online. Available at: https://antipodeonline.org/ (accessed on 20 August 2024).

Manyame-Tazarurwa, K.C. (2011) *Health Impact of Participation in the Liberation of Zimbabwe by Zanla Women Ex-combatants in the Zanla Operational Areas*. Bloomington: Author House.

Manyonganise, M. (2022) 'When a Pandemic Wears the Face of a Woman: Intersections of Religion and Gender during the COVID-19 Pandemic in Zimbabwe', in Sibanda, F., Muyambo, T. & Chitando, E. (eds.), *Religion and the COVID-19 Pandemic in Southern Africa*. London: Routledge, pp. 232–243.

Manyonganise, M. (2023) *Daring Patriarchy: A Biblical Engagement with Gender Discourses on Political Participation in Post-colonial Zimbabwe*. Bamberg: University of Bamberg Press.

Margolis, D.R. (1993) 'Women's Movements around the World: Cross-cultural Comparisons'. *Gender and Society*, 7(3), 379–399.

McFadden, P. (2005) 'Becoming Postcolonial: African Women Changing the Meaning of Citizenship'. *Meridians*, 6(1), 1–22.

Mizrahi, T. and Greenwalt, J. (2017) 'Gender Differences and Intersectionality in Community Organising'. *Journal of Community Practice*, 25(3-4), 432–463.

Molyneux, M. (2002) 'Analysing Women's Movements'. *Development and Change*, 29(2), 219–245.

Naples, N. (2009) 'Teaching Intersectionality'. *International Feminist Journal of Politics*, 11(4), 566–577.

Nhongo-Simbanegavi, J. (2000) *For Better or Worse? Women and ZANLA in Zimbabwe's Liberation Struggle*. Harare: Weaver Press.

Pyles, L. (2009) *Progressive Community Organising: A Critical Approach for a Globalising World*. London: Routledge.

Ranchod-Nilsson, S. (2006) 'Gender Politics and the Pendulum of Political and Social Transformation in Zimbabwe'. *Journal of Southern African Studies*, 32(1), 49–67.

Ray, R. and Korteweg, A.C. (1999) 'Women's Movements in the Third World: Identity, Mobilisation, and Autonomy'. *Annual Review of Sociology*, 25, 47–71.

Rupp, L. (2011) Transnational Women's Movements. Available at: https://ieg.ego.eu (Accessed on 31 October 2022).

Shields, A.P. (2021) 'Midwife for Power: Towards a Mujerista/Womanist Model of Community Organising', *Gateways*, 14(2), 1–16.

Smith, M. K. (2001) *Community. In The Encyclopedia of Informal Education*. Available at: www.infed.org/community/community.htm. (Accessed on 20 August 2024).

Stall, S. and Stoecker, R. (1998) 'Community Organising or Organising Community'. *Gender and Society*, 12(6), 729–756.

Staples, L. (2004) *Roots to Power: A Manual for Grassroots Organising*, Second Edition. Westport, CT: Praeger.

Staples, L. (2012) 'Community Organising for Social Justice: Grassroots Groups for Power'. *Social Work with Groups*, 35, 287–296.

Stewart, S. and Taylor, J. (1995) 'Women Organising Women – Doing it Backwards and in High Heels'. *IDS Bulletin*, 26(3), 79–85.

Toyana, M. (2020) *Hashtags and Spectacles: Zimbabwe's Feminist Activists find Online Avenues to Tackle the Government's COVID-19 Clampdown*. Essay Series: African Journalism and the Media in the time of COVID-19.

Van Eerdewijk, A. and Mugadza, T. (2014) *Resilience in Adversity: The Changing Face of Women's Activism in Zimbabwe, 2000–2014*. Hague: Hivos.

Win, E. (2004) 'When Sharing Female Identity Is Not Enough: Coalition Building in the Midst of Political Polarisation in Zimbabwe'. *Gender and Development*, 12(1), 19–27.

Win, W. (2005) 'Joyce no cause for Rejoicing'. *Sister Namibia*, 17(1), 22.

7 Women, Religion, Socio-Cultural Beliefs and the HIV/AIDS and COVID-19 Pandemics in Zimbabwe

Tabona Shoko and Tracey Chirara

Introduction

The influence of religion and cultural belief systems on gender relations become more pronounced during pandemics. Observations during the HIV/AIDS and COVID-19 pandemics to some extent lead to the conclusion that the Zimbabwean culture in general and the local religious beliefs in particular may act as catalysts for some forms of violence against women during such emergencies. The pattern of gender-based violence (GBV) during pandemics is largely similar, and this chapter has opted to use the HIV/AIDS pandemic in its discussions. Culture and religion are widely recognised as important factors in understanding of health risk perception and myth in the general fight against the HIV pandemic in Zimbabwe (Mapingure et al., 2021). The spread of the human immunodeficiency virus (HIV) and acquired immune-deficiency syndrome (AIDS) in Zimbabwe is influenced by the inferior status of women who are negatively portrayed in culture and religion as prone to commit immoral sexual acts. Women are continuously stigmatised in Zimbabwe in the context of HIV and AIDS. The pandemic affects all aspects of life, including the social, political, religious and economic (Nenge, 2011). While the HIV pandemic might be thought of as belonging to the past, the harsh reality is that many people continue to be infected and many deaths are being recorded in the contemporary period. Therefore, the focus on HIV and AIDS in this chapter is justified.

Assumptions about religion and culture as factors in the spread of HIV and AIDS have persisted, despite a lack of empirical evidence. The preponderance of evidence suggests that culture as a singular determinant in the African epidemic of HIV and AIDS falls flat when disabused of its biased and ethnocentric assumption (Sovran, 2013). The effects of the spread of HIV and the impact of AIDS are enormous, ranging from physical suffering, emotional, spiritual, but also family and communities are severely affected socially and economically (Owino, 2010). HIV and AIDS statistics in many countries of the developing world, including Zimbabwe, continues to show a gender skewed state of infection with women more than men increasingly and apparently being more infected (Kang'ethe and Chikono, 2014). Realistically, HIV and AIDS prevalence in Zimbabwe is higher

DOI: 10.4324/9781003494546-8

for women than men hence, and as such, the country displays or embraces the state of feminisation of HIV and AIDS (Kang'ethe, 2013).

HIV can be spread by sexual contact with infected persons, injections and sharp equipment which touch blood if used without proper sterilisation and from a mother to her unborn baby or through breast feeding. HIV causes AIDS which is a group of diseases that occurs when HIV affects a person's immune system. If the virus gets into the blood stream of a person, it attacks the white blood cells. There is an assumption that HIV and AIDS are a result of sexual transgressions, but there are hundreds of thousands of people infected and affected not because they were immoral (Murthy, 2015). This chapter acknowledges strides being done to curb HIV and AIDS, but advocates for the empowerment of women so that they can advocate for their rights in the context of HIV and AIDS.

Factors Influencing the Spread of HIV and AIDS in Zimbabwe

In Zimbabwe, infection for women is driven not only by biological factors but also by social, religious, political, cultural and economic inequalities that limit women's ability to avoid exposure to HIV and AIDS (Nenge, 2011). In Zimbabwe, women in most instances are involved in the role of being care-takers even of HIV and AIDS patients and this makes them to be at a vulnerable position. Familial and societal burdens need to be fairly distributed, and overburdening women in the care of AIDS patients is arguably a form of GBV. In the event that the parents succumb to HIV and AIDS, girl children are often forced to perform adult care, taking duties such as feeding and bathing the sick and cooking for the rest of the family. The girl (some of them very young) is exposed to HIV and AIDS as she would be nursing and dressing wounds of patients probably without protective clothing (Kang'ethe, 2010). In Zimbabwe care-giving is in the hands of women, and patriarchy has had a huge contribution of the quagmire.

Religio-cultural practices in Zimbabwe contribute to the prevalence of HIV and AIDS there. Today practices that include lobola, stigmatising people with diseases such as AIDS and some cultural definitions of normative behaviour have been incorporated into modern societal norms, leaving women vulnerable to infections (Nenge, 2011). People living with HIV and AIDS are treated as social outcasts and discriminated against in society. In Africa, cultural constructions of HIV and AIDS based on beliefs around the epidemic, sexuality and religion have thus played a vital part in the development of HIV-related discrimination (Murthy, 2015). Culturally sanctioned gender relations have an especially prominent role in the HIV and AIDS epidemic in sub-Saharan Africa where the HIV rate in women substantially exceeds those in men (UN AIDS, 2008). In most instances, AIDS-related discrimination can hinder the uptake of HIV and AIDS interventions.

Some religio-social and cultural practices and factors that fuel the spread of HIV and AIDS among women in Zimbabwe include but are not limited to patriarchy, inheritance, polygamy and female genital mutilation.

Patriarchy

Patriarchy is a system entrenched in Zimbabwe's cultural practices. Women have a limited say in decision-making as well as in sexual matters. Patriarchy legitimises men's domination of women and this increases the latter's vulnerability to HIV and AIDS. Women are experiencing a whole range of effects of patriarchy and gender inequality, which increases their vulnerability to HIV (Madiba and Ngwenya, 2017). Women are regarded as minors and do not have equal status as men (Nyoni, 2008).

Patriarchy and stigma against women have emerged as major challenges in fighting HIV and AIDS (Nenge, 2011). Patriarchy implies a system in which the father or a male member who is considered the head of the family controls all economic and property resources and makes all the major decisions in the family and maintains control over all members of the family and those related to it (Arisunta, 2010). Traditional practices, religious beliefs and colonial influences have greatly limited women's power. The status of women under traditional patriarchy has been associated with their capacity for reproduction and jobs that extend those bodies into household places to take care of children and male relatives (Nenge, 2011).

Masculine sexual behaviours associated with patriarchy are often reinforced beginning at the childhood and adolescence stages. Similarly, boys are often taught that 'real' men already know about sex and see no need to inform themselves about safe sex (Sovrana, 2013). The patriarchal nature of Zimbabwean society has often meant that women understand life as troublesome. Social norms and values tend to privilege men. This forces women to become second-class citizens. It is men who are expected to be heads of families, organisations and communities (Kang'ethe, 2014). Patriarchy has played a significant role in determining the state of feminisation of HIV and AIDS. This is because patriarchy makes the female gender more vulnerable to the virus in that it stifles her sexual independence as well as her capacity to negotiate for safer sex (Kang'ethe and Chikono, 2014). Apart from being vulnerable to HIV infections, women carry the greater burden of care giving (Chitando, 2011).

Most cultures in Zimbabwe, especially the ones that still value traditional norms, expect and indicate that married women are expected to be sexually passive and submissive to their husbands or male partners. Women, therefore, do not adequately afford to negotiate for safer sexual practices, neither do they have the power to initiate sex or refuse when they do not want (Kambarami, 2006).

Sexually transmitted diseases are often stereotyped as '*zvirwere zvevakadzi*' (meaning women's diseases) and this sometimes includes HIV and AIDS. Although a sizeable number of women are now formally and informally employed, cultural and religious norms expected of a 'noble woman' still follow them at their work places (Nenge, 2011). Issues to do with masculinities in the context of HIV and AIDS raise concern on social cultural ideologies and behaviours of men. Dangerous and negative masculinities emerge following a misconception of what most males will refer to as being a 'real man' and these have made them vulnerable to HIV while at the same time spreading women's vulnerability to the HIV.

For instance, polygamy has become an issue of concern, and officially practiced, if not, a common fashion among men (Owino, 2010). Africans are often believed to be more culturally tolerant of sexual indulgence and having multiple sexual partnerships than other parts of the world (Packard and Epstein, 1991). This, however, has been shown to be a misleading position.

Forms of coercion usually supported by African culture are used by men as a means of punishing or controlling their partners, and these are clear cases of GBV. These include forced polygamous unions, when the husband takes another wife or other wives and forces all the wives to accept this new situation. In these ways cultural and religious beliefs disempower women and make them accept a subservient role, even to the detriment of their well-being, dignity, status and lives (Nenge, 2011). In doing this, women become vulnerable to HIV and AIDS. Women living with HIV experience higher levels of violence due to stigma attached to women and HIV. The trend of 'small houses' is closely linked to patriarchy, and women do not refuse sex to their husbands even if he is coming from his 'small house' (concubine). Due to this, women become more and more vulnerable to HIV.

More so, these patriarchal norms influence the bride's father to demand exorbitant payment from the son-in-law to demonstrate his suitability as husband. *Lobola* becomes an expression of power by men in keeping women distanced from power and decision-making because they have no part in the decision-making. They also have no power to negotiate as they look up to their male partners for decisions (Nenge, 2011). The bride price makes women lose control over their well-being, and also lose power to negotiate issues to do with sex since they are viewed as assets bought by men. If women find themselves in a subordinate position to their male sexual partners, particularly, with the threat of violence, they may be unable to refuse unsafe sexual practices, to insist on condom usage, to resist rape and to control their male partners' faithfulness (Niens and Lowery, 2009). Some religio-social and cultural norms in Zimbabwe approve promiscuity for men. Many men deal with women as sexual objects and do not allow them to make reproductive health decisions. Women are expected to make their husbands happy, and *lobola* helps the African husbands to own the bodies of their wives (Nyoni, 2008).

The preponderance of available evidence suggests that male circumcision is protective against HIV acquisition in men. Although the exact interaction remains obscure, the foreskin is thought to facilitate transmission because it has a higher density of target cells for the virus, is more prone to trauma during sexual intercourse and is more susceptible to other communicable diseases that are known to act as co-father for HIV infection, including syphilis and herpes (Halperin and Bailey, 1999). Circumcision importantly does not prevent HIV transmission reliably on the individual level, but rather in population statistics. Thus, individual risk remains a very real concern for circumcised men, who could easily negate the benefits of circumcision by increasing their exposure through unprotected sexual intercourse with greater number of partners (Sovrana, 2013). In doing this, women who are partners to these men become vulnerable to contracting HIV. Violence against women promotes the spread of HIV and makes women more vulnerable to HIV infection. Rape exposes women and girls to HIV infections and place women on the receiving end of the HIV infection (Gabaitse, 2008). Women in Zimbabwe are also exposed to HIV through inheritance. This issue is discussed further.

Inheritance

Widow inheritance has been implicated in the spread of HIV and AIDS because it encourages the formation of extended sexual networks (Nyindo, 2005). In other settings, sexual contact with a widow is encouraged through sexual cleansing rituals in which penetrative intercourse is thought to chase away the spirit of the deceased and thereby prevent misfortunes amongst the living (Nkwi, 2005). Other common alternative practices to sexual cleansing include sliding over a partially naked person, administering herbs, hair cutting and offering prayers (Malungo, 2001). Since HIV is potentially transmitted after widow inheritance or during sexual cleansing rituals, the practice poses a risk to the individuals involved. Given the present state of knowledge, however, the population-level risk associated with widow inheritance and sexual cleansing is difficult to determine. Furthermore, levirate may not decrease risk if widows would remarry or engage in sex with other partners anyway (Sovrana, 2013). Widow inheritance, or levirate marriage, usually by a brother of the deceased husband, helps to maintain the social and economic welfare of widows and orphans. The family of the deceased may also desire continued control over the widow and dowry, as well as any wealth accumulated by the deceased (Mabumba et al., 2007).

Children are highly valued by both men and women in most African societies. Childbearing in the era of HIV can be risky, since there must not be any condom use for pregnancy to take place. Women can take risks of engaging in unprotected sex for the sake of becoming pregnant even if it would lead them to contracting HIV. For them, as long as one can bear a child, other issues come later (Baloyi, 2019). A woman is expected to give birth even when her husband has died. She is inherited by her husband's brother so as to bear children (Mogotlane et al., 2007). Childbearing is very important in African society, including Zimbabwe. In ethnic groups such as Korekore, Ndebele, Shona, Ndau, fertility is highly valued (Nyoni, 2008). Inheritance makes women vulnerable to HIV and AIDS. There is also a trend of inheritance in Zimbabwe which is not 'official' whereby some married men (relatives of the deceased or strangers) have sexual relations with widows without proper marriage. Both these men and women involved in this sexual web are exposed to HIV and AIDS. Polygamy is also a driving factor behind the spreading of HIV.

Polygamy

Polygamy is a common practice among the African people and African societies. Polygamy is valued because it is a sign of prosperity, wealth and good economic status. It also has a bearing on the reproductive status of women since having children in marriage enhances a woman's status. If the husband is found to be barren, his young brothers could provide children for him by forcing themselves on their in-law. The practice results in the wife becoming the property not only of her husband but also of his extended family. *Lobola* weakens the personhood of women under the guise of preserving tradition. It leaves the woman vulnerable to HIV and AIDS as she is forced to have sex with more than one man (Nenge, 2011). Culturally, having multiple (chain) sexual partners portrays men as 'real men' and like a bull, a man should not be confined to one pasture and cow. According to Shoko (2012), most men display a 'macho' attitude of risk-taking by indulging in unprotected sex in the belief that a 'real man' is distinct by scars such as sexually transmitted infections (STIs). Many African cultures sanction male, while restricting female, promiscuity (Owini, 2010). Women in such cultures are vulnerable to be infected with HIV and AIDS and other STIs and sexually transmitted diseases (STDs).

In some polygamous families, violence can be perpetuated by the husband. Sexual violence and religious and cultural beliefs regarding women make women vulnerable to HIV infection. Domestic violence can contribute to HIV infection when the husband or partner blames the woman for bringing the disease into the home (Nenge, 2011). Younger women, on average, may also be less likely to insist on safe sexual practices, such as the use of a condom, when negotiating sexual encounters, particularly with older men in these polygamous families (Hallet et al., 2007). Females under the age of 19 years are more likely than older women to experience forced first sex as well as physical and sexual violence at the hands of a partner (UNAIDS 2010). In Zimbabwe, having sex at a younger age correlates with higher lifetime numbers of sexual partners, a lack of school education and engagement in transactional sex work. These young women, however, are more unlikely to use condoms. Overall, women with early debut were more likely to be HIV positive at a rate of 54.6% compared with 38.2% for those with a later debut (Pettifor et al., 2004). Young women may be vulnerable to HIV and AIDS, especially if involved with some older persons who have been sexually active before and this is the case in many polygamous marriages in Zimbabwe.

The fear of ending their marriages from promiscuous husbands has caused many women to remain silent about their HIV status, and thus not seek counselling or treatment (Nenge, 2011). Polygamy alone does not spread HIV since a polygamous family in which all partners are faithful is no more threatening than a monogamous marriage in the same circumstance (Gausset, 2001). Although theoretically polygamy does not increase vulnerability to HIV if all the partners are faithful, studies on human sexual behaviour indicate that in most cases there are extra-marital sexual activities that may take place in polygamous unions (Chitando, 2009). However, some scholars have argued that polygamy is a cultural practice that should be considered an HIV intervention practice if it adheres to sexual discipline because it helps prevent and reduce unfaithfulness on men, thus reducing STDs and HIV (Owino, 2010). This matter remains debatable as it requires further examination. Even though polygamy is practiced according to the customary law, it should be done in a way that will not result in detrimental effects on women (Mulaudzi, 2005). Women in polygamous marriages are vulnerable to HIV when polygamy and promiscuity are practised at the same time, hence faithfulness in polygamy is recommended.

Female Genital Mutilation

Female genital mutilation is also a practice that has been implicated in the spread of HIV, although steps have been taken to limit its impact. Female genital cutting is predisposed to HIV infection through a few mechanisms. The surgery is traditionally performed in various ways, ranging from removal of the clitoral prepuce to radical excision of the vulva subsequent to partial closure of the vaginal introitus. HIV can be transmitted directly when using septic tools or through the transfer of blood from the practitioner into the open wounds of the female (Hardy, 1987).

After the procedure, the altered anatomy is often thought to enhance exposure to the virus during sexual intercourse. The scar tissues and abnormal anatomy resulting from female genital mutilation would increase vagina trauma, which in turn compromises the protective function of the vaginal lining for women (Yount and Abraham, 2007). Although the practice may be impugned on other grounds, claims that female genital mutilation confers vulnerability to HIV transmission, according to evidence, likely reflects cultural biases rather than biological facts (Sovrana, 2013). If there is a serial use of unsterilised instruments and equipment, women become vulnerable to HIV and AIDS. In order to salvage women from the yokes of HIV and AIDS, there is urgent need to educate and to empower them.

Empowering Women in the Context of HIV and AIDS

The existing strategies for preventing HIV infections, namely, abstinence, mutual monogamy between HIV-negative partners, condom use and treatment of STIs are not easy for some women because they lack access to HIV prevention information and autonomous control over their sexual relationships (Nenge, 2011). Poverty and HIV and AIDS go side by side. Factors that exacerbate the spreading of HIV and AIDS include poverty, malnutrition, unemployment, illiteracy and inadequate healthcare (Murthy, 2015). HIV and AIDS is generally perceived as a gendered epidemic needing a response by women. This is because women are at a greater risk of being infected and affected (Shoko and Mapuranga, 2020).

Poverty, unemployment and the scourge of HIV and AIDS characterise the socio-economic profile of some southern African countries, including Zimbabwe. Due to harsh socio-economic backgrounds, some young girls end up indulging in sex for money (Kang'ethe, 2014). Many women are dependent upon men to provide for them; poor women are forced to barter sex in exchange for financial gain and this may further expose them to HIV infections. It is this syndrome that makes women unable to negotiate safe sex with the fear of offending men and thus losing their source of material support (Gabaitse, 2008).

Women should be empowered to own their sexuality and stand their ground when it comes to sexual matters. Traditionally, women are constructed to be passive when it comes to issues of sex and sexuality. Women's sexuality is determined by the socio-cultural norms which deny them control over their own sexuality. Women are not expected to refuse the sexual advances of their male partners (Alexander, 2005). It is high time that women negotiate for safer sex and even the use of condoms. Women should find other alternative ways to keep their households instead of being abused sexually for material gain.

Culturally, women's reproductive powers do not belong to them. They belong to their partners who decide whether the couple uses a condom or not. Because of this they are not able to negotiate, influence and discuss safer sex in the home and this obviously makes them to be vulnerable to HIV and AIDS infections. Women who insist on using condoms are subjected to violence and are thought to be of loose character. Therefore, it is only in affirming both women and men as equal sexual partners who can equally decide on when and how to have sex that HIV infection rates can be reduced and effective prevention made possible (Gabaitse, 2008).

Leadership

Patriarchal attitudes also exist in the corporate world, and few women are allowed to occupy leadership positions (Kambarami, 2006). In the Constitution of Zimbabwe (Constitution of Zimbabwe Amendment Act (No. 20), 22 May 2013) there is a spectrum of well-established laws which are in place to empower women, but observably due to custom and the perpetual patriarchy, women are still often neglected. Women need jobs, and, just as their male counterparts, they need power and other privileges (Muchemwa and Muponde, 2007). There is a need for the emancipation and empowerment of women from all the risky practices entrenched in their culture through involving them in HIV-prevention strategies that are culturally relevant (Baloyi, 2019). Women should also occupy key leadership posts from grassroots level so as to tackle issues of HIV and AIDS and come up with sustainable strategies and solutions to curb this pandemic.

Educating Women in the Context of HIV and AIDS

Women need to be educated, and awareness strategies need to be initiated at grassroots levels. The campaign infrastructure to educate people on various prevention strategies is still weak. This is a clear revelation of rigidity within social institutions which compromise women's livelihoods in the face of HIV and AIDS. In these circumstances, women become the most infected and affected gender. Most HIV positive women as well as healthcare workers do not have adequate information on the mother to child transmission of HIV and the prevention thereof (Kang'ethe, 2014).

HIV and AIDS have thus been highly gendered. It is vital to craft strong and responsible programmes and strategies that are likely to curb the wide spread of HIV and AIDS (Kang'ethe, 2014). Women should actively participate in HIV and AIDS education and prevention programmes. They need to be empowered to veto marriage plans, to divorce their husbands if necessary and also to insist on the use of protection (Sovran, 2013).

There is also need for a more holistic approach to curb the spread of HIV that includes the alignment of laws, advocacy, human rights education, awareness raising on legislation, a change in patriarchal mind-sets and political will. Most harmful cultural practices are perpetuated by and for men and the affected parties almost always are women. Nevertheless, not all men are culprits (Sithole and Dziwa, 2019). A lot of people are infected because there is no proper and open sexuality education. HIV and AIDS must force us to break this culture of silence about sex and sexuality in order to break the stigma, to exercise care and prevent the virus from spreading. Religious leaders, children and parents must openly talk about and discuss sexuality as it relates to their life (Gabaitse, 2008). Among married couples issues of condom use should no longer be a taboo, and initiating for condom use should be discussed between men and women.

Conclusion

More education on HIV and AIDS is needed among women. In some rural areas where some people have lower literacy levels, education on HIV and AIDS is still wanting. It is critical for such education to be increased and ensure that all social institutions are gender mainstreamed and also ensure that all processes in institutions respect gender equity. Women should be given more space and this would widen their scope of negotiating for reproductive sexual health. All policies in combating HIV and AIDS should be gender neutral to address the needs of women (Kang'ethe and Chikono, 2014).

The practice of making women submissive in Zimbabwe causes some women to seem to be ignorant and non-assertive and at times they cannot voice their opinions. As a result, they lack negotiation skills in relation to safer sex. Many women do not have opportunities for open communication regarding HIV and condom use. The authority of males in Zimbabwe results in women failing to have full control or a say regarding most matters including sex (Nyoni, 2008). Women need to have a say in issues to do with sex including initiating condom use. There should be a paradigm shift from the cultural practices that reinforce patriarchy. Instead of inheriting them, there is need to support widows financially and materially without engaging in sexual intercourse. If intercourse is insisted, there is a need to go for HIV testing before engaging in sex between the widow and the inheritor.

There is need for a deconstruction of the texts that support patriarchy as one strategy to employ in the fight against HIV and AIDS in Zimbabwe (Nenge, 2011). There is need for a deconstruction of dangerous and aggressive masculinities and reconstruct them into peaceful and harmonious masculinities (Owino, 2010). There is a need to examine the various cultural practices that hinder or exacerbate the spreading of diseases. Patriarchy and stigma are challenges in the fight against HIV and AIDS in Zimbabwe. This chapter gives a comprehensive understanding of HIV and AIDS amongst women in Zimbabwe. It is important to highlight that this study focused on the religio-social and cultural beliefs among women in Zimbabwe that fuel the spread of HIV and AIDS as a form of violence that needs to be challenged in order to promote women's rights.

References

Alexander, E.M. (2005). Beyond inequalities. Women in Botswana. Southern African Research and Documentation Center. Gender and Development in SADC, Women's NGO Coliation (Botswana), Botswana WNGOC/SARDC.

Arisunta, C. (2010). *Women land rights and HIV/AIDS in Zimbabwe: The case of Zvimba communal area in Mashonaland West province.* Master's dissertation, University of Fort Hare, South Africa.

Baloyi, L. F. (2019). Vatsonga cultural practices and their impact on the health of widows and significant others. Thesis submitted in accordance with the requirements for the degree of Doctor of Philosophy in Nursing in Health Studies, University of South Africa.

Chitando, A. (2011). *Narrating gender and danger in selected Zimbabwe women's writings on HIV and AIDS*, Doctor of Philosophy and Literature, University of South Africa, South Africa.

Chitando, E. (2009). *Troubled but not destroyed African theology with HIV and AIDS.* World Council of Churches Publications: Geneva, Switzerland.

Gabaitse, R. (2008). Dual relevance: The Department of Theology and Religious Studies, University of Botswana's Response to HIV and AIDS. In E. Chitando (ed.), *Mainstreaming HIV and AIDS in theological education: Experiences and explorations.* World Council of Churches Publications: Geneva, Switzerland.

Gausset, Q. (2001). AIDS and cultural practices in Africa: The case of the Tonga (Zambia). *Social Science and Medicine*, 52(4): 509–518.

Hallet, T. B., James, J.C., Lewis, B.A., Lopman, C.A., Nyamukapa, P., Mushati, M.W., Garnett, C.B., and Gregson, S. (2007). Age at first sex and HIV infection in rural Zimbabwe. *Studies in Family Planning*, 38(1): 1–10.

Halperin, D. T. and Bailey, R. C. (1999). Male circumcision and HIV infection: 10 years and counting. *Lancet*, 354(9192): 1813–1815.

Hardy, D. B. (1987). Cultural practices contributing to the transmission of human immunodeficiency virus in Africa. *Review of Infectious Diseases*, 9(6): 1109–1119.

Kambarami, M. (2006). *Feminity, sexuality and culture: Culture and female subordination in Zimbabwe.* ARSRC, University of Fort Hare, South Africa.

Kang'ethe, S. M. (2010). The dangers of involving children as family care givers of palliative care and home based care to advanced HIV/AIDS patients in Botswana. *Indian Journal of Palliative Care*, 16(3): 117–122.

Kang'ethe, S. M. (2013). Exploring feminization of HIV/AIDS and millennium development Goals (MDGs) with examples from Botswana, South Africa. *Journal of Human Ecology,* 49(3): 211–217.

Kang'ethe, S. M. (2014). Exploring social works gaps in Africa with examples from South Africa and Botswana. *Journal of Social Sciences* 4(3), 423–431.

Kang'ethe, S. M. and Chikono, G. (2014). Exploring feminisation of HIV/AIDS in Zimbabwe, A literature review. *Journal of Human Ecology*, 47(2): 139–145.

Mabumba, E., Mugyenyi, P., Batwala, V., Mulogo, E. M., Miremba J., Khan, F. A., and Liljestrand, J. (2007). Widow inheritance and HIV/AIDS in rural Uganda. *Tropical Doctor*, 37: 229–231.

Madiba, S. and Ngwenya, N. (2017). Cultural practices, gender inequality, and inconsistent condom use increase vulnerability to HIV: Narratives from married and cohabiting women in rural communities in Mpumalanga province: South Africa. *Global Health Action*, 10(13): 23–45.

Malungo, J. R. (2001). Sexual cleansing (kusalazya) and levirate marriage (kunjilila mungada) in the era of AIDS: Changes in perceptions and practices in Zambia. *Social Science and Medicine*, 53(3): 371382.

Mapingure, M., Makandawire, Z., Chingombe, I., Cuadros, D., Mutenherwa, F., Mugurungi, O., and Musuka, G. (2021). Understanding HIV and associated risk factors among religious groups in Zimbabwe. *BMC Public Health*, 21: 375. https//doi.org/10.10.1186/512 889-10405-8.

Mogotlane, S. M., Hazell, E., and Mthembu, B. (2007). Women's cultural perspectives on reasons for HIV/AIDS prevalence in a rural area in Kwazulu-Natal Province. *South Africa Journal of Nursing and Midwifery*, 9(2): 35–43.

Muchemwa, K. Z. and Muponde, R. (2007). *Manning the nation: Father figures in Zimbabwean literature and society*. Harare: Weaver.

Mulaudzi, F. M. (2005). Attitudes, beliefs and practices on the HIV and AIDS of Vhavenda in sexually transmitted infections. *Indilinga African Journal of Indigenous Knowledge Systems*, 4(1): 323–339.

Murthy, J. (2015). HIV/AIDS in Africa: Implications and challenges for African churches. *Reflexus-Ano ix*, 4(2): 318–339.

Nenge, R. T. (2011). Redefining the status of women searching for context in Zimbabwe in the face of HIV and AIDS: Reinterpretation of 1Timothy 2 vs 8-15. *Boleswa Journal of Theology, Religion and Philosophy*, 3(3): 152–171.

Nien, L. and Lowery, D. (2009). Gendered epidemiology: Sexual equality and the prevalence of HIV/AIDS in Sub Saharan Africa. *Social Science Quarterly*, 90: 1134–1144.

Nkwi, P. N. (2005). The impact of cultural practices on the spreading of HIV/AIDS: An anthropological study of selected countries in sub Saharan Africa. *Discovery and Innovation*, 17: 21–35.

Nyindo, M. (2005). Complementary factors contributing to the rapid spread of HIV in Sub Saharan Africa: A review. *East African Medical Journal*, 82(1): 40–46.

Nyoni, C. (2008). *Socio-cultural factors and practices that impede upon behavioral change of Zimbabwean women in the era of HIV/AIDS*. Unisa: Pretoria.

Owino, K. (2010). *Masculinities, HIV and AIDS in South Africa – Evaluating the present, mapping the future: Towards a transformative missociological paradigm (a theology of hope)*. A paper presented at a Ph.D. seminar arranged by Broken Women Healing Traditions, on comparative theology and feminist theory: Engaging African and Nodic contexts. University of Oslo, Faculty of Theology, Oslo, Norway, 25–27 May 2010.

Packard, R. M. and Epstein, P. (1991). Epidemiologists, social scientists and the structure of medical research on AIDS in Africa. *Social Sciences and Medicine*, 33(7): 771–783.

Pettifor, A. E., van der Straten, A., Dunbar, M. S., Shiboski, S. C., and Padian, N. C. (2004). Early age of first sex a risk factor for HIV infection among women in Zimbabwe. *AIDS*, 18(10): 1435–1442. DOI:10: 1097/01.aids.0000131338. 61042.b8

Shoko, T. (2012). Karanga men, culture and HIV and AIDS in Zimbabwe. In E. Chitando and S. Chirongoma (eds.), *Redemptive masculinities: Men, HIV and religion,* EHAIA Series. World Council of Churches Publication[s]: Geneva, Switzerland, pp. 91–112.

Shoko, T. and Mapuranga T. P. (2020). Church women's organizations: Responding to HIV and AIDS in contemporary Zimbabwe. In E. Chitando (ed.), *The Zimbabwe Council of Churches and Development*. Palgrave Macmillan: Cham, pp. 149–162.

Sithole, L. and Dziwa, C. (2019). Eliminating harmful practices against women in Zimbabwe: Implementing articles of the African women protocol. *African Human Rights Law Journal*, 19, 568–590. http://dx.doi.org/10.17159/1996-2096/v19n2a1.

Sovran, S. (2013). Understanding culture in Sub-Saharan Africa. *Journal of Social Aspects of HIV/AIDS*, 10(1): 32–51.

UNAIDS (2010). *United Nations AIDS report on the global AIDS epidemic*. World Health Organization: Geneva.

Yount, K. M. and Abraham B. K. (2007). Female genital cutting and HIV/AIDS among Kenyan women. *Studies in Family Planning*, 38(2): 73–88.

8 Media Framing of COVID-19 Gender-Based Violence in Zimbabwe

The Case of *the Herald*, *Daily News*, and *NewsDay* (2019–2022)

Chipo Musoko

Introduction

Media organisations are capitalist ventures in nature and have dual roles to play in society, including generating revenue for shareholders and being purveyors of information. However, some stories the print media publish and deem newsworthy or 'juicy,' may be sensational and damaging to society. Journalists often claim that disseminating such information is in the public interest. Over the years, women in Zimbabwe have borne the brunt of negative publicity making news, mostly for all the wrong reasons, including as victims and perpetrators of gender-based violence (GBV). While women continue to suffer from all forms of abuse which some scholars blame on sex and gender, the media are often blamed for not doing enough to bring their plight to the fore. However, Annan-Yao (in Annan-Yao et al., 2004: 2) believes that the girl child in particular experiences discrimination right from the womb. While men generally have more physical prowess than women, their tendency towards verbal and/or physical abuse of their female counterparts should not be interpreted as a birth right (Hudson-Weems, 2004: 94). The media as mirrors of society tend to reflect on the abuse of women but at times do it in such a way that makes the women even more vulnerable. This was glaring during the government-induced COVID-19 lockdown (March 2020–June 2022) in Zimbabwe when women experienced high levels of GBV, particularly from intimate partners. This was exacerbated by restricted movements which resulted in women being confined for extended periods of time in the home with their abusers. The media captured most of these abuses through stories where women were mostly victims of violence compared with their male counterparts who were perpetrators. According to Padare Men's Forum/Enkundleni, 20% of married men are emotionally, financially, and sexually (denied conjugal rights) abused by their spouses (*Daily News*, 12/21). Therefore, this chapter discusses the findings of a study on how the print media in Zimbabwe (*The Herald, Daily News*, and *News Day*) covered GBV stories during the lockdown and whether there were any ethical violations.

DOI: 10.4324/9781003494546-9

Methodology

The researcher visited the National Archives (NA) for two weeks between 9 November 2022 and 18 January 2023 to search for GBV stories between intimate partners (excluding other forms of violence) in *The Herald*, *Daily News*, and *NewsDay*. Articles covering the period November 2019–March 2022 were analysed using qualitative content analysis. However, it was difficult to draw a sample of articles on GBV without reviewing the whole population of newspapers as cases were infrequent. In the case of *NewsDay*, articles sampled only covered the period November 2019–March 2020 (122 newspapers). The researcher could not access copies of the paper for the whole period under review as its publisher, Alpha Media Holdings, stopped supplying copies to the NA citing COVID-19 and reduced sales. Hence results of *NewsDay* cannot be generalised. However, in the case of *The Herald* (726) and *Daily News* (743), newspapers covering the period November 2019–March 2022 were reviewed. A total of 1591 newspapers were reviewed out of which only 307 stories (*The Herald*: 124, *Daily News*: 155, and *NewsDay*: 28) on GBV between intimate partners were analysed. Focus was on hard and soft news, opinions and letters to the editor.

Feminism, Africana Womanism

Theories underpinning this study include feminism and Clenora Hudson-Weems' Africana womanism (2004), an ideology grounded in African culture which focuses on the unique experiences, struggles, needs, and desires of African women. It critically addresses the dynamics of the conflict between the mainstream feminist, the black feminist, the African feminist, and the Africana womanist (Hudson-Weems in Nnaemeka, 1998: 155). It priorities race, class, and gender and is encompassing unlike the feminist theory which Hudson-Weems calls 'racist,' while labelling black feminism and African feminism as 'insufficient' titles for women.

Feminism is a movement committed to the elimination of male-gender power and privilege, or sexism (Warren, 1997: 3–4). "Something is a feminist issue if an understanding of it helps one understand the oppression or subordination of women." It is divided into three broad phases (Delamont, 2003: 2). Of interest to this study are the First Wave and Third Wave feminisms, which according to Delamont (2003: 3) are concerned with among others tackling violence and ensuring that female voices and experiences are treated as seriously as male. Arndt (2002: 71) describes feminism as a worldview and way of life of women and men who as individuals, groups, and/or organisations actively oppose existing gender relationships based on the discriminating hierarchies and ratings. Hudson-Weems (2004: 95) attributes a large part of sexist behaviour to societal norms, making it, fairly difficult for men in general to avoid being sexist to some degree. "This is because of the way we are taught and trained and the roles men and women are assigned to in society. Men continue to hold the most powerful positions in society."

Socialisation is at the heart of women's oppression. I argue that socialisation of African children has contributed to the creation of gender disparities between men and women hence perpetuating GBV. For example, during shopping a boy child is often encouraged to get a toy gun and the girl a doll which symbolises motherhood and all the attendant issues. This is where the power dynamics start to shift as the gun symbolises power, control, and manhood. Similarly, at home, girls are urged to do house chores and cooking, while boys are encouraged to focus on "manly" duties. Women socialise boys and girls to accept conditions of exploitation of females by males through the values they transmit. Boys then grow up with a superiority complex, while girls are made to accept and internalise an inferior position in society. Girls accept the domination role attributed to men (and boys) by society, become submissive to men, and aim to fulfil social roles as wives and mothers, sometimes at incredibly rather early ages (Annan-Yao in Annan-Yao et al., 2004: 2).

As social reproducers, girls are automatically educated to become the future caretakers of the family. Consequently, they are taught to appropriate the multiple roles their mothers play in the family. These roles range from food production and preparation to the portage of water and fuel over long distances, as well as household chores (Annan-Yao in Annan-Yao et al., 2004: 3). Annan-Yao argues that this deprives girls of any potential to participate in public life. However, Makaudze and Gudhlanga (2012: 167, cited in Muwati et al. 2012:103) believe that African traditional ways of socialising children do not encourage or promote masculine oppression and denigration of women.

> Instead, masculinities are socialized into a scheme in which the valuing of women's dignity, presence and significance is non-negotiable. Thus, it is erroneous to blame African men for purportedly sidelining and oppressing modern African women without unravelling the celebrated indigenous ways of managing gender interaction.

Chabata and Mashiri (cited in Muwati et al., 2012: 103) believe that the woman has an important role to play in the family referring to her as the 'axis' and an engine with which the family runs. They dismiss the notion of patriarchy and domesticity belaboured in feminist intellection which they argue are applied out of context. Makaudze and Gudhlanga cited in Muwati et al. (2012: 163) concur that the role of women in the kitchen is misunderstood by Westerners and feminists. "When young girls work around the home and the kitchen, it is not confinement. The Shona have an adage, *Musha usina mai hauna mapfihwa* (A home without a mother has no hearthstones/fireplace)." They further argue that the kitchen or the mother is thus a symbol of stability. "The kitchen from which the feminists desire to escape is invariably a school for young boys and girls as they are exposed to the cultural dictates of society by elderly, experienced and knowledgeable mothers." Thus, they don't see the kitchen as a symbol of oppression and exploitation but of life, culture, family stability, and education.

Curtin (in Warren, 1997: 87) says patriarchal cultures tend to locate women's practices on the border between nature and culture. "These involve caring for others, e.g. mothering, cooking, health care, and certain kinds of simple, traditional agricultural labour that are low paid or unpaid, such as weeding and tending to livestock." Kopytoff (in Oyewumi, 2005: 139) highlights many responsibilities of women in the home including childbearing and rearing, socialisation, and education of children, providing a physically and psychologically encouraging ambience at home. Women are also responsible for the management of the social life and calendar of the family unit, housekeeping. They also have to present to the world attractive and physically cared-for house, children, husband.

At the centre of gender discrimination is colonialism, which according to Seidman (1984: 421 cited by Furusa in Mguni et al. 2006: 2), brought its own gender ideology along with new economic relationships. This ideology constructed roles that Zimbabwean women were expected to play within the context of established institutions and policies. According to Seidman, the white settlers' male dominant colonial ideology codified the position of Zimbabwean women into 'minors' under control and guidance of their fathers and husbands.

Colonialism bracketed the Zimbabwean woman into restricted roles of wife and mother. Her performance space was the home, with her major staging area as the kitchen (Seidman, 1984: 22). However, confining the woman to the kitchen creates a host of problems for her as she is often excluded from decision-making fora such as *padare/dare* (traditional men's forum) where only men converge. The kitchen role is glorified, yet the 'heat' in it creates problems for women resulting in some rebelling and seeking to emancipate themselves, hence the growth of the feminist movement. The kitchen represents oppression and subjugation for many women in Zimbabwe and can be used as a symbol of oppression in the workplace too. The subjugation dates back to the colonial era where women were not even allowed to obtain birth certificates for their children in the absence of the father of the child.

While the role of women in the home is celebrated in the Shona culture, it also perpetuates patriarchy, hence the man claims ownership of a woman after paying *roora* (bride price). I believe that patriarchy plays a role in how women are treated by their male counterparts, both in the home and workplace. Patriarchy is often used to suppress and oppress women under the guise of submissiveness. This often causes violence both in the workplace and at home which then plays out in the media.

In the artificiality of male domination and patriarchy, the woman is placed in a vulnerable and peculiar position of subjugation, fulfilling her assigned role of servant and underling (Hudson-Weems in Muwati et al., 2012: 2). Hudson-Weems further argues that the male assumes the role of a dispassionate dictator be it overt or covert. This assessment in critical as it helps to understand the gender dynamics in Zimbabwe and how they play out in the media which are dominated by men who exert too much power. This has resulted in gender issues not receiving adequate attention and space in the press. They are often tucked deep inside the papers, while political and controversial stories get prominence.

Sofola (in Nnaemeka, 1998: 59) blames the Europeans and the Arabs for treating women as inferior while institutionalising the superiority of men.

> The first level of damage was done when the female lines of authority and socio-political power were destroyed and completely eliminated by the foreign European/Arabian male-centred systems of authority and governance. That was the first death blow to our psyche and the beginning of the de-womanization of African womanhood.
>
> (Sofola in Nnaemeka, 1998: 53–54)

The author argues that the woman "became and remained only an extension of her husband, as was/is the case in the Western world, and a mere shadow in the Arab culture." Sofola describes a woman as gradually growing to be irrelevant, ineffective, redundant, and dull, good only as an ornament, a wall flower – if allowed to be by her egocentric, almighty husband (p. 61).

Foreign cultures are castigated for igniting and fuelling a perpetual gender conflict that has now poisoned the erstwhile healthy social order of traditional Africa (Sofola in Nnaemeka, 1998: 62). The African perception of the gender question is thus healthier, positive, and allows for a wholesome development of human society (pp. 53–54). Sofola posits that the woman has always had a vital place within the African cosmology with the 'dual-sex system' of socio-political power-sharing fully developed by African people based on the perception of womanhood as the divine equal of man in essence, daughter, mother, and wife. Failing to realise that gender applies to both men and women has resulted in Zimbabwe being largely representative of the country's patriarchal setup (Tapfumaneyi, 2005, cited in Chikafa-Chipiro, 2016: 62). Tapfumaneyi argues that the media relegate news on GBV to the periphery with cases being covered as isolated based on court proceedings or police reports and not human rights issues. This confirms what my study also established, namely, that journalists tended to rely more on police and court reports when writing about GBV instead of gathering news directly from survivors and perpetrators.

Nzengwu (2003: 99) cited by Furusa (in Mguni et al., 2006: 18) calls Western perspectives on gender, "dramatic sites of violence in which the activities, actions, and humanity of others are violated" and where "cultural rights and cultural personhood" are denied space. However, Aidoo (in Nnaemeka, 1998: 40–41) dispels claims that African women are not powerful citing some of the most outstanding women soldiers and military strategists, many of whom died in the struggles. These include Queen Nzingha (1582–1663), who tried to prevent the Portuguese from overrunning Angola; Yaa Asantewaa, queen of the Asante (Ashanti Ghana), who led an insurrection against the British but was defeated; Winnie Mandela, Sibongile Mkhabela, Albertina Sisulu, Zodwa Sobukewe (South Africa), and the spirit medium, Mbuya Nehanda (Zimbabwe), who mobilised her people against the British invasion and was subsequently executed. "Given such a heroic tradition, it is no wonder that some of us regard the docile, mendicant, African woman of today as a media creation" (Aidoo, 1998: 41–42, cited in Nnaemeka 1998: 40–41).

Aidoo (1998: 46, cited in cited in Nnaemeka 1998: 40–41) also dismisses the notion that feminism is a foreign ideology, imported into Africa to ruin good African women arguing that African women were feminists long before feminism. Hudson-Weems advocates for women's unity and to have each other's back.

> Once women 'get themselves together,' their male counterparts would have little choice but to follow. Women would no longer be pitted against each other and thus, physically and emotionally abusive male–female relationships would decline significantly. Their support of each other would aid in uplifting their self-esteem, indeed, a necessary ingredient in their refusal to be physically and/or emotionally disrespected by their male companions.
>
> (Hudson-Weems, in Muwati et al., 2012: 4)

I concur with this view, hence the need for women in the media to fight in the corner of their female counterparts when reporting about GBV. Often times the media portray women as victims or blame them for being abused or retaliating. But very few articles dig deeper to identify causal factors such as extreme provocation, neglect, abuse – verbal, physical, and sexual.

Although Africana womanism has its shortcomings, it treats both men and women as equal, unlike the feminist theories which treat the former as an enemy hence failing to bring men on board when it comes to fighting for gender equality. This has presented challenges in Zimbabwe where gender issues are often associated with women hence often shunned by both men and the media. Therefore, the media play a significant role in perpetuating gender discrimination and patriarchy, masculinity, and general oppression and abuse of women which both feminists and Hudson-Weems are fighting to eradicate. Hence, for one to understand the portrayal of both men and women in the media, there is also need to understand how they operate.

The Media versus Audiences

The best way to explain why the media do what they do and how audiences respond to them is by looking at various theories such as the social construction theory popularised by Berger and Luckmann (1966), the hypodermic needle theory (Harold Lasswell, 1927), the uses and gratifications theory (Blumler, 1974 and Katz,1940), and the gate-keeping theory (Kurt Lewin, 1947). These theories have their strengths and shortcomings too but they give a clear perspective of how the media operate and the audiences' response to them.

Social Construction Theory

The theory conceptualises people's realities as a consequence of their experiences and interactions with others with news being a construction of reality. Burr (1995) argues that within a particular worldview, some forms of action are natural(ised), others made unthinkable. The media are known to generally give their audiences a version of reality that is not the reality itself. This theory is pertinent to this study as it helps to explain how GBV was framed in the media. In other words, GBV became a constructed 'reality' through story angling, choice of headlines (particularly screaming and misleading ones), selection and positioning of stories, sources,[1] and language used among others. Editors also contributed to the filtering of news that entered their 'media gates' to ensure that they conformed to set editorial – written or unwritten – policies.

The Gate-Keeping Theory

The theory describes the process in which news travels through a series of checkpoints or gates before it reaches the public (Griffin, 1994). The gate-keeping concept, despite its usefulness and its potential for dealing with many different media situations, has a built-in limitation in its implication that news arrives in readymade and unproblematic event-story form at the 'gates' of the media, where it is either admitted or excluded (McQuail, 1987).

According to Hermida et al. (2012), as a result of social media, editorially, the traditional gate-keeping function of the media is weakened, as a significant proportion of news consumers turn to family, friends, and acquaintances to alert them to items of interest. Essentially, a person's social circle takes on the role of news editor, deciding whether a story is important, interesting, or entertaining enough to recommend.

In the context of GBV, the news that the audiences received had been carefully selected through the gate-keeping process to include or exclude certain information in order to suit particular narratives. Hence certain voices were heard, while others were silenced in the stories. It was established that the official voice of the government, UN agencies, the European Union, and non-governmental organisations (NGOs) were largely prominent in GBV stories compared with those of ordinary people and survivors.

The general assumption is that the audiences are powerless to resist media messages. So, when a journalist writes a particular story, they expect the audiences to react to it in a particular way. For example, the headline "*Woman scalds hubby over salt*" (*NewsDay* 30/01/20) compels the reader, without even reading the story, to sympathise with the husband and jump to the conclusion that the woman is the villain. This notion is supported by the hypodermic needle theory.

Hypodermic Needle Theory

The theory, also known as the magic bullet theory, credits the media with considerable power to shape opinion and belief, change habits of life, mould behaviour actively more or less according to the will of those who could control the media and their contents (Bauer & Bauer, 1960, cited in McQuail, 1987).

The theory regards the media as omnipotent and having strong effects over an atomised, passive, and powerless audience. It presumes direct behavioural effect on an individual in line with the intended goal of the communicator.

According to McQuail (2000), in Europe the use of the media by advertisers and the First World War propagandist, dictatorial states in the inter-war years and by the new revolutionary regime in Russia, all appeared to confirm what people were already made to believe – that the media could be immensely powerful. Windahl (1992) argues that the purpose of a great deal of effects research has been to study how to use the media to influence people to do what they might not otherwise do.

The basic idea behind the magic-bullet theory is that every member of the audience receives messages in a uniform way and that immediate and direct responses are triggered by such stimuli (DeFleur & Ball-Rokeach, 1989). The theory isolates audience from one another and are vulnerable targets easily influenced by mass communication messages (Severin & Tankard, 1988). Media audiences are often regarded as powerless to resist pervasive media messages. This has thus reduced audience to media victims. Although the magic-bullet theory has been challenged by many scholars, it remains relevant in helping understand how audiences interact with media messages to give them meaning.

However, Abercrombie and Longhurst (1998) challenge this theory, saying that the audience does not simply respond to the media message; it interacts with it in a variety of different ways. In addition, the messages contained in the media are not always simple and straightforward, rather they are complex and reasonably diverse. Individuals in the real social world do not simply respond to messages, as if to an injection or stimulus.

The way GBV was framed in the newspapers under study reflects how the media wanted their audiences to perceive it, particularly when women were presented largely as perpetrators and 'victims' of GBV. Hence this theory is relevant to this study in that the messages that were being perpetuated by the media were not innocent but intentional. Their objectives were, among others, to convince the audience that GBV existed, to curb it, and to some extent consciously or unconsciously perpetuate negative stereotypes about women. In some instances, the women were presented as the perpetrators of violence, yet most of them were not interviewed to hear their side of the story. Hence audiences are not passive recipients of media messages but can use different filters to deduce meaning from them, which the uses and gratifications theory seeks to address.

Uses and Gratifications Theory

The uses and gratifications theory (UGT) states that people have the power to selectively expose themselves to media messages in order to gratify certain needs. These needs range from entertainment, escapism, to sexual needs. According Stevenson (2002), the UGT is premised on the view that audiences are active, autonomous, and unique. This school of thought also proposes that individuals selectively expose themselves to media messages but they have selective perception and retention, retaining only the information that is useful for their gratification. It emphasises what people do with the media as opposed to what media do to people (Stevenson, 2002).

According to Fiske (1990) examining cultural theory established that the guerrilla activities of audience provide a means of resistance to the dominant power bloc. These include channel hoping or switching off the TV or radio completely. Notions of an all-powerful media having "tranquilizing effects on defenceless, atomized, passive audience are therefore dismissed."

Bennett (1986) cites the Gramscian perspective, where the audience is not entirely sovereign but have the capacity to negotiate or interrogate the media discourses presented to them. Autonomy of the audience and their capacity as active producers of meaning come into question if we look at globally disseminated news material (Curran & Gurevitch, 1996). For example, people only get to see edited versions of the ongoing at the time of writing Russia–Ukraine, Gaza, and Sudan wars, among others. Although the UGT was also challenged by various scholars, the upside of it is that it seeks to re-empower the audiences. In the context of GBV, it can be concluded that it is not everyone who believes the stories they read in the papers. People have the power to choose what to believe or discredit. They can rely on alternative sources such as the Internet or even opinion leaders which Katz and Lazarsfeld (1955) talk about in their two-step flow theory. Captivating headlines on GBV may persuade a reader to buy a paper, but some would still question their credibility. In order to understand how the media in Zimbabwe covered GBV stories during the lockdown, there is a need to unpack the GBV concept.

Gender and Gender-Based Violence

Many people tend to confuse gender and sex, yet the latter is biologically determined while the former is socially prescribed. According to Annan-Yao (in Annan-Yao et al., 2004: 1), gender is a socially constructed term depicting the system of relations between women and men. It designates behaviours, attitudes, roles, status, and other processes that govern relationships among the sexes in a given socio-cultural, socio-economic, and/or socio-political context.

By the early 1980s, 'gender' as a category of analysis had come to distinguish the biological, which initially referred to male and female, from the cultural, which was associated with masculine and feminine (Eileen in Cole et al., 2007: 192). Eileen in Cole et al. (2007:192cites Joan Scott (1988: 2) who argues that gender is the social organisation of sexual difference. "But this does not mean that gender reflects or implements fixed and natural physical differences between women and men; rather gender is the knowledge that establishes meaning for bodily differences."

The Convention on the Elimination of All Forms of Discrimination against Women (CEDAW), an international treaty adopted in 1979 by the United Nations General Assembly, defines GBV as violence that is directed against a woman because she is a woman or that affects women disproportionately. GBV also refers to harmful acts directed at an individual based on their gender. It is rooted in gender inequality, the abuse of power and harmful norms "GBV is a serious violation of human rights and a life-threatening health and protection issue" (UNHCR, n.d.).

GBV includes physical, sexual, mental, or economic harm inflicted on a person because of socially ascribed power imbalances between males and females. It also includes the threat of violence, coercion, and deprivation of liberty, whether in public or private (UNICEF, n.d.). It takes numerous forms including intimate partner violence, sexual violence, and 'honour' crimes. The World Bank classifies GBV or violence against women and girls as a global pandemic that affects one in three women in their lifetime. In some countries, violence against women is estimated to cost countries up to 3.7% of their GDP – more than double what most governments spend on education (World Bank, 2019).

Violence against women – particularly intimate partner violence and sexual violence – is a major public health problem and a violation of women's rights (World Health Organization, 2021). At least 27% of women aged 15–49 years who have been in a relationship have been subjected to some form of physical and/or sexual violence by their intimate partner. "Violence can negatively affect women's physical, mental, sexual, and reproductive health, and may increase the risk of acquiring HIV in some settings." Zimbabwe witnessed high cases of GBV during the COVID-19 lockdown (March 2020–June 2022), most of which were captured by the media.

COVID-19 and GBV

Emerging data on GBV and COVID-19 showed a sharp increase in violence against women and girls. Globally, there was a 30% increase in reported cases of GBV. For every 3 months the lockdown continued, an additional 15 million extra cases of GBV were expected (UNFPA, n.d.). According to the African Union Commission, UN Women, OHCHR, and UNFPA (n.d.), since the outbreak of the pandemic, emerging reports showed that several types of violence against women and girls intensified. "In Africa too, there have been reports of abuse such as intimate partner violence, sexual harassment, child marriage, female genital mutilation, domestic and sexual abuse of women and girls which are exacerbated particularly under lockdowns."

In Zimbabwe at least 68% of women have experienced GBV, while 46% of the country's men have perpetrated violence against females, according to the Southern African Development Community Gender Protocol Barometer 2020 (*Daily News*, 08/20). According to civil society organisations, the country recorded over 75% increase in GBV cases since the lockdown, while gender-based organisations reported 4100 cases by 2020 (*Daily News*, 06/20). In 2020 alone, the Women's Coalition in Zimbabwe said the Zimbabwe Republic Police Victim Friendly Unit recorded 340 GBV cases, Musasa Project 953, Zimbabwe Women Lawyers Association 210, Padare/Enkundleni 67, Family Support 91, Adult Rape Clinic 56, GBV one-stop centres 241, and National GBV hotline 2276.

The national GBV hotline, run by Musasa, recorded more than 6800 GBV-related calls from the beginning of the lockdown on 30 March 2020 until end of December 2020, which was 40% higher than pre-lockdown figures (*Daily News*,

12/21). The cases reported on the GBV hotline increased from 1930 in 2019 to 5507 in 2020 (*The Herald*, 11/21). According to Musasa Project, during the lockdown, the organisation received the highest number of cases of GBV against women and children with cases jumping from 30 to 140 per day (*Daily News*, 04/20). The home became an 'incubation hub' for GBV, resulting in Musasa Project in partnership with the United Nations Population Fund increasing its hotlines from one to five. The organisation normally provided support to about 500 GBV survivors each month but recorded more than 700 cases in the first week of lockdown (*Daily News*, 08/20). Some of the domestic violence cases were captured by the media and are analysed in the findings.

Media Coverage of GBV under Lockdown in Zimbabwe

The study established that there was a surge in the cases of GBV reported in the country during the COVID-19 lockdown (March 2020–June 2022) when movement was restricted throughout the country. A Bulawayo Magistrate, Lizwe Jamela, painted a grim picture saying that "not a day goes by without dealing with a domestic violence case …" (*Daily News*, 02/20). This was buttressed by stories written in *The Herald, Daily News*, and *NewsDay*. It should be noted that like any other cases, some GBV stories went unreported, hence the stories analysed here are not representative of all violations that transpired in the country during the lockdown. They, however, mirrored the situation on the ground.

The newspapers made a lot of GBV 'noise' mainly during the 16 days of activism against GBV (25 November–December 10), the International Day for Women (8 March), and Mother's Day (14 May), but outside these periods stories were few to none. Stories headlined "16 Days of Activism start" (25/11/21) became common but meaningless. It would have been prudent for the journalists to write features on GBV instead.

It was also established that most articles on GBV were written by male journalists, yet women bear the brunt of abuse hence their stories would have been best articulated by their counterparts. This is why the government of Zimbabwe established a Women's Affairs Ministry to ensure that women's issues receive adequate attention.

The newspapers' lead[2] stories were mainly political (covering the parties Zanu-PF, CCC, and MDC-T), especially in the *Daily News*. The media also tended to focus more on high-profile divorce and criminal cases. In December 2019 alone, the paper carried at least nine stories on VP Chiwenga and ex-wife Marry Mubaiwa divorce and criminal trial, with the majority of them being lead stories. Similarly, in December 2019, *The Herald* carried six stories on Chiwenga and Mubaiwa.

Ordinary women were largely not given voices to speak on GBV. They mostly made news as beneficiaries of community or empowerment projects by the government, NGOs, and international organisations. Most positive stories on women were based on government events (especially those covered by *The Herald*), corporate events, UN agencies, women's organisations, and sponsored columns. The *Daily News* and *NewsDay* being tabloids, tended to write more sensational stories with screaming headlines, probably to sell their papers. One such was carried by the *Daily News* titled "Juicy details in T Freddy trial" (07/01/22). The story was about the alleged sexual abuse of a radio presenter by a popular pastor.

The study revealed that the media were generally not writing much about GBV. From 1591 newspapers reviewed, only 307 stories on GBV between intimate partners were identified. Stories on actual GBV cases were fewer (105) in all newspapers compared with the high number of general stories (202) on it. All the papers relied heavily on police and court reports, as well as officials instead of interviewing survivors, perpetrators, and witnesses. Most stories tended to lack balance as they were based on single or two sources only. Hence, this confirms the theory that news is a constructed reality.

NewsDay carried a total of 28 articles on GBV (general stories and actual violence between intimate partners). Between November and December 2019, the paper published 19 articles on GBV between intimate partners; 14 focused on general GBV news, while 5 were actual cases. Between January and March 2020, the paper published nine articles on GBV, with two being general articles, while seven were on actual violence. Most were just general GBV stories and the paper wrote very few features on it, yet these would have enabled the journalists to speak to more people and write detailed and analytical pieces compared with hard news stories.

During the period under review, the *Daily News* carried a total of 155 stories (general and violence between intimate partners) on GBV. Between November and December 2019, the paper published 15 articles on GBV between intimate partners of which 12 focused on general GBV news, while 3 were actual cases. In 2020, the paper published 52 stories on GBV: 41 were general and 11 actual violence. In 2021 the paper published 77 stories on GBV, where 53 were general and 24 actual violence. Between January and March 2022, the paper published 11 articles on GBV: 4 were general news, while 7 were on actual violence. The challenge is that the general stories were largely based on official voices, while the remainder were to a greater extent based on police and court reports, hence lacked balance.

The Herald published a total of 124 stories on GBV (general and violence between intimate partners). Between November and December 2019, the paper published 14 articles on GBV between intimate partners: 12 focused on general news about GBV, while 2 were actual cases. In 2020, the paper published 42 stories on GBV, with 25 being general news and 17 actual violence. In 2021 the paper published 65 articles: 37 were general and 28 on actual violence. Between January and March 2022, the paper published three articles on GBV of which two were general news, while one was on actual violence.

Hence *The Daily News* led in terms of its coverage of GBV relating to intimate partners compared with *The Herald*. However, all papers tended to focus more on general stories on GBV instead of the actual violence which demanded more coverage in order to expose perpetrators and to help seek justice for survivors. The media could have played a critical role of educating audience about GBV, not just through reporting about incidents or events, but digging deeper and writing in-depth features such as 'how to deal with GBV,' 'how to report GBV,' 'signs of an abusive relationship,' etc.

Voices in GBV Stories

In all the three papers, GBV stories were largely based on official comments including government, UN agencies, churches, and civic society organisations, instead of including ordinary people, particularly survivors to tell their own stories. Others were based on events such as the launch of the GBV campaign or Women's Day. There was little to no initiative on the part of most journalists to look for independent GBV stories and sources. The journalists and editors used their gate-keeping roles to include and exclude certain voices. Hence the media to a greater extent failed the survivors, particularly women who happen to be the worst affected by GBV.

The voices in most stories published in the *NewsDay* were officials, including church leaders, government officials, particularly Minister of Women's Affairs, the Gender Commission, NGOs, and politicians, yet survivors were barely heard apart from court and police stories which were told from the perspective of these institutions. *The Herald* mostly quoted government officials, NGOs, civic organisations, UN agencies, and the First Lady who dominated news on success stories about women and fighting GBV. However, the survivors' voices were largely missing. Most stories written by the paper were events-based and tended to quote senior government officials. Journalists did not take the initiative to do independent stories outside the 16 Days of Activism or events they were invited to cover, especially by government and other organisations, including corporates. For example, the story headlined "Take lead in fighting GBV, men urged" (05/12/19) quoted the Judicial Service Commission and the UN, but not the men.

The *Daily News* also used many official sources in its stories, including the government, Women's Coalition in Zimbabwe, UN, International Labour Organisation, Employers Confederation of Zimbabwe, Zimbabwe Congress of Trade Unions, and the European Union. For example, the story headlined "Men suffering GBV in silence" (30/11/21) only quoted the Anti-domestic Violence Council and Padare, but not ordinary men; hence it lacked balance and fairness. Another story titled "Churches urged to speak against gender violence" (06/11/19) only quoted the Zimbabwe Council of Churches to the exclusion of other sources. The story was based on an event which brought together congregants and development partners, yet none of them were interviewed. Another story headlined "Men must take part in drive against gender-based violence" (26/11/19) was based on the launch of 16 Days of Activism and only quoted two sources – Women's Affairs Minister and the UN Resident Coordinator.

Multiple Sourcing in News Stories

The Herald largely used multiple sources in some of its stories, which is commendable. These included a GBV story headlined "PR practitioner Moyo dies" (27/05/20). The journalist quoted various sources, including the National Police Spokesperson, Zimbabwe Institute of Public Relations, a family member (anonymous), and an eye witness. Another story titled "Elders urged to deal with GBV" (22/05/20) quoted the First Lady, two chiefs, three elderly people, and the MP for Shurugwi North, hence the story was balanced. The story headlined "Doctor kills children, attempts suicide" (05/01/21) had many voices – the police, neighbours, and a high school friend of the perpetrator. In the story, "Businessman guns down wife, boyfriend" (24/04/21) many people were interviewed – witnesses and the father-in-law. The journalist also visited the scene, a departure from basing stories on just police or court reports. In the story "Man locks family inside, petrol bombs house" (08/05/21), the journalist quoted the police and also interviewed the survivor (wife). "Gender-based violence cases increase under lockdown" (28/09/21) is one of a very few stories where survivors were given a voice. The journalist quoted the Women Action Group Director and five victims who narrated their ordeals. The story "Domestic dispute ends in tragedy" (15/10/21) quoted eye witnesses and the son of the deceased. In the story titled "First Lady lends an ear to survivors" (11/01/22), three GBV survivors were quoted, which was commendable. The story published by *The Herald* titled "Killer hubby commits suicide" (01/11/21) quoted the police, sources, and sister of the deceased, which shows balance.

The Daily News hardly used multiple sources in its stories. One of the few articles identified was headlined "Scorned wife sets house on fire" (05/08/21) where the Bulawayo Fire Brigade acting chief executive and a witness were quoted.

GBV Stories Based on Police Reports

The *Daily News* wrote many stories based on police reports. The paper failed to go beyond the police reports; hence their coverage was not fair and balanced. However, very few stories quoted other sources. For example, the story headlined "Wife kills self over hubby's infidelity" (23/12/21) gave a voice to relatives of the deceased. This was a departure from the usual stories quoting officials, the police, and court officials or documents.

The Herald wrote more stories based on police reports. In the story titled "Soldier guns down wife, kills self" (05/11/19), the only other source quoted was the Zimbabwe National Army Public Relations Deputy Director. And in the article titled "Woman hires boyfriend to kill hubby" (15/07/20), the journalist quoted the police and 'police sources,' though they were not named. Hence their existence was questionable. However, in one article titled "Man kills wife, hides body on mountain top" (21/10/21), the journalist at least quoted the Ward Councillor, the man's sister, and 'unnamed sources.' These should have been identified since both the perpetrator and victim were dead.

NewsDay also wrote stories based on police reports: again, there was no initiative on the part of the journalists to interview other sources. It should be noted that journalists often rely on police-check,[3] when they have no other viable diaries.[4] Some of the stories tend to be gruesome and the media enjoy publishing such as they sell the papers and attract advertisers.

GBV Stories Through the Eyes of the Courts

Most stories carried by the papers were based on court reports without interviewing the survivors or other sources. For example, the *Daily News* carried at least 19 stories based on just court reports. This showed lack of initiative as the journalists relied heavily on court reports without quoting other sources, survivors, perpetrators, and witnesses.

At least 18 stories were sampled that *The Herald* wrote based solely on court reports. The courts are also a source of easy news which the journalist can access effortlessly by visiting them. There is nothing wrong with journalists covering courts but they should have gone beyond just reporting what was said in court and instead used the cases as basis for further investigations. Interviews with the affected people and other sources should have been conducted before writing the stories. This reduced journalists to mere court parrots.

Negative Publicity of Women in the Media

The papers carried many stories that portrayed women in negative light compared with men hence the bias towards them. Most of these stories were based on the courts and police reports discussed earlier where women were largely victims or perpetrators of GBV. However, there were some stories that were glaringly negative. Other stories, though not linked to GBV that generally portrayed women in bad light included, "Chipinge granny (66) up for stock theft" (*NewsDay*, 06/02/20). There was no need to emphasise that the woman was old by calling her 'granny' and even stating her age as it had no correlation to the crime committed. A headline "Chipinge woman up for theft," would have sufficed. Another story headlined "Of Zoey pole dancing and bedroom lessons" (*NewsDay*, 09/02/20) did not in any way benefit audiences but rather sought to demean women.

A story carried by *The Herald* headlined "Woman in fake marriage saga" (27/11/19) was given unnecessary prominence and large acres of space, including a screaming headline. Similarly, a story headlined "Husband snatcher wins peace order," carried negative connotations because the journalist labelled the woman, a 'husband snatcher.' Other negative stories included "Social media affair, woman raped" (*The Herald*, 10/12/19), implying it was the woman's fault that she got raped.

The *Daily News* story headlined "Mash Central women accept violence" (9–15/02/20) written by a male journalist was misleading and it appears it was meant to sell the paper. Since the story was based on a UN study on GBV, the journalist could have focused on the high number of women facing GBV in the provinces surveyed. The paper published a comment headlined "GBV against men is real"

(01/12/21) but the opinion piece tended to bash women. The paper also quoted only one source, Padare/Enkundleni/Men's Forum director. Apart from that the journalist stereotyped women, calling the problematic ones by their totems – "*Chihera, Sokostinas, MaMoyo* who are all well known for the verbal diarrhoea they spew from their mouths." Other insensitive stories about women carried by the paper included "Marry is a witch, claims Chiwenga" (15/01/20), "Wife still wants to kill Chiwenga" (17/12/19), "Radio presenter begged for sex – T Freddy" (14/01/22).

In the few stories where men experienced GBV, the media tended to portray them as victims, for example headlines such as "Woman scalds hubby with cooking oil" (*The Herald*, 01/06/21), "Men suffering GBV in silence" (*Daily News*, 30/11/21), and "More men reporting GBV" (*The Herald*, 04/10/21). However, from the stories analysed, men were the greatest offenders. This is buttressed by feminist theories' assertion that men tend to exert domination over women because of various reasons including socialisation, culture, and power. Hence it is necessary to adopt Hudson-Weems' strategy of involving men to eradicate GBV.

Positive Stories on GBV

The media carried many positive stories on GBV and on women in general, although most of them were mainly based on events such as the 16 Days of Activism against GBV commemorations, Women's Month, and Mother's Day. During these periods the media were awash with positive stories on women. *The Herald* must be commended for carrying many positive stories on women, although the majority of them were based on officials especially the government. The stories included "Culture of silence in domestic violence and abuse a killer" (23/10/21), "Bring up children well to end GBV" (02/12/21), "Take lead in fighting GBV, men urged" (05/12/19).

Among opinion pieces carried by *The Herald* aimed at eradicating GBV was one titled "Delivering justice to survivors of SGBV through DNA evidence" (UNICEF, n.d.). The story headlined "Galvanising masculinity to end gender-based violence" (25/11/21) was good, although it was published when the 16 Days started. Journalists should make GBV noise all year around and not only when it's being commemorated. Other positive opinions were "EU supports efforts to tackle GBV in Zim" (EU, 30/11/21), "Why working with men, boys is key in ending GBV" (UNFPA, 14/12/21), "Diplomats fight to end domestic violence" (25/03/22), "Devise strategies to curb lockdown domestic violence" (Comment, 15/04/20).

Most positive articles in the *Daily News* were on eradicating GBV and also letters to the editor. The highlights were "GBV major factor behind HIV prevalence in women" (07/02/20), "Prioritise GBV fight in Covid-19 lockdown" (14–20/06/20), "Abuse of women at startling levels" (04/08/20), "Promote men, women dialogue to curb gender-based violence" (14/06/21), "GBV going out of control" (Editorial, 20/09/21), "Media must amplify GBV issues: Govt" (07/12/21). However, the article "ZGC, IOL fight GBV at the workplace" (28/11/21) cited only one senior government official; the Zimbabwe Gender Commission Chairperson and no workers were interviewed.

Positive opinions in the *Daily News* included "Let's end sexual violence" (29/11/19), "Act on water crisis to stop violence against women" (09/12/19), "We all need to tackle GBV" (05/12/19). Though opinions are a positive development, none were written by ordinary people. In the article, "Traditional leaders told to fight GBV" (21/08/20), only official voices were heard – Heal Zimbabwe Trust and Women Coalition of Zimbabwe. The journalist should have interviewed traditional leaders and survivors too.

NewsDay carried the following positive stories on women "Reproductive justice for Zimbabwean women" (07/02/20) and "Archaic 1929 properties law discriminating against women" (18/02/20).

Ethical Violations in GBV Coverage

Some journalists from all three newspapers violated ethical principles of truthfulness, balance, fairness, accuracy, and objectivity in their reportage of GBV. Most articles lacked balance and were one-sided either based on police reports, the courts, or officials.

An article published by *The Herald* headlined "More men now reporting GBV" (04/10/21) quoted authorities and not victims or men in general. And the story "GBV increases in Guruve" (05/10/21) only quoted two women who were not even survivors. *The Herald*'s story headlined "16 Days of Activism start" (25/11/21) was largely based on senior officials, Deputy Minister of Women's Affairs, and Acting UN Resident Coordinator. Another story "Gender-based violence must stop" (06/04/21) was based on an event by the Women's Action Group to commemorate Women's Day in Bindura. The journalist only quoted the Provincial Nursing Officer (guest of honour) and Women Action Group Director. An article titled "End harmful cultural practices to win GBV war" (25/11/21) quoted only two people – Women Action Group Executive Director and a 'Ms Masiiwa.' No other sources were interviewed, including religious leaders. The story "Killer doctor's wife speaks on 'fit of rage'" (08/01/21) quoted one source – his wife. The article titled "First Lady re-engages men over domestic violence, drug abuse" (30/03/22) quoted only the First Lady yet she was speaking at meeting with men, an opportunity that could have been used to allow them to speak for themselves. The paper carried a story titled "Call for multifaceted approach to end GBV" (22/11/21) based on the "Love Shouldn't Hurt" campaign by Population Solutions and the Swedish Embassy. Only two sources were interviewed – the Deputy Minister of Women's Affairs and Swedish Embassy Deputy Head of Mission. The story was also a repeat of a similar one on 19/11/21 titled "Joint approach key in GBV fight," though the headline was different. Hence the ethical principle of truthfulness was violated.

NewsDay also violated ethics, for example, in the story headlined "Cop stabs children during fight with wife" (26/11/19), which quoted 'police sources' but did not name them. Hence its credibility is questionable because of the absence of an official voice. Most stories in the *NewsDay* were based on one source, particularly the police, hence the paper violated the ethical principle of balance. A feature story titled "Community initiative against GBV pays off" (08/03/20) apart from one victim who narrated her story, the journalist focused more on officials –the Director of Musasa Project, Bubi matron, National Prosecuting Authority, and UNFPA Regional Director. More survivors should have been interviewed.

The *Daily News* carried several letters on GBV, which is commendable. However, some letters to the editor were written by one person and repeated over several months, hence the paper lost credibility, particularly where authors differed but the content was similar. These included one titled "Lockdown exposes domestic violence traits" (Alois, 20/04/20) and "Take gender-based violence seriously" (Nomatter, 11/08/20). Some of these letters were repeated on different dates, giving the false impression that they were written by different people. For example, a letter by 'Murawo' titled "Let's put an end to domestic violence" (13/01/22) was repeated several times and this showed lack of initiative by the media house to look for alternative letters. It raises questions as to whether this letter was written by a reader or the paper. Another letter headlined "Report domestic abuse" (11/03/22) reportedly penned by 'Alex' had similarities to Murawo's which was repeated five times between July and November 2021. A letter "Promote men, women dialogue to curb gender-based violence" (15/03/22) was written by 'Apostle.' Another letter titled "Promote men, women dialogue to curb gender-based violence" (02/11/21) was similar to the one written by 'Apostle,' but this time they added an initial 'J.' The same letter with a similar headline and content to that by 'Apostle J' was published under a different name, 'Murevi,' on 12/11/21. This is unethical and the paper violated the ethical principle of truthfulness.

In as much as feminist theories and the Africana womanism seek to address gender issues across the globe, the battle to end GBV in Zimbabwe is far from being won because of how the media continue to perpetuate gender stereotypes, blaming survivors and capitalising on GBV to sell news. It confirms the notion that women only make news when they either do wrong or when bad things happen to them. The media as the fourth estate have an obligation to bring issues affecting society to the fore, but there is need to give voice to the voiceless which they failed. Regurgitating court and police reports was also rampant and served no purpose while paying lip service to GBV by reporting it during commemorations or when NGOs or government had spoken about it. This showed lack of initiative on the part of the journalists.

Conclusion

The pen is indeed mightier than the sword. The stories analysed revealed that the journalists had an upper hand in terms of telling the GBV story, with some positive and others negative, thereby reinforcing the theory that audiences are passive recipients of media messages. However, this may not necessary be true as audiences have the power to use Stuart Hall's three readings of media messages, namely the dominated, negotiated, and oppositional reading. The study exposed many ethical violations with most stories lacking truthfulness, balance, and fairness. Women were also negatively portrayed across the media, with many screaming headlines meant to sell the papers and appease the advertisers and shareholders. However, the media must be commended for shining the spotlight on GBV, even though in most cases it was around the period to commemorate GBV, Women's Month, and Mother's Day.

Media houses need to employ more female journalists in the newsrooms to ensure that women get fair coverage, even though this cannot be guaranteed. Women are usually not seen as news editors, chief sub-editors, or editors. Only in rare cases will management consider women for these posts. Women are more likely found in positions of assistantship (Ogundipe-Leslie, 1994: 170). However, in Zimbabwe, although promotion of female journalists has improved over the years, more women need to occupy senior managerial and editorial posts. More female journalists must be allowed to write about GBV, since women are the ones who mostly bear the brunt of violence. Journalists should use their power to report on GBV responsibly and in a fair, balanced, and objective manner to ensure that audiences are educated about its dangers and help save lives. They should also give voices to marginalised and ordinary women to speak about GBV and they must also write more success stories. Reporters should interview survivors and not just rely mainly on police, court, and official reports. There is a need to train journalists including citizen journalists on ethics and professionalism. I concur with Makaudze and Gudhlanga (2012: 168) that gender education needs to be given priority in the curriculum on the basis of African cultural values. GBV stories should be written all year round and not only when commemorating the 16 Days against GBV. From the study, it was established that there was a sudden surge in stories and columns on GBV during commemorations. The Zimbabwe Media Commission, Zimbabwe Union of Journalists, Voluntary Media Council, and other stakeholders need to train and conscientise journalists on media ethics. Such empowerment will position the media more strategically to respond to GBV during future pandemics.

Notes

1 People who are interviewed by journalists to supply them with information/news.
2 Main story on the front page of a paper.
3 This is whereby a journalist contacts the police to get news on crimes and other events.
4 Diaries are story ideas that are presented by journalist(s) to and approved by the News Editor.

References

Abercrombie, N. & Longhurst, B. 1998. *Audiences – A Sociological Theory of Performance & Imagination*. London: Sage Publications.

African Union Commission (AUC), UN Women, OHCHR and UNFPA. n.d. *Gender-based Violence in Africa during the COVID-19 Pandemic*. Policy paper. https://esaro.unfpa.org/sites/default/files/pub-pdf/gbv_covid_report_final.pdf (accessed on 22.03.23).

Annan-Yao, E., Bashaw, Z. N., Ishengoma, C. G., Mookodi, G., Ongile, G., Pereira, C., Phalane, M., Ssewakiryanga, R., Tamale, S., & Uroh, C. O. 2004. *Gender, Economies and Entitlements in Africa*. Dakar, Council for the Development of Social Science Research in Africa.

Arndt, S. 2002. *The Dynamics of African Feminism*. New Jersey: Africa World Press.
Bennett, T. 1986. *Popular Culture & Social Relations: The Turn to Gramsci*. London: Open University Press.
Berger, P. L. & Luckmann, T. 1966. *The Social Construction of Reality*. New York: Anchor Books.
Burr, V. 1995. *An Introduction to Social Constructionism*. London: Routledge.
Chikafa-Chipiro, R. 2016. Discoursing Women, Christianity and Security: The Framing of Women in the Gumbura Case in Zimbabwean Media. *Agenda: Empowering Women for Gender Equity* 30(3), 60–69.
Cole, C.M., Manuh, T. & Miescher, S. F. (eds.) 2007. *Africa After Gender*? Bloomington: Indiana University Press.
Curran, J. & Gurevitch, M. 1996. *Mass Media and Society*. London: Arnold.
Daily News. 2019–2022. *Articles on GBV*. Harare: Associated Newspapers of Zimbabwe.
DeFleur, M. & Ball-Rokeach, S. 1989. *Theories of Mass Communication*. New York: Longman.
Delamont, S. 2003. *Feminist Sociology*. London: Sage Publications.
Fiske, J. 1990. *Introduction to Communication Studies* (2nd ed.). London: Routledge.
Griffin, E. 1994. *A First Look at Communication Theory*. New York: McGraw-Hill.
Hermida, A., Fletcher, F., Korell, D., & Logan, D. 2012. Share, like, recommend: Decoding the social media news consumer. *Journalism Studies*, 13(5–6), 815–824.
Hudson-Weems, C. 2004. *African Womanist Literary Theory*. New Jersey: Africa World Press.
Katz, E. & Lazarsfeld, P. F. 1955. *Personal Influence the Part Played by People in the Flow of Mass Communications*. Minneapolis, MN: The Free Press.
McQuail, D. 1987. *Mass Communication Theory – An Introduction* (2nd ed.). London: Sage Publications.
McQuail, D. 2000. *Mass Communication Theory* (4th ed.). London: Sage Publications.
Mguni, Z., Furusa, M. & Magosvongwe, R. (eds.). 2006. *African Womanhood in Zimbabwean Literature – New Critical Perspectives on Women's Literature in African Languages*. Harare: College Press Publishers.
Muwati, I., Mguni, Z., Gwekwerere, T., & Magosvongwe, R. (eds.) 2012. *Rediscoursing African Womanhood in the Search for Sustainable Renaissance*. Harare: College Press Publishers.
NewsDay. 2019–2022. *Articles on GBV*. Harare: Alpha Media Holdings.
Nnaemeka, O. 1998. *Sisterhood, Feminisms and Power: From Africa to the Diaspora*. New Jersey: Africa World Press.
Ogundipe-Leslie, M. 1994. *Re-Creating Ourselves: African Women & Critical Transformations*. New Jersey: African World Press.
Oyewumi, O. (ed.) 2005. *African Gender Studies*. New York: Palgrave.
Severin, J. & Tankard, J.W. 1988. *Communication Theories*. New York: Longman.
Stevenson, N. 2002. *Understanding Media Cultures: Social Theory & Mass Communication*. London: Sage Publications.
The Herald. 2019–2022. *Articles on GBV*. Harare: Zimpapers.
UNFPA. n.d. *Gender-based Violence and Covid-19 Actions, Gaps and the Way Forward*. https://esaro.unfpa.org/sites/default/files/pub-pdf/gbv_covid_report_final.pdf
UNHCR. n.d. www.unhcr.org/gender-based-violence.html# (accessed on 22.03.23).
UNICEF. n.d. *Gender-based Violence in Emergencies*. www.unhcr.org/what-we-do/protect-human-rights/protection/gender-based-violence (accessed on 11.11.22).
Warren, K. J. (ed.) 1997. *Ecofeminism – Women Culture Nature*. Bloomington & Indianapolis: Indiana University Press.

Windahl, S., Olson, J. T., & Signitzer, B. 1992. *Using Communication Theory – An Introduction to Planned Communication*. London: Sage Publications.

World Bank. 2019. *Violence against Women and Girls*. www.worldback.org/en/topic/socialsustainability/brief/violence-against-women-and-girls (accessed on 22.03.22).

World Health Organization. 2021. *Violence against Women*. www.who.int/news-room/fact-sheets/detail/violence-against-women (accessed on 22.03.22).

9 Stay-at-Home, a Double-edged Consequential Policy

The Case of Zimbabwean Women during the COVID-19 Pandemic

Agber Thaddeus Igbalumun, SJ

Introduction

Stay-at-Home, also known as lockdown, was one of the non-pharmaceutical interventions (NPI) identified by the World Health Organization (WHO) to curtail the spread of COVID-19 pandemic. Other NPIs included wearing of face masks, social distancing, school closure, no mass gathering, and so on. However, stay-at-home was seen by the WHO as the cornerstone for an effective mitigation of the COVID-19 pandemic. However, the effectiveness of the stay-at-home approach in mitigating the virus is debatable. There are others who argue that stay-at-home was the best approach or response towards COVID-19 because of its mode of transmission, that is, through respiratory droplets and contact routes, but there are others who also argue that stay-at-home was not the best approach or response towards the effective mitigation of COVID-19 pandemic. Those who hold this view claim that the negative effects of stay-at-home such as domestic violence, poverty, mental health disorders, and so on were worse than the virus itself. The stay-at-home policy can therefore be seen as a double-edged consequential policy whose negative impacts seem to supersede its intended purpose. This chapter does not intend to take a position on this debate but to stand as a bridge between these two extreme positions. Discussions in this chapter are based on available literature on the effects of lockdowns on Zimbabwean women during the peak of the COVID-19 pandemic. Even though much focus is on Zimbabwean women, studies from across Africa and other parts of the world are used, as women's experiences during peak periods of COVID-19 were largely the same across Africa and the world over.

The stay-at-home approach should not be taken as a cornerstone for an effective mitigation measure of the COVID-19 pandemic and other related contagious pandemics if it is not supported with appropriate ways of limiting its negative impacts. Most importantly, research on the impact of the COVID-19 pandemic shows that the virus has more negative impacts on women than men. Perhaps, this could be linked to the patriarchal society which sees women as underdogs and a commodity to be used by men. It also reveals a general trend of gender inequality. This chapter will therefore examine how Zimbabwean women were greatly affected during the COVID-19 pandemic lockdown, particularly in the areas of domestic violence and mental health. It shall thereafter offer some recommendations that

DOI: 10.4324/9781003494546-10

would complement the stay-at-home approach and limit its negative impacts. Thereafter comes the conclusion.

Methodology

The content of this chapter is based on the data from the available literature relevant to the impacts of the COVID-19 pandemic on Zimbabwean women in the aspect of domestic violence and mental health disorders. The review basically involved articles from official publications such as journals, encyclopaedia, and statistics from reputable organisations such as WHO, Child Trends, and others. The chapter employed recursive abstraction as an interpretive technique while conducting secondary data analysis. The question of the validity of the literature was addressed as the main challenge to ensure the reliability or the credibility of the review. Also, a reference check, conformability, and balancing were employed to ensure the validity of the review. However, the limitation of the methodology and technique used in this chapter may ignore or omit pertinent information and even the ongoing dialogue on the subject matter. However, the recommendations will be generalised in order to encompass what might have been omitted as a result of the limitation of this methodology.

Conceptual Analysis

Stay-at-home is used in this chapter interchangeably with the word, lockdown to mean the restriction of the movement of all people. According to James Fowler (2021: 2), stay-at-home was an order by most governments that required citizens to shelter in their residence with very few exceptions. This implies that citizens of different states were not allowed to move freely for fear of being infected or spreading the virus. For this reason, both the infected and non-infected persons were subjected to the stay-at-home policy. However, the strictness of this policy was dependent on each state or nation. For instance, Edouard Mathieu et al. (2020) observed that some countries such as the United States, Ukraine, and Japan observed absolute lockdown such that no one was allowed to leave the house. Also, countries such as Zimbabwe, India, Madagascar, China, Italy, and Ghana, amongst others, observed stay-at-home with some exceptions such as grocery shopping, daily exercise, and essential trips. However, some countries including Nigeria, the Democratic Republic of Congo, Brazil, Chile, South Sudan, Algeria, and Chad, amongst others, had no clearly defined measures about the stay-at-home policy. Most interestingly, some countries such as Argentina, Peru, Namibia, Niger, and Burkina Faso had no data regarding the stay-at-home policy. This does not mean that they did not experience lockdown. Perhaps, they experienced it in some ways but not as stringently as the United States and others. But the bottom line is that almost every country or state experienced lockdown in one form or the other.

When stay-at-home is referred to as a double-edged consequential policy, it simply means that stay-at-home has two effects, that is, it can be good as well as harmful. Stay-at-home may be considered a good policy if it curbed the spread of COVID-19, which was its intended purpose. Adversely, stay-at-home may be considered a harmful policy if it gave rise to other factors that impacted negatively on the lives of citizens. These factors include domestic violence, food insecurity, depression, and other forms of mental health disorders. Some scholars such as Nyabeze and Chikoko (2021) argue that the impacts which came as a result of COVID-19 lockdown were more devastating than the virus itself. In their words,

> The implementation of the COVID-19 lockdown measures on street vendors was more than the pandemic itself according to some proponents as its effects had more devastating effects in a country that has inadequate social protection coverage that would sustain the informal sector during the COVID-19 lockdown.
>
> (2021: 232)

Nyabeze and Chikoko were arguing in the case of Zimbabwe and for them, the country does not have a structure that supports informal traders such as street vendors who rely solely on daily income from their hustle. This means that stay-at-home or lockdown in this case can be seen as a harmful policy since it worsened the lives of some citizens.

COVID-19 is used in this chapter to mean the coronavirus. It belongs to the family of Coronaviridae, which infects both animals and humans. Human coronaviruses can cause mild disease similar to a common cold, while others cause more severe disease. The species which is under discussion, COVID-19, has not been previously diagnosed in humans until it was identified in Wuhan, China, in 2019 (World Health Organization, 2020). According to the WHO, COVID-19 is primarily transmitted between people through respiratory droplets and contact routes. This droplet transmission basically occurs when an infected person with symptoms such as coughing or sneezing is in a close proximity of one metre with a non-infected person (World Health Organization, 2020). Due to its channel of transmission (contact with the droplets of an infected person), the WHO identified social distancing, stay-at-home, and other measures that would limit human interaction as the overall protective measures to extinguish coronavirus.

There are many controversies about the word 'Africa', but this chapter uses the word 'Africa' to mean a place or geographical area. Geographically, Ladipo Mabogunje et al. (2020) describe Africa as follows:

> the second largest continent after Asia, covering about one-fifth of the total land surface of the earth. The continent is bounded to the west by the Atlantic Ocean, to the north by the Mediterranean Sea, to the east by the Red Sea and the Indian Ocean, and to the south by the mingling waters of the Atlantic and Indian oceans.

Therefore, this chapter uses the concept 'African women' to mean all women living in Africa who share common African traditional values. Cecil Blake (1993: 3) outlines some of these African traditional and cultural values as follows: 'respect for elders, acceptance of the supremacy of the hierarchical structures, performance of certain rituals in respect for ancestors, performance of rituals for various occasions ranging from farming to death and burial ceremonies, sibling relationships, etc.' Perhaps, the values of *Ubuntu* such as compassion, empathy, solidarity, respect, and dignity are also worth mentioning as shared cultural values of Africans. This then means that the connotation of the concept 'African women' in this chapter implies women with shared African traditional values and who live in Africa.

Literature Review

COVID-19 impacted the world in different aspects of life. However, in this chapter I shall focus on the aspect of mental health and domestic violence, as noted previously. To begin with mental health; researches show that there was an increased incidence of mental health disorders amongst women during the COVID-19 lockdown. Mental disorders, according to David Murphey et al. (2013: 1) 'are diagnosable conditions characterised by changes in thinking, mood, or behaviour (or some combination of these) that can cause a person to feel stressed out and impair his or her ability to function.' According to El Mostafa Rezrazi (2020: 2),

> the spread of the virus has created a widespread state of anxiety and plunged many people into existential states of distress, particularly because of the great number of uncertainties and also because of the media and audio-visual coverage by the media.

Chang-Lan Xia et al. (2022: 2–3) assert that there was an increased psychological distress level such as depression, anxiety, worry, sleeplessness, and stress after a few months of lockdown in the United States, Germany, and the United Kingdom. They maintain that females were more vulnerable to mental health disorders because the rate of common mental health disorders in women is much higher than the rate in men. For instance, the research carried out by the WHO shows that the rate of unipolar depression in women is twice as common as it is in men (quoted in Chang-Lan Xia et al., 2022: 2). This shows psychological differences in gender and the vulnerability of each gender to mental health disorders.

Chang-Lan Xia et al. (2022: 2) maintain that, 'a cross-sectional study regarding health care workers during the COVID-19 pandemic in China was conducted. The result illustrates that the female gender tended to experience more severe depression, anxiety, and distress.' In a comprehensive study carried out by Chang-Lan Xia et al. amongst 613 married women who were living and working in the Guandong province of China, 85% experienced income declines during COVID-19 lockdown. According to the study, about 88.9% of married women were at high risk of experiencing mental distress and only 0.3% were comfortable during the lockdown. Some women felt depressed, tired out, found it difficult to calm down, hopeless, worthless, and so on. The study shows that women whose income dropped during the lockdown were more nervous than women whose income did not drop. Also, women who had more responsibilities to their families during the lockdown were more tired than those who had none or less family responsibilities (Xia C.L. et al., 2022: 6–9). The result of this study shows that financial instability and family responsibility were associated with the negative effects of COVID-19 lockdown policy on women in the Guandong province of China.

In Africa, a similar study was carried out by Mathew Nyashanu et al. amongst women living in the Copperbelt province of Zambia. The Copperbelt province is considered as the backbone of the Zambian economy. It covers the mineral rich, farming, and bush areas of Southern Zambia (2021: 119). The result of the research shows that many women who were living in the Copperbelt province experienced domestic violence, loss of employment which led to financial instability, stress of managing children indoors, fear of COVID-19 infection, loneliness, and poor access to health services (2021: 122). The findings of this research are indicators or causes of mental health disorders. Nyashanu et al. (2021: 125), argue that, 'loss of employment is one of the triggers of mental health distress especially when there is no potential chance of getting another job…Such a situation can be worse in female headed single-parent families'. The research reveals that many women lost their jobs during COVID-19 lockdown, especially women who were working in food markets and tourism. This left them in dire need of money to purchase food for their families and also to provide the basic needs of the family. Nyashanu et al. observe that women who went through this situation were at high risk of developing mental illness.

Another indicator of mental health disorders which was observed from the study of Nyashanu et al. amongst women living in the Copperbelt province of Zambia is 'loneliness'. Loneliness and isolation, according to Kim et al., are triggers of mental health distress especially for people who are living alone or lacking some sort of social interaction with others (quoted in Nyashanu et al., 2021: 126). The research reveals that 'participants reported loneliness due to family social isolation during COVID-19 lockdown leading to boredom, stress, and anxiety' (2021: 126) . The boredom, stress, and anxiety here are clear symptoms of mental health illness which shows that women who were living in the Copperbelt province of Zambia were negatively impacted by the lockdown or stay-at-home policy.

In addition to the mental health disorders which women experienced during the time of COVID-19 lockdown, there was also an increased level of domestic violence on women. Domestic violence according to Abdul and Ishrat (2016: 1698) 'is an interpersonal violence which takes place in domestic settings, family relationships and intimate relationships'. This form of violence includes physical, psychological, sexual, and other forms of attack on one's intimate partner. It is often called marital assault, woman battery, wife-beating, intimate violence, spousal abuse, etc. these terms are sometimes used interchangeably to convey a particular meaning. For example, some people use the term 'wife abuse' to imply that most of the victims of domestic violence are women. However, this does not refute the fact that men also can become victims of domestic violence. Domestic violence is basically an attempt to dominate and control the other partner in either marital or dating relationship. This chapter, however, uses the term domestic violence in the sense of wife or woman abuse to signify the abuse or violence on women during the time of COVID-19 lockdown.

In the Zimbabwean context, scholars such as Nyabeze and Chikoko (2021) acknowledged an increased level of domestic violence on women during COVID-19 lockdown. They observe that the pandemic increased gender-based violence. Their argument is based on the report from the Musasa Project. According to them, the Musasa Project, which is aimed at providing temporary shelter to the victims of gender-based violence, recorded an increased number of 1200 cases, doubling the usual number of 500–600 cases. According to the Musasa Project, these cases were mostly victims of domestic violence, which was manifested in sexual, physical, economic, and psychological abuse. They also observed that economic insecurity and poverty were the major causes of domestic violence during the stay-at-home period (Nyabeze and Chikoko 2021: 236). Similarly, the research carried out by Mathew Nyashanu et al., amongst women living in the Copperbelt province of Zambia, also shows an increased level of domestic violence during the pandemic. According to the research, many participants reported an upsurge of domestic violence during the pandemic due to prolonged lockdown in closed spaces, which sometimes led to arguments and quarrels. In the words of one of the participants,

> I am experiencing domestic violence nearly every day since we are spending most of the time with my husband. I am subjected to ridicule and sometimes beating for no apparent reason in front of my children. I am really stressed. We need time to go out of the house and relax somewhere away from each other.
> (2021: 122)

These reports show how women were negatively impacted during the pandemic.

Furthermore, another research carried out by Mahlangu et al., amongst women living in the Gauteng province of South Africa, also shows that women faced different kinds of emotional abuse during COVID-19 pandemic lockdown. According to the study, 43.7% of the women who participated in the study experienced emotional violence (2022: 2). This percentage is approximately half of the women that participated. Which seems to show that in every ten women living in Gauteng province, five women experienced one form of emotional abuse or the other. The research reveals that some women experienced emotional violence from their partners such as shouting, manipulation, and insults. This emotional violence was experienced by most women in the low socio-economic status whose spouses lost their job and were faced with both financial and food insecurity. But some women in the high socio-economic status also experienced some form of emotional violence from their spouses such as increased stress and aggression. In the words of one of the participants,

> My husband was working for a company which was affected by a ban on alcohol sales. They did not get paid if they did not work… We had fights because there is a lack of income in the house. We don't fight physically; he gets harsh when he

> responds. It is more the verbal exchanges, angry responses, and a cold shoulder after arguments, but not physical.

(Mahlangu et al., 2022: 4)

This shows that financial and food instability were the cause of this emotional violence. However, other causes such as loneliness and even fear of the pandemic itself cannot be underestimated.

In addition, the report from the UN Women report reveals that one in three of the women worldwide experienced physical or sexual violence from their spouses or intimate partners. According to the report, the outbreak of COVID-19 and its lockdown measures show an increasing level of domestic violence against women and girls. The research conducted by Sithembiso Ndlovu et al. also shows that there was an increased level of domestic violence on women during the COVID-19 pandemic lockdown in Zimbabwe. They attributed the rise in the level of domestic violence to the change in income and the existing income gap, more time spent at home, and frustration because of lockdown restrictions (2022: 61). This research also raises the issue of income instability as the cause of domestic violence during the COVID-19 lockdown. Which means that income plays a key role in the peaceful co-existence amongst family members. In other words, the peaceful atmosphere in some families depends on the income of those families. According to the research by Ndlovu et al. (2022: 60), more than 40% of gender-based violence cases are physical assault and about 38% are related to intimate partner violence (IPV), which is a form of abuse or aggression that occurs in a romantic relationship. The increase in IPV could be linked to boredom, living in an enclosed system that forms different kinds of negative emotions, and so on. Ndlovu et al. also identified high consumption of alcohol as the cause of gender-based violence. According to them, even though the government banned the consumption of alcohol, there were still numerous places where the consumption of alcohol prevailed (2022: 65). This means that an excessive consumption of alcohol during the COVID-19 pandemic lockdown was a contributing factor to IPV in Zimbabwe and other nations.

Discussion and Recommendations

In view of the literature given previously, it is clear that financial instability which was due to the loss of jobs by people in low socio-economic status was the major cause of domestic violence during COVID-19 pandemic lockdown. Other factors such as loneliness, stress of managing children, fear of COVID-19 infection, poor access to health services, and also financial instability amongst others were observed as the primary causes of mental health disorders during the pandemic. Considering the numerous challenges associated with the COVID-19 lockdown or stay-at-home policy, it is important to note that this policy should not be considered as a cornerstone for an effective mitigation of COVID-19 pandemic or any other related pandemic. However, the stay-at-home policy can become an effective way of mitigating such pandemics if and only if it is supported with appropriate ways of limiting its negative impacts. Some of these ways include online jobs, online learning, online shopping, and also the subsidisation of the internet subscription by the government. In other words, shifting from physical to digital or virtual space during lockdown is rather the cornerstone for an effective mitigation of any pandemic that would necessitate stay-at-home. The findings in this research therefore suggest the need for Africa to adopt these modern ways of living if they are to implement stay-at-home policy in any subsequent pandemic.

Most importantly, it is no longer a fantasy or an illusion but a reality that the world is gradually moving to virtual space, especially for things that are virtually-compatible. COVID-19 pandemic for instance accelerated that movement. I shall use online jobs also known as 'work from home' (WFH) to support this claim. This research uses online jobs because from the previous literature, it is clear that loss of jobs by people from low socio-economic status was one of the primary causes of domestic violence and mental health disorders. But this does not undermine other areas of life which are online-compatible such as online learning, online shopping, and others. In times of pandemic such as COVID-19 that necessitate stay-at-home, the most effective way of coping and mitigating such pandemic is to move to the virtual world where the pandemic cannot move to. This will facilitate virtual socialisation while keeping physical distance.

Studies show that many developed countries were able to shift their working environment from physical to virtual space. For instance, the study carried out by Kosteas Vasilios et al. (2022:14) shows that 35.5% of US workers were working from home or online during the pandemic, which is close to the 37% of US jobs which are compatible with working at home. This means that over 90% of people who work with such organisations or companies were fully engaged during the period of stay-at-home. This also means that their jobs were intact and their income was not affected to a large extent. The same research shows that there was an increased rate of 'work from home' jobs in Japan, with an increase from 6% in January 2020 to 17% in June of the same year. Also, 13.3% of Brazilian workers started working from home in the second quarter of the pandemic, which was close to 14.8% of Brazilian jobs which are compatible with working from home. Another country which also shows this equivalent number or a close ratio between those who are working online and the jobs that can be done online is Costa Rica. The research shows that 10.6% of Costa Rican workers were working from home which is close to 13.8% of jobs which can be done from home (2022: 16). This research shows how COVID-19 accelerated the migration from physical working space to the online working space. This means that people who were part of these organisations were fully engaged during the time of stay-at-home, and their income was not affected. This, therefore, means that financial instability would not be the cause of their mental health disorders or reason for them to engage in domestic violence. Similarly, if African countries could create more online jobs to enable people to work from home during the time of any crisis that would necessitate lockdown, then financial instability and loneliness will neither be the cause of domestic violence nor mental health disorders.

Conclusion

This chapter has critically discussed the impacts of the COVID-19 pandemic lockdown or stay-at-home policy on Zimbabwean women. The chapter focused on two important aspects: domestic violence and mental health. According to the research in this chapter, the COVID-19 pandemic lockdown increased the rate of domestic violence and mental health illnesses amongst Zimbabwean women and women from other parts of Africa and the world in general. The research used different literature reviews on the subject matter to support this claim. The chapter acknowledged loss of jobs, which led to financial instability, loneliness, fear of the pandemic amongst others as the major causes of domestic violence and mental health illnesses. Based on the negative impacts the stay-at-home policy has on women; the research refuted the claim that stay-at-home policy is a cornerstone for an effective mitigation of COVID-19 and other related pandemics.

The chapter argued that for stay-at-home policy to be considered a cornerstone, it must be accompanied with other ways of limiting its negative impacts. The chapter suggested moving from physical to online or virtual space as an effective way of containing such pandemics. This involves moving from physical working spaces to virtual or online working spaces where online jobs will be created for jobs that are online-compatible as it is done in many developed countries. Also, moving from a physical classroom to an online classroom. In fact, it involves absolute migration from the physical space to the online space for whatever is online-compatible. This, therefore, means that any country that does not have these facilities or structures to deal with any pandemic that necessitates stay-at-home should not even think of implementing the stay-at-home policy, since its negative impacts supersede its intended purpose.

References

Abdul, RN. and Ishrat., BN. (2016). Domestic violence: its causes, consequences and preclusions strategies. *Ijariie,* 2(2), pp. 1697-1705. www.researchgate.net/publication/325102675_DOMESTIC_VIOLENCE_ITS_CAUSES_CONSEQUENCES_AND_PRECLUSIONS_STRATEGIES

Blake, C. (1993). Traditional African values and the right to communicate. *African Media Review,* 7(3): 1-17. https://typeset.io/pdf/traditional-african-values-and-the-right-to-communicate-heas2px6km.pdf

Edouard, M., Ritchie, H., Rodes-Guirao, L., Appel, C., Gavrilov, D., Giattino, C., (2020). Coronavirus pandemic (COVID-19). Our World in Data.org. https://ourworldindata.org/coronavirus [4 September 2022].

El Mostafa, R. (2020). *COVID-19 and Mental Health: The Impact of Lockdown on Mental Health*. Policy Centre for the New South, pp. 1–5. www.policycenter.ma/sites/default/files/2021-01/PB_20-64_Rezrazi%20EN.pdf

Fowler, H. J., Hill, S.J., Levin, R., and Obradovich, N. (2021). 'Stay-at-home orders associate with subsequent decreases in COVID-19 cases and fatalities in the United States'. *Plos One,* pp. 1–15. https://journals.plos.org/plosone/article?id=10.1371/journal.pone.0248849

Kosteas, V. D., Renna, F., and Scicchitana, S. (2022). 'COVID-19 and working from home: toward a new normal?' GLO Discussion Paper No. 1013, Global Labour Organization (GLO), Essen. www.econstor.eu/bitstream/10419/248570/1/GLO-DP-1013.pdf

Mabogunje, A. L., Gardiner, R. K., Nicol, D. W., Middleton, J. F., Clarke, A., Kröner, J. I., Smedley, A. S., et al. (2020). *Encyclopedia Britannica.* [12 January 2021]. Africa | History, People, Countries, Regions, Map, & Facts | Britannica.

Mahlangu, P., Gibbs, A., Shai, N., Machisa, M., Nunez, N., and Sikweyiya, Y. (2022). Impact of COVID-19 lockdown and link to women and children's experiences of violence in the home in South Africa. *BMC Public Health*, 2–11. https://bmcpublichealth.biomedcentral.com/articles/10.1186/s12889-022-13422-3

Murphey, D., Barry, M., and Vaughn, B. (2013). *Mental Health Disorders*. Child Trends. No.1. https://cms.childtrends.org/wp-content/uploads/2013/03/Child_Trends-2013_01_01_AHH_MentalDisordersl.pdf

Ndlovu, S., Mulondo, M., Tsoka-Gwegweni, J., and Ndirangu, J. (2022). COVID-19 impact on gender-based violence among women in South Africa during lockdown: a narrative review. *African Journal of Reproductive Health,* 26(7), pp. 59–71. www.ajol.info/index.php/ajrh/article/view/229785

Nyabeze, K., and Chikoko, W. (2021). Socio-economic impact of COVID-19 lockdown measures on the informal sector livelihoods in Zimbabwe. *African Journal of Social Work,* 11(4), pp. 231–239. www.ajol.info/index.php/ajsw/article/view/215263

Nyashanu, M., Thamary, K., Gemma, N., Maureen, M., and Wendy, N. (2021). COVID-19 lockdown and mental health: exploring triggers of mental health distress among women in the Copperbelt province, Zambia. *International Journal of Mental Health,* 51(2), pp. 117–130.

World Health Organization. (2020). Mode of transmission of virus causing COVID-19: Implications for IPC precaution recommendations. Scientific Brief. www.who.int/news-room/commentaries/detail/modes-of-transmission-of-virus-causing-covid-19-implications-for-ipc-precaution-recommendations [4 September 2022].

Xia, CL., Wei, AP., Huang, YT. (2022). The COVID-19 lockdown and mental wellbeing of females in China. *International Journal of Environmental Research and Public Health*, pp. 1–19. www.ncbi.nlm.nih.gov/pmc/articles/PMC9100609/

10 Structural Violence and/as a Pandemic in Crisis Communication

Has the Media Done Justice to Women's Sexual Reproductive Rights?

Nyari Kachepa and Nehemiah Chivandikwa

Introduction

Effective, efficient, and sufficient crisis communication is an imperative in managing pandemics such as COVID-19 (Gianella, 2022; Mackay et al., 2021; Mcnamara, 2021). Crisis communication refers to the collection, processing, and dissemination of information required to address a crisis such as the COVID-19 pandemic (Kiptnness and Okoye, 2021; Mcnamara, 2021; Anasah, 2022). Yet crisis communication scholarship suggests that during the peak of the COVID-19 pandemic, guiding principles of effective crisis communication were inconsistently applied and combined (Mackay et al., 2021: 1). These weaknesses in crisis communication may cause complacency and negligence among organizations and state institutions, whose activities and responses to the pandemic must be persistently reported on to ensure accountability (Gianella, 2022). Ineffective crisis communication affects trust in health systems and local, state, and global governance systems and institutions, and ultimately, this weakens the capacity of the public to respond and protect themselves (Mackay et al., 2021). Hence media on crisis communication needs to be a watchdog on the governance of public and state institutions, because disasters and crises are structural in nature, in the sense that pre-existing unsafe conditions make disasters and pandemics hit harder (Singer and Rylko-Bauer, 2020; Svistova, 2022). Yet regrettably, the media and public health officials tend to ignore or overlook structural dimensions of a pandemic (Svistova, 2022). Weak and toxic governance of social organizations, the state and global institutions, trigger inequalities which make marginalized groups vulnerable to pandemics. This is structural violence. Structural violence is essentially, the everyday (unnoticeable/invisible), oppressive social, political, and economic structures of governance or social organizations that cause pain, suffering, sickness, disability, and death to affected marginalized populations (Farmer, 2005; Nandagira et al., 2020). Such oppressive systems are violent, because they cause suffering and injury to innocent people (Farmer, 2005). Structural violence is characterized by interlocking axes of oppression such as gender, class, religion, politics, racism, and global inequalities (Farmer, 2005; Nandagira et al., 2020).

To the degree that structural violence causes pain or worsens the pain caused by natural pandemics (Nandagira et al., 2020), the study theorizes that structural

DOI: 10.4324/9781003494546-11

violence is a human-made and avoidable 'pandemic'. To date, this concept has never been deployed as an analytical lens in women's sexual reproductive health crisis communication, within the context of pandemics in Zimbabwe. Consequently, this study deploys this concept to examine how and the degree to which select media organizations made visible the way structural violence negatively impacted and shaped women's access to sexual reproductive health products and services, during the COVID-19 pandemic. This study comes in a Zimbabwean COVID-19 context, where structural challenges worsened the gendered impacts of COVID-19 (Sibanda et al., 2022; Dzinamarira et al., 2021; Mhiripiri and Midzi, 2021), which was complicated by prevalent misinformation and disinformation (Simba and Ngcobo, 2020). The study then interrogates how select media channels (television, Facebook, and YouTube) reported and projected the images and narratives of women's sexual reproductive rights in relation to abortion, pregnancy, contraceptives, and general maternity services during the period 2020–2022. The following section focuses on questions that guide the study.

Main Question

To what extent did select media channels in Zimbabwe implicate structural violence in their coverage of women's sexual reproductive health–related suffering, during the COVID-19 pandemic?

Sub-questions

a What media formats were deployed in disseminating information on different forms of bodily suffering and how do the images depicted relate to principles of crisis communication in a COVID-19 pandemic context?
b To what extent (if at all) did the select media channels critically link/relate women's sexual bodily suffering to oppressive axes of power in Zimbabwe and beyond?

Through an analysis of 11 purposely selected Facebook, television, and YouTube videos, the study shows how, during the COVID-19 pandemic, Zimbabwean women's sexual reproductive bodies embodied both local and global sociopolitical and socioeconomic axes of oppressive power – the violence of injustices, the violence of inequalities and misgovernance, that is rarely noticed in everyday habituated circumstances (see Nandagira et al., 2020). Identifying documentaries, news, drama, and talk shows as the dominant media formats that were deployed, the study acknowledges the commendable efforts of the media in aligning with principles of crisis communication, such as cultural congruency, use of experts, call to action, and accuracy in depicting injuries, deaths, and illnesses that occurred as a result of the COVID-19 pandemic. While the application some of the principles of crisis communication were commendable, the study notes that most of the media channels did not sufficiently make 'visible' the interlocking axes of national, social, and global axes of oppressive power that exacerbated the impact of COVID-19 on women's sexual reproductive health.

Literature Review: Crisis Communication Media, Women, and Structural Violence in the COVID-19 Pandemic

Four significant themes emerge from the emergent literature on crisis communication: media, structural violence, and the COVID-19 pandemic. Both Zimbabwean (Sibanda et al., 2022; Dzinamarira et al., 2021; Mhiripiri and Midzi, 2021; Murewanhema et al., 2022) and international literature (Nandagira et al., 2020; Singer and Rylko-Bauer, 2020) emphasize the gendered dimensions of the COVID-19 pandemic in which women were the most disadvantaged in relation to access to sexual reproductive products and services. Second, existing literature notes that the COVID-19 pandemic intensified other social catastrophes that feed on the ruins of inequalities which condemn women to sickness, injuries, deaths, and related sufferings (Manyonganise, 2022; Singer and Rylko-Bauer, 2020). This means the COVID-19 pandemic exacerbated already existing inequalities that put women at sexual reproductive health risk during the crisis (Macnamara, 2021). Third, in the Zimbabwean context, there is a perception that the media did not sufficiently report gender inequalities that negatively impacted women, as the media insufficiently exposed gender injustices and did not eloquently articulate the aspirations of the marginalized women (Tshuma et al., 2022). Here the expectation is that the media should deploy principles of crisis communication to build trust in institutions, reduce risks, and empower women sociopolitically and demand good governance to create an enabling environment to combat pandemics such as COVID-19 (Macnamara, 2021). Fourth, in the COVID-19 context, structural violence was globally a 'secondary disaster' (Svisvota, 2022), because the pandemic revealed perpetuated and produced structural violence (Svisvota, 2022) in devastating ways that prompted the need to activate the media towards transformative discourses, so that media narratives can force/motivate public health, the state, and global institutions to strengthen the health delivery systems to protect personal and public health (Gianella, 2022; Macnamara, 2021). This relates to the crisis communication, principle of producing people-centered media narratives (Mackay et al., 2021), that prioritizes marginalized and vulnerable people's interests as opposed to profits of elite political interests (Svisvota, 2022).

This study contributes to the previous literature by deploying the development communication framework and the structural violence lens in analyzing the way selected media channels reported and reflected on the experiences of Zimbabwean women in relation to access to sexual reproductive health services and products in the context of the COVID-19 pandemic.

Methods

This is analytical research with a qualitative approach. The study deployed YouTube algorithm search using the following keywords: women, reproductive health during COVID-19 pandemic in Zimbabwe, pregnancy, abortion, contraceptives, sexual violence, and maternal health. On Facebook, the authors used the search column and typed the same words. There were three major inclusion criteria. The first one was that the video had to be based on Zimbabwe. The second criterion was that the video should have been broadcast during the period 2020–2022, which was perceived as the peak of the COVID-19 pandemic. Third, the researchers were looking for videos that had some clear reference to some form of sexual reproductive bodily suffering, and at least some indirect reference or comment on the surrounding legal, political, global, and social and institutional systems or governance structure, in which the video functions. The researchers also did a qualitative analysis of the depiction of bodily suffering and the extent to which each video commented on or referred to axes of oppressive power. In the data analysis, the study adopts a development communication framework, which essentially means that the role of media is beyond passively disseminating information from sources. In this regard, the media has to adopt transformative approaches where the media becomes a center for the circulation and interrogation of subversive and transformative knowledge and information (Choudhury, 2011; Mcphail, 2009). This framework then fits into crisis communication and the structural violence lenses, which seek to provide crisis messages to assist communities to cope and survive a disrupted system, polity, or community (Anasah, 2022). In this way, crisis messages can equip and prepare communities against impeding dangers. The following sections focus on the results that emerged from the aforementioned methods.

Results

Subsequent sections will present summaries of media formats used, and a summary of the content of each video. Lastly, the section offers a descriptive analysis of how each video reflected and commented on the bodily suffering of women in relation to structural violence.

Media Formats and Principles of Crisis Communication

This section presents a summary of the formats used by different organizations in relation to the principles of crisis communication to answer sub-question (a), namely, "What media formats were deployed in disseminating information on different forms of bodily suffering and how do the images depicted relate to principles of crisis communication in a COVID-19 pandemic context?"

Most media channels focused specifically at the peak of lockdowns. The results are presented in Table 10.1 followed by a brief explanation.

Table 10.1 Summary of formats during 2020–2022

Format	*Dominant principles of crisis communication observed*
Documentary	5 (Empathetic, cultural congruency, and use of experts)
Drama	1 (Use of experts and cultural congruency)
News	4 (Consistency and use of experts)
Talk show	1 (Empathetic, call to action)

The table shows that documentaries and news were the most dominant formats. Television stations (both local and foreign) used the news format to highlight the challenges facing women in relation to their sexual reproductive health rights. The major principles of crisis communication that were observed include being empathetic, the use of experts, and cultural congruency. These principles, as will be highlighted in subsequent sections, did not only make the communication of the COVID-19 pandemic ethically sound but they also enhanced the vivid illustration of the level of sexual reproductive health suffering that the women experienced. The select media narratives were generally consistent, accurate, and provided expert views and statistics on the rate of infection, deaths, hospitalization, and relevant cultural views on abortion and maternity services witnessed during the pandemic. For example, Tables 10.2 and 10.3 show that Amakhosi Media, Hawks News, eNCA, Bustop TV, and BBC depicted vivid narratives and images of

Table 10.2 Summary of content: Facebook, YouTube, and television programs and channels during 2020–2022

Channel	*Title*	*Format*	*Organization*
YouTube https://youtu.be/Xy8AhvCUEkQ	Maternal health in the time of COVID-19 in Zimbabwe	Documentary	Amakhosikazi Media
Facebook https://fb.watch/gzAslzlAtH/	Inside Zimbabwe's backyard abortion clinics	Documentary	The News Hawks
YouTube https://youtu.be/pGAWgFtJ9zk	Amai vanobvisa nhumbu! (Is abortion a sin or a crime?)	Documentary	Bustop TV
ZBC TV https://youtu.be/MbHk2k5QZG0	Exclusive: ZBC exposes illegal abortion clinic in Harare	Feature news	ZBC
BBC News www.bbc.com/news/world-africa-58130891	Outrage after Zimbabwean girl, 14, dies giving birth at a church shrine	Text	BBC
YouTube https://youtu.be/ze-v7TwKiQ	Abortion in Zimbabwe: A legal overview	Documentary	Katswe Sisterhood
Facebook https://fb.watch/gzBJa9B5z-/	Contraceptive	Drama	Geraldine Rache Drama
Facebook https://fb.watch/gzBXVFkL4v/	Digital conversation on access to sexual reproductive services for adolescents and young women in Zimbabwe	Talk shows	My Age Zimbabwe

Table 10.2 (Continued)

Channel	*Title*	*Format*	*Organization*
YouTube www.youtube.com/watch?v=t7ORp0mFgtI	Zimbabwe health: Concerns for pregnant women and girls	News	eNCA
YouTube www.youtube.com/watch?v=CNLpxfaWMbs	Impact of COVID-19 on women and girls in Zimbabwe	News	SABC
YouTube https://youtu.be/f7HEZx4vSIM	Teen pregnancy during the COVID-19 2020–2022	Documentary	Africa News Channel

hunger, maternal death, bleeding, deaths on shrines, with verified statistics of more than 5000 deaths, more than 400 unwanted child pregnancies, and other facts and figures relating to maternal services and sexually transmitted diseases (STDs) that were witnessed during the short COVID-19 period under discussion. In general, the media narratives provided factual and technical information on the causes and possible solutions to the impact of COVID-19 on Zimbabwean women's sexual reproductive health. To this extent, the media narratives give credence to Paul Farmer's theorization that the knowledge of suffering cannot be effectively conveyed in pure facts and figures (Farmer et al., 2006). The deployment of stories and biographies of specific girls and women provided convincing details on the extent of suffering that the women experienced. Table 10.2 provides background details of each of the media channels under discussion.

All the 11 videos generally outline the social, economic, and health challenges that affected women in Zimbabwe. The major focus was on pregnancy and abortion and the challenges that prevented women from accessing healthcare. These findings resonate with wider studies (see Murewanhema et al., 2022; Tiew et al., 2022; Mittal and Singh, 2020; Singer and Rylko-Bauer, 2020) which show the gendered impact of COVID-19, because while the virus does not discriminate, the impact of COVID-19 does discriminate (Igbinoba et al., 2020), as it brings several challenges such as violence against women, unwanted pregnancies, and limited access to female reproductive health facilities. Indeed, as the 11 videos attest, Zimbabwean women faced many disruptions that affected their health potential and denied them the right to access even basic reproductive health facilities. Media narratives from the aforementioned channels resonate with crisis communication scholarship, which suggests that at the peak of the COVID-19 pandemic most health institutions suspended some essential services and in the process effectively curtailing women's rights to reproductive healthcare (Senol and Polat, 2022). Yet the crucial issue here is the degree to which the aforementioned media narratives, biographies, and images of suffering women were embedded in the larger matrix

Table 10.3 Depiction of female sexual reproductive bodily suffering/harm and comments/link with axes of oppressive power

Title	*Channel*	*Nature of bodly harm and suffering depicted*	*Direct comment on structural violence*	*Indirect/implicit reference on power axis*
Maternal health in time of COVID-19 in Zimbabwe	YouTube: Amakhosikazi Media	- Pain of women in labor - Thirteen-year-old giving birth on the floor - Child dying from lack of attention - Woman having a still birth due to lack of proper care - Hygiene challenges due to lack of water	- No direct comment or reference to structural violence	- Low salaries - No protective wear - Transport delays - Poor sanitation - Staff shortage - No editorial comment from interviewer
Inside Zimbabwe's backyard abortion clinics	Facebook: The News Hawks	- Use of crude instruments to abort pregnancies - Hunger	- No direct reference to structural violence	- Reference and brief analysis to the Abortion Act - Expensive medical bills - No reference from interviewer on governance
Amai vanobvisa nhumbu! (Is abortion a sin or a crime?)	YouTube: Bustop TV	- Abortion-related suicides	- No direct reference to structural violence	- Expensive access to legal abortion - Cultural fears–related abortions - Reference to Abortion Termination Act
Exclusive: ZBC exposes illegal abortion clinic in Harare	YouTube: ZBC TV	- Bleeding women - Dead fetus	- No direct reference to structural violence	- Unnamed health institutions supplying drugs and protective wear
Outrage after Zimbabwean girl, 14, dies giving birth at a church shrine	Web News Text: BBC	- Maternal mortality at religious shrines	- Call the law to deal with religion-related violence against women and girls	

			- Interviewer makes broad reference to relevant laws	
Abortion in Zimbabwe: A legal overview	YouTube: Katswe Sisterhood	- Bleeding women - Deaths	- No direct reference to structural violence	- Discussion of the termination of pregnancy act - Mentioning of UN human rights protocols
Contraceptive	Facebook: Geraldine Rache Drama	- Mentioning of Sexually transmitted infections (STIs)	- No direct reference to structural violence	- Cultural taboos on sexuality
Digital conversation on access to sexual reproductive health services for adolescents and young women in Zimbabwe	Facebook: My Age Zimbabwe	- Teenage pregnancies - Sexually transmitted infections - Unplanned pregnancies during COVID-19 period	- No direct reference to structural violence	- Reference to amendment of the Public Health Act
Zimbabwe health: Concerns for pregnant women and girls	YouTube: eNCA	- Obstetric fistula - Hundreds of girls dropping out of school due to pregnancy during COVID-19 era - Hunger - Untreated obstetric fistula	- Mentioning of inequalities which lead to death, diseases, and hunger - Privileges of the elite highlighted	None
Impact of COVID-19 on women and girls in Zimbabwe	YouTube: SABC News	- Hunger - Rudimentary sanitary wear - Four hundred pregnant girls dropping out of school due to unplanned pregnancies during COVID-19 era	- Hard hitting sarcastic comment on minister of finance who fails to fund the local health system	none
Teen pregnancy during the COVID-19 2020–2022	YouTube: Africa News	- COVID-19 lockdown–induced pregnancies and hunger - Five thousand child pregnancies between 2020 and 2021		- No contraceptives - Older men refusing paternity

of culture, history, and political economy (Farmer, 2005), and that is the focus of the next section.

Media Coverage of COVID-19 Pandemic: Linking Women's Suffering to Axes of Oppressive Power in Zimbabwe and Beyond

This section answers sub-question (b), namely "To what extent (if at all) did the select media channels critically link/relate women's sexual bodily suffering to axes of power in Zimbabwe and beyond?" The section briefly summarizes the nature of women's bodily suffering and harm that was brought about by the COVID-19 pandemic. Focus is on how each video reported and commented on the sexual reproductive bodily harm/suffering that the women experienced, and the degree to which they critically linked that suffering to local, regional, and global oppressive axes of power. As is curiously evident, in Table 10.3, all the local videos do not have direct reference and comment on local Zimbabwean institutional everyday forms of restrictions and oppressions that affected women's access to sexual reproductive care and services. Only foreign channels, namely, SABC eNCA, and BBC news, critically refer to the Zimbabwean axes of power that caused the bodily suffering of women. For instance, the SABC report gave a hard hitting and sarcastic comment on the Zimbabwean Minister of Finance, for failing to fund the health sector, against the background in which the minister had boasted that he would adequately fund the health sector. The report mocked the financial mismanagement which was affecting the sexual health of women. The BBC report on the other hand challenged the legal violence of the country, by making a passionate call for authorities to craft laws that punish religious leaders who engender the sexual reproductive health of women by denying them access to modern medical services. The apparent silence of local media channels on this legal violence could be linked to the larger democratic context, in which there seems to be media restrictions in disseminating information that is critical of the state (see Tshuma et al., 2022). It is evident that most local media channels did not critically link the suffering of women to both local and international axes of oppressive power. The only exceptions are private media organizations, such News Hawks and Magamba TV. These two organizations articulated 'mild' legal criticisms of the Abortion Act. Most local media channels were silent on what the state and other related institutions did/did not do to protect women against the gendered impact of COVID-19. Table 10.3 provides details on how and the degree to which each media channel critically linked the plight of women to oppressive axes of power.

Discussion

The COVID-19 pandemic was a global crisis which deserved systematic coverage, especially on women's sexual reproductive health in Zimbabwe. COVID-19 disrupted women's access to safe abortion, menstrual health, contraception, pregnancy, and maternal health among others. The data presented previously has established that the COVID-19 pandemic brought about a disproportionate distribution of sexual reproductive bodily pain, injury, suffering, and deaths. The analysis from the videos shows that pain, injury, and deaths were distributed mainly to low-income women, rural girls, young school girls, and sex-workers. These bodily sufferings are indirectly caused by institutional systems relating to culture, religion, sexism, weak legal systems, weak governance, corruption, and global inequalities which do not bring equitable global healthcare and funding (see Singer and Rylko-Bauer, 2020). There is limited literature focusing on media as effective strategy for crisis health communication in Zimbabwe. Yet the media was "… perhaps our only window to understand the corona virus crisis and women's place in it …" (Kiptnness and Okoye, 2021: 3). The media channels show bodily sufferings of women during the COVID-19 pandemic, and these bodily sufferings include deaths of children, bleeding, STDs, untreated wounds, untreated obstetric fistula, rudimentary sanitary wear, dead fetuses, and unwanted pregnancies. Second, the media narratives are quite significantly accurate and detailed in showing the immediate and visible COVID-19-related bodily sufferings. To this extent, all the videos achieved the informative functions and observed several principles of crisis of communication, such as credibility, clarity, accuracy, respect, promotion of action, and cultural congruence (see Ansah, 2022). Indeed, the videos clearly showed how the COVID-19 pandemic disrupted women's sexual reproductive health.

However, one of the key principles of crisis communication which has not been sufficiently observed is the principle of people-centeredness, which is that the media (as a watchdog of democracy and good governance) has to articulate the impact of pandemics from sociopolitical points of views that benefit and protect marginalized social groups such as women during pandemics (Ansah, 2022; Tiew et al., 2022; Tshuma et al., 2022). This view relates to the development communication framework (Choudhury, 2011) and the structural violence theoretical lenses (Farmer et al., 2006), which view injustices and inequalities as major causes of human suffering. Hence, major challenges in the way select media channels discussed in this study communicated the COVID-19 pandemic relate to the degree to which the videos did not sufficiently make visible the social injustices, oppressions, and the inequitable impact of the COVID-19 pandemic (see Nandagira et al., 2020). For instance, the local media in particular did not seize the opportunity to demonstrate the intersectionality of axes of oppression (Farmer, 2005), in that most of the white garment churches which do not allow women to seek modern health services are very close to the state and the ruling party (see Manyonganise, 2022). Consequently, both the private and public channels hardly mentioned that connection which resulted in the suffering of women. The deaths of women giving birth at religious shrines were caused by the 'unholy' union of the church and the state which denies them justice, freedom of choice, and religious liberty. Further, the local media did not sufficiently demonstrate and comment on the institutional forms of restrictions and misgovernance that are captured succinctly in a pastoral letter by Zimbabwean bishops. These include theft of personal protective equipment (PPE), forcing doctors to work without sufficient protective equipment, legal violence, financial mismanagement, and the disjointed approaches to the COVID-19 pandemic (see Manyonganise, 2022), which denied women access to financial resources and related health services. All local videos lost the opportunity to link the bodily suffering of women to these forms of violence of injustices and forms of violence of inequalities and misgovernance (see Mittal and Singh, 2020).

While all foreign channels (eNCA, SABC, and BBC) managed to unmask some axes of oppressive power, within Zimbabwe, they fell short in linking health disparities in the country to globalizing capitalism (Mcphail, 2009), which has created a global health funding scheme whose approval systems are not transparent and disadvantage countries from the Global South (see Tiew et al., 2022). One of the practical ways of transforming global inequalities is to promote local health systems and practices. One key issue that some of the videos bring to the fore is the question of local or traditional herbalists, traditional midwives, and indigenous health knowledge systems within a health crisis. The videos tend to denigrate and demonize the traditional herbalist, 'abortionist', and midwife. While indeed, there are reports of deaths happening at their centers of health, it is not ideologically sound to dismiss them, because they may have some local solutions to women's sexual health. Indeed, the ZBC TV video shows that the woman who carried out abortions did so in the context of an apparent collapse of conventional health services due to the restrictions imposed by the COVID-19 pandemic. Given this restrictive context, perhaps the media could have considered setting the agenda by advocating for the empowerment and capacitation of traditional herbalists, midwives, and other healthcare providers. In any case, success stories from Gambia, Zambia and Kenya show that community distribution of misoprostol tablets by community health workers led to reduced adverse outcomes from post-partum hemorrhage (see Murewanhema et al., 2022).

To this degree, the dissemination of COVID-19-related women's sexual reproductive health crisis messages by both local and foreign media was not adequate, value-laden, purposive, goal-oriented, interventional, and positive (Choudhury, 2011). This means instead of just telling audiences to adjust to the current global and local governance systems, the media needed to go further and seek to expose the achievements and shortcomings of cultural organizations, public health institutions, the state and global institutions in protecting women and mitigating the gendered impact of COVID-19. This can make these governance institutions accountable, and prepare them for future pandemics. This is crucial because effective leadership, just sociopolitical systems, and good governance are key factors in creating enabling environments that protect women from adverse health hazards during pandemics (Mackay et al., 2021). This calls for people-centered, transformative and subversive crisis communication, which current Zimbabwean health crisis communication scholarship and media institutions are yet to embrace.

Conclusion

The study concludes that the media performed a critical and commendable role in the dissemination of information relating to the impact of the COVID-19 on women's sexual reproductive health during COVID-19. Specifically, the media observed several principles of crisis communication to raise awareness, suggest solutions, and the direction to take during the COVID-19 pandemic. However, to a large extent, select media channels on Zimbabwe did not sufficiently implicate structural violence in their coverage of women's sexual reproductive health–related suffering during the COVID-19 pandemic. This everyday violence of institutional governance systems is a theme that media practitioners, researchers, and development communicators cannot ignore if the media is to do justice to its significant roles – relating to providing information, education, awareness, and as a watchdog of democracy, good governance, and development. The authors contend that structural violence offers additional analytical lenses to analyze and inform practices in crisis health communication, in the context of the disruptions and injustices that happen to women's sexual reproductive health. Structural violence draws attention to the usually invisible but powerful axes of internalized oppressions that (we have theorized as everyday 'pandemics') cause bodily diseases, pain, injury, and death on a scale that maybe too enormous to qualify and quantify. The larger implication is to call the attention of the media and crisis health communicators on the need to investing in ideological commitment – raising awareness of the dynamics of the axes of oppressive power (every 'pandemics'), which always complicate the search for solutions to stability – before, during, and after a pandemic. Given their enormity, everyday 'pandemics' require sustained focus and challenge in media coverage of pandemics.

References

Ansah, P. O. (2022). COVID-19 dialogue on Facebook: crisis communication relationship between Ghanaian authorities and citizens. *Journal of International Crisis Communication and Risk Communication Research,* 5(10): 57–86.

Choudhury, P. S. (2011). Media in development communication. *Global Media Journal – Indian Edition,* 2(2): 1–13.

Dzinamarira, T., Nachipo, B., Phiri, B., & Musuka, G. (2021). COVID-19 vaccine roll-out in South Africa and Zimbabwe: urgent need to address community preparedness, fears and hesitancy. *Vaccines,* 9(250): 1–10.

Farmer, P. (2005). *Infections and inequalities: The modern plagues.* University of California Press: Berkeley, CA.

Farmer, P. E., Nizeye, B., Stulac, S., & Keshavyee, S. (2006). Structural violence and clinical medicine. *PLOS Medicine,* 3(10):1686–1691. Available at https://journals.plos.org/plosmedicine/article?id=10.1371/journal.pmed.0030449

Gianella, C. (2022). The Peruvian response to the COVID-19 pandemic: the role of evidence-based governance and structural violence. WIDER Working Paper, 2022/81, 118:138. United Nations World Institute for Economic Development Research, WIDER, unu.edu.

Igbinoba, A. O., Soola, E. O., Omojola, O., Odukoya, J., Adekeye, O., & Salau, O. P. (2020). Women's mass media exposure and maternal health access, in Ota, Nigeria. *Cogent Social Sciences,* 6(1). http://doi/10.1080/23331188.2020

Kiptnness, E. M. & Okoye, J. B. (2021). Media coverage of the novel corona virus in Kenya and Tanzania: content analysis of newspaper articles in Africa. *Cogent Public Health,* 8(1). www.tandfonline.com/doi/full/10.1080/2331205X.2021.1956034

Mackay, M., Calongeli, T., Gillis, D., McWhirter, J., & Papadopuulos, A. (2021). Examining social media crisis communication during early COVID-19, from public health and news media for quality, content and corresponding public sentiment. *International Journal of Environmental Research and Public Health*, 18(15), 7986. doi: 10.3390/ijerph18157986

Manyonganise, M. (2022). When a pandemic wears the face of a woman: intersections of religion and gender during the COVID-19 pandemic in Zimbabwe. In Sibanda, F., Muyambo, T. & Chitando, E. (eds.), *Religion and the COVID-19 pandemic in Southern Africa*. London: Routledge, pp. 232–242.

Mcnamara, J. (2021). New insights into crisis communication from an "inside" emic perspective during covid-19. *Public Relation Inquiry,* 10(2): 23702622021.

Mcphail, T. L. (ed.) (2009). Introduction. In Mcphail, T. L. (ed.). *Development communication: Reframing the role of the media*. West Sussex, UK: Wiley-Blackwell, pp. 1–20.

Mhiripiri, N. A., & Midzi, R. (2021). Fighting for survival: persons with disabilities' activism for the mediatisation of COVID-19 information. *Media International Australia*, 178(1): 151–167. https://doi.org/10.1177/1329878X20967712

Mittal, S., & Singh, T. (2020). Gender based violence during covid-19 pandemic: a mini review. *Frontiers in Global Women's Health,* 1(4): 1–7

Murewanhema, G., Musuka, G., Gwanzura, C., Makurumidze, R., Chitungo, I., Chimene, M., Tungwarara, N., Dzinamarira, T., & Madzyire, M. G. (2022). Maternal sexual and reproductive health in marginalized areas: renewing community's involvement strategies beyond the worst COVID-19 pandemic. *Environmental Research and Public Health*. 19(1): 1–12. doi: 10.3390/ijerph19063431

Nandagira, R., Coast, E., & Strong, D. (2020). Making structural violence visible. *International Perspective on Sexual Reproductive Health,* 46(1): 83–89.

Senol, D. & Polat, F. (2022). Effects of the pandemic on women's reproductive health protective attitudes, a Turkish example. *Reproductive Health,* 19(106): 1–9. doi: 10.1186/s12978-022-01412-y

Sibanda, F., Muyambo, T. & Chitando, E. (2022). Introduction: religion and public health in the shadow of COVID-19 pandemic in Southern Africa. In Sibanda F., Muyambo. T & Chitando E. (eds.), *Religion and the COVID-19 pandemic in Southern Africa*. London: Routledge, pp. 1–24.

Simba, H. & Ngcobo, S. (2020). Are pandemics gender neutral? Women's health and COVID-19. *Frontiers in Global Women's Health,* 1: 570666. doi: 10.3389/fgwh.2020.570666

Singer, M., & Rylko-Bauer, B. (2020). The Syndemics and structural violence of the COVID-19 pandemic: anthropological insights on a crisis. *Open Anthropological Research,* (7): 7–32.

Svistova, J. (2022). US systematic violence amid the COVIS D-19 disaster: a conceptual critical disaster model. *Cultural and Radical Social Work*, 11(2): 295–312.

Tang, J. W. (2020). Covid-19: Interpreting scientific evidence-uncertainty confusion and delays. *BMC Infectious Diseases*, 20(653): 1–4. doi: 10.1186/s12879-020-05387-8]

Tiew, A., Pizzarossa, L., Jastaniah, B., & Jayaweera, R. T. (2022). The impact of COVID-10 on safe abortion access in Africa: an analysis through a framework of reproductive justice and the lens of structural violence. *Frontiers in Global Women's Rights*, 3: 1–7. 3389/fwg 2022 958710.

Tshuma, B. B., Tshuma, L., & Ndlovu, N. (2022). Media discourses on gender in the time of COVID-19 pandemic in Zimbabwe. In Dralega, C. A., & Napakol, A. (eds.), *Health crises and media discourses in Sub-Saharan Africa*. Springer: Cham, pp. 267–281. https://doi.org/10.1007/978-3-030-95100-9_16

11 The Media and Dynamics of COVID-19 Vaccine Acceptance and Hesitancy among Harare Central Prison Camp Female Participants

Glory Ruvarashe Chirara and Nehemiah Chivandikwa

Introduction

This research aims at demonstrating the dynamics of COVID-19 vaccine acceptance and hesitancy amongst Zimbabwean female participants in Harare Central Prison Camp (HCPC). The focus is on how television formats in mainstream media in Zimbabwe, in this case, The Zimbabwe Broadcasting Television Corporation (ZBC-TV), complexly linked with and or informed, select women's responses to vaccine's acceptance and hesitancy. In general, chief factors that inform women's decision-making to vaccinate or not are media literacy, political consciousness, and corporal agency (see Mukenge, 2020). During pandemics, ZBC-TV acts as a medium for risk communication and employs different strategies to keep the nation well-informed (see Muchetwa et al., 2021). This study therefore examines how the use of infomercials and advertisements to endorse the vaccine complexly linked with or influenced vaccine hesitancy or acceptance among female participants. Penafiel-Saiz (2019) suggests that mainstream media is an effective means of communication about the vaccines as it makes use of models from different backgrounds, race, economic status as a way of trying to reach all categories of female populations. However, due to sociological, biological, and physiological factors, the vaccine can face both hesitancy and acceptance. This study's research site was Harare Central Prison Camp (HCPC), which is located in Newlands, Harare. The study is guided by the following research questions:

Main Question

What dynamics influence COVID-19 vaccination acceptance and hesitancy as advertised in ZBC-TV formats?

DOI: 10.4324/9781003494546-12

Sub-questions

- What factors might influence the way women may be persuaded by television advertisements and infomercials to accept COVID-19 vaccine?
- What dynamics may inform the way a television media format may cause vaccine hesitancy among women?
- How are the above dynamics implicated in risk communication for women in a pandemic context?

In answering these questions, the study draws on interview materials with selected female participants on media testimonials, infomercials, sermons, advertisements, chain messages, and musical interludes formats that were used to push the vaccine and anti-vaccine drive. Some of the most common factors that influenced vaccine acceptance are trust in the vaccines, and media used fear of the pandemic through the use of fear appeals as well as information adequacy. Hesitancy among participants was influenced by mistrust in vaccines and information source, interaction with social media, and information inadequacy. These variables relate to women's agencies and capabilities in media literacy, political consciousness, and gender identity politics, which then directly and indirectly inform the way the women accept or reject vaccines. Overall, the study theorizes that the safety of women in a pandemic will largely depend on how their media literacy, political and health agencies are continuously reinforced before, during, and after a pandemic.

Literature Review: Context of COVID-19 Vaccine Acceptance and Hesitancy

In Zimbabwe, researchers have established that national television and newspapers were used to promote and gain the approval of the vaccines by the public. They further note that the role of mainstream media was to disseminate information on the vaccines so as to convince those who were hesitant to accept the vaccine (Dzinamarira et al., 2022; Muchetwa et al., 2021). Elsewhere, commenting on television and vaccine messages, Piltch-Loeb et al. (2021) and Penafiel-Saiz (2019) argue that television campaigns for vaccines should be accurately and efficiently disseminated to promote healthy behaviours. This is crucial so that communication of COVID-19 vaccines gains more relevance amongst citizens when the advertisements and campaigns acknowledge biases and misunderstandings (Piltch-Loeb et al., 2021), since the fundamental role of media in general and in television (advertisements and infomercials in this case) is to create awareness so as to shape the perceptions and attitudes of people towards the vaccine (Mackay et al., 2021).

COVID-19 Vaccination Acceptance and Hesitancy

Vaccination hesitancy in Zimbabwe is caused by sociocultural, psychological, religious and behavioural factors (Chirara, 2022; Dzinamarira et al., 2022; Dzinamarira et al., 2021; Muchetwa et al., 2021; Muyambo et al., 2023). Hesitancy varies from individuals to societal levels (WHO, 2021), and it is also related to interaction with social media (Kagarakupi and Ndoma, 2022; Murewanhema et al., 2022). Mistrust in vaccines maybe due to their abundance (Kugarakuripi and Ndoma, 2022). Information inadequacy has been noted as another major setback promoting vaccine hesitancy affecting the marginalized communities in Africa and abroad (see Chaudhuri et al., 2022).

Further, Yoda and Katsuyama (2020) and Piltch-Loeb et al. (2021) assert that the information channel used to disseminate information about the vaccines influence acceptance. Acceptance is also influenced by the viewer's trust in the medium used to disseminate information about the vaccines as sufficient and transparent information about the vaccine's safety (Piltch-Loeb, 2023). Willingness to vaccinate against COVID-19 was influenced by accessibility, perceived benefits, and awareness on the consequences of not being vaccinated (Yoda and Katsuyama, 2020). In addition, different experiences with COVID-19 and advertisements result in fear-driven acceptance. The previous scholarship also highlights that positive health-promoting behaviours are not always due to willingness. For example, Yoda and Katsuyama (2020) established that threat = susceptibility + severity, hence the more fear appeals are used in advertisements, the more increase in health-promoting behaviours.

The previous literature is critical in risk communication for pandemics, because the literature shows that there are complex attitudes, subjective norms, and social norms (Fishbein and Ajzen, 2010), which may influence people to take adaptive actions to survive pandemics. Consequently, health and risk communicators need to use persuasive communication to influence positive health change, and to do this, they need to understand the aforementioned complex variables. Persuasive communication in risk communication is affected by several factors. For example, inconsistency, language discourse, and lack of transparency affect effective risk communication in Zimbabwe (see Mukenge, 2020; Chikonzo, 2018; Makuyana, 2013). This is reinforced by WHO (2020), which notes that effective risk communication engages the community at every level of a pandemic for consistent engagement with the public. Risk communication–driven campaigns must be able to convince the public on the dangers of a new infection (Yoda and Katsuyama, 2020). In addition, other studies on women and pandemics/epidemics have revolved around the use of television, print, and social media as effective tools of promoting healthy behaviours to curb the transmission of HIV/AIDS (see Mukenge, 2020; Chikonzo, 2018).

This research is unique as it takes a new dimension on the theme of women and pandemics. The study examines the dynamics that influence COVID-19 vaccine acceptance and hesitancy, as complexly linked with and/or influenced by television advertisements and infomercials in Zimbabwe. Most vaccination messages that were aired on ZBC-TV were 'neutral' in terms of gender representation, and this study examines how women's consumption of COVID-19 television advertisements and infomercials could be complexly linked to their acceptance and hesitancy to take vaccines. Specifically, the unique contribution of the study is the theorization that the safety of women in a pandemic will largely depend on how their media literacy, political and health agencies are continuously reinforced before, during, and after a pandemic. This presents new insights into interpretations of health, security, and violence in the context of pandemics.

Methodology

This is a television ethnographic research that deploys qualitative methods. Ethnography is a qualitative research design method that seeks to understand factors that influence individuals or society's perspectives concerning any issue, in this case, the reception of vaccination advertisements. Mudavanhu (2015) submits that ethnography is the standard and correct method to discover audience reception of media texts. Health communication is vital and its reception, especially on TV, needs the researcher to be on the ground – understanding different dynamics that stimulate human behaviour. Hence the researchers integrated with females at Harare Central Prison for at least a year. Purposive sampling was deployed where the researchers intentionally selected individuals and settings to understand the various dynamics that influence their perceptions. This design seemed to tally with television ethnography, and the researchers got to gain detailed information. The researchers deployed conceptual content analysis to analyse the relationship between the text and meanings in the advertisements. Makuyana (2013) explains that content analysis examines the text, pictures, and narratives that are used in a television show or text. Ethnographic interviews, questionnaires, and observations were used as data collection tools. The study draws on interview materials with selected female participants on media testimonials, infomercials, sermons, advertisements, infomercials, chain messages, and musical interludes formats that were used to push the vaccine and anti-vaccine drives.

Theory of Reasoned Action

The theory of reasoned action (TRA) was developed by Fishbein and Ajzen in 1967 (Fishbein and Ajzen, 2010). This theory is a modification of the theory of planned behaviour. Both theories agree that a person's attitudes and behaviours shape the way they make sense of healthy behaviours. The TRA is used in health promotion to measure or analyse how an individual's intention to respond to a health service is embedded in their behaviours, inspiration, evaluation of perceived benefits, behavioural belief, normative beliefs, amongst other factors. This research focuses mainly on concepts of behavioural intention and evaluation. For behavioural intention to be positive, referent groups must clearly inform the benefits of taking action so as to influence an individual's attitudes (Fishbein and Ajzen, 2010; Yzer, 2017). Evaluation means that when a health service is advertised, an individual or group of people in a family or society evaluates the potential outcomes. The clearer the outcomes of performing a certain behaviour, the more a person is inspired to take action. Evaluation can be intrapersonal or interpersonal and it involves weighing the information from an advertiser and its perceived outcomes. For service-providers to instil willingness to take action, they should accurately and effectively endorse the outcomes of performing a behaviour. Evaluation includes establishing behavioural beliefs which allow an individual to assess the consequences of taking action (Fishbein and Ajzen, 2010). A person's intention to perform a certain behaviour is influenced by their attitudes and motivation from referent groups. The attitude of an individual towards a healthy behaviour is influenced by their evaluation of the perceived outcomes, hence the more positive the attitude, the greater the chances of performing a conduct (Yzer, 2017). The referent groups are regarded as a social norm by this theory and these groups may be families or influential individuals in a society. Due to contextual dynamics, the attitude of a person towards a prominent person, be it a doctor, musician, or socialite, can influence them to take a positive or negative action. This theoretical framework will be deployed to analyse data that will emerge from the research questions outlined earlier.

Research Findings and Discussion

COVID-19 is a global pandemic and it is the role of every government to keep its citizens informed on the new developments regarding the pandemic (WHO, 2021). While the advertisements on ZBC-TV were risk communication–driven, the dissemination of vaccine-related information instilled hesitancy among a number of female participants. The need to feel safe and healthy can be a factor that can cause vaccine acceptance amongst women. Moreover, the political consciousness of advertisements and media literacy can cause both hesitancy and acceptance in women (Matenga, 2022). This research used responses from seven questionnaire participants and five interview respondents. Three participants who responded to interview questions also responded to the questionnaire. Out of five interview participants, three were hesitant and two were vaccinated. From the seven questionnaire respondents, five were hesitant. This discussion will use the integration analysis. In light of these details, subsequent sections will focus on the factors that the researchers identified as the chief causes of vaccine acceptance–hesitancy among the select women under consideration in this study.

Media Literacy

Media literacy refers to the ability by a viewer to analyse the messages, texts, and pictures in a media content, whether a newspaper, television, radio, or social media, (Yoda and Katsuyama, 2020). Media literacy comes in two broad categories, which are old and new media. Mainstream media is the old media that has been in existence for long. However, when looking at COVID-19 vaccine information, both mainstream and social media played a role in disseminating information to the people. It is against this background that media literacy extends its boundaries to new media literacy (NML). NML requires an individual to critically examine content deployed by mainstream media vis-à-vis social media. During the vaccination phase of COVID-19, various messages about anti-vaccines and those that supported the initiative stormed both mainstream and social media. The different levels of media literacy informed the decisions made by women.

Women who were hesitant displayed high levels of media literacy. Their interaction with various sources of media increased their literacy as they assessed information from all their sources of information (ZBC-TV included) before making decisions to either vaccinate or not. Worldwide vaccine acceptance was affected by the reception of chain messages on Facebook, Twitter, and WhatsApp spreading anti-vaccine information (Chirara, 2022). Catalan-Matamoros and Peñafiel-Saiz (2019) and Penafiel-Saiz (2019) note that national televisions can influence the decisions and impact the perceptions of the public's response to vaccines against controversies instilled by other sources of information. One respondent, RR, noted that her vaccine hesitancy was due to how ZBC-TV failed to comment on chain messages that were received by people through WhatsApp, Facebook, and Twitter. The participant, therefore, questioned the authenticity of advertisements on ZBC-TV and this resulted in hesitancy. Below is an extract from a participant who displayed high levels of media literacy

Box 11.1 Extract from a questionnaire

Q: Are there any other factors that influenced you to or not get vaccinated?

J: ZBC-TV advertisements were not open-minded like what WhatsApp was doing. They chose not to create an independent advertisement to address the myths on COVID-19 vaccines. I learnt about various side-effects of the vaccines through Twitter and WhatsApp. Yes, they might not be true, but I was concerned with why Mahomva[1] shunned that specific topic every Friday. I noticed from their health ministry website that most citizens wanted clarity. So why vaccinate now?

Box 11.2 Extract from interviews, 9 January 2022

GRC: For how long have you been watching ZBC-TV?

Jane (55: retired teacher): For a while now (chuckles). It's been a while since I last subscribed to my DSTV.

GRC: Ok, so what is your general comment on ZBC-TV advertisements vs the chain messages you mentioned earlier on?

Jane (55): I have always relied on ZTV, especially on health matters because they report health matters related to Zimbabwe, but then my sixth sense cannot allow me to ignore the messages I received on my Facebook. I gained more information and what I read was devastating and I could not trust ZBC alone because it lacked that vision of taking us through those messages. So maybe I will vaccinate later on but not now.

The previous extract shows that despite their consistent engagement with ZBC-TV, women in HCPC have adopted to NML as they weigh all the information before making decisions. Penafiel-Saiz (2019) suggests that national televisions, rather than social media, should be influencers of vaccine acceptance. In addition, Dzinamarira et al. (2021) explain that through their persuasive tone and appeals, television advertisements should gain the public's approval more than any other source of information. However, from the current research findings, women with low media literacy were more likely to uncritically embrace or accept the vaccine. Low media literacy can be informed by an individual's past experience with the broadcaster (see Matenga, 2022; Piltch-Loeb et al., 2021; Penafiel-Saiz, 2019). Two interview participants who claimed that they were persuaded by television media formats to accept the vaccine noted that their past experiences and reference to the health services advertised on ZBC-TV before proved to be beneficial. Hence the participants quickly accepted the vaccine advertisements. However, they further noted that ZBC-TV did not entirely frame the vaccine messages on their own, but partnered with various stakeholders to disseminate messages to its viewers, hence, this reinforced their trust in the vaccines.

Media literacy enables the viewer to access, process, critique messages, and adopt critical thinking on information received. This also includes understanding media politics (Ansah, 2022; Mckay et al., 2021). Elsewhere, studies have shown that a high media literacy rate is associated with vaccine acceptance and that low media literacy is associated with vaccine hesitancy. For instance, Austin, Baron, and Domgaard (2021) argue, that in the United States, equity gaps and disproportionate COVID-19 effects expose non-white races to disinformation from the media and that such social groups with low media literacy have less knowledge about COVID-19 and vaccines. What this means is that generally media literacy can protect marginalized communities such as women.

However, it is clear that the current research strongly associates relative media literacy to vaccine hesitancy and high risk to COVID-19 infection. It seems this correlation maybe linked to other contextual complexities, such as the fact that the women with relative high media literacy are extremely conscious of the restrictive political dynamics that control ZBC, and therefore, they tend to distrust most of the information that is broadcast on that channel. Second, it is clear that the media-literate women tend to be very critical of the messaging in the adverts and testimonials, which are not anchored and informed by major principles of health risk communication, such as transparency, evidence, participation, equity, proportion, flexibility, and testing (Ansah, 2022). This is also consistent with the reasoned action theory, which posits that for a health advertiser to instil willingness to action (vaccination), there is need for accuracy and credibility in the risk communication. A clear example is in Box 11.1, where a female viewer who is relatively media literate complains that ZBC adverts lack 'open-mindedness' (transparency) in which she expects detailed information on the pros and cons of the vaccines. This is very crucial, because as a result, she trusts social media platforms which are generally expected to be less credible sources of the pandemic. Such challenges are avoidable if the health communicators apply the principle of participation, which simply means that pandemic risk communication for women is crafted from the perspectives of women. The next section focuses on political ideology, which in Zimbabwe is to some extent linked to media literacy.

Political Ideology

Vaccine hesitancy and acceptance amongst women was also informed by their political consciousness. In this study, political consciousness refers to the realization that there are various administrations behind the production of infomercials and advertisements. The aim of the administration is either to clarify or foster vaccine uptake among viewers. ZBC-TV screened advertisements from the Ministry of Health Child Welfare and Care (MoHCC), as well as testimonials from prominent figures in Zimbabwe who once contracted COVID-19. In these testimonials, prominent figures narrated their ordeals to fear-drive viewers into vaccine acceptance. Moreover, in other testimonials, they feature religious leaders, like Prophet Makandiwa and Abdul Mahammad Ali of the Islamic society – an initiative to push for vaccine uptake.

Two female participants were vaccinated because of their trust in the information channel and the various administrations that sponsored vaccine advertisements. Through observations from intensive interactions with participants, the researchers noted that both women are politically affiliated to the ruling party, hence their trust in vaccine advertisements. Piltch-Loeb et al. (2021) established that in Singapore, those who received information about the vaccine from their national televisions were willing to vaccinate compared with those who relied on other sources of media. This observation applies to the two women from HCPC. ZBC-TV partnered with not only MoHCC, but 'trusted' stakeholders like OK, Maisha, and Delta Beverages which have had long-lasting relationships with the public. These various stakeholders are people's choice brands and their partnership was used by ZBC-TV to assure the viewers that they are safe. One participant, Amai Shalo, proudly noted that ZBC-TV is a ZANU-PF media house, hence there was no way they would misinform the public.

However, female participants who were hesitant demonstrated their resentment to vaccine adverts that they suspected of being associated with the political interests of the ruling ZANU-PF party. Participants noted that the use of well-known people to persuade citizens to get vaccinated by the ZBC adverts was an act of propaganda that was used to endorse the vaccine. A typical example of such adverts is the testimonial advert, COVID Chronicles by ZBC-TV. The advert featured politically prominent people like Ms Henrieta Rushwaya (former CEO of ZBC), and other reporters who shared how their tragic experiences with the pandemic pushed them to get vaccinated. The next extract shows how some select audiences viewed such adverts.

The aforementioned details clearly show how political ideology and consciousness shaped and informed women's attitude and evaluation of health risk communication messages from ZBC-TV. Theoretically (within the theory

Box 11.3 Extract from an interview held in HCPC, 22 January 2022

GRC:	So how do you rate (evaluate) the adverts aired on ZBC-TV?
BT (female, social worker, 32):	I don't know how I can explain it but let's just say they tried hard to push for the vaccine to an extent of featuring Makandiwa achiti (saying) vaccine is not the mark of the beast but whatever he said there was a publicity stunt considering how numbers then increased. I hope I don't sound judgemental (laughs).
GRC:	In other words, you are saying its propaganda?
BT:	(smiles broadly) Definitely, *iwewe ndiwe unotoziva materms acho* (you are the one who knows the right terms to use).

of reasoned action), politicians are the reference groups (Yzer, 2017) whom women may rely on to adopt health-protecting behaviour during a pandemic. The participants trusted and distrusted political influencers according to their political affiliation and consciousness. What this means is that the media has to work hard as a watchdog, to influence elite politicians and state functionaries to earn the trust of women, to prepare them not only for the current pandemic but even other future pandemics, because in Zimbabwe and elsewhere vaccine safety and perceptions of risks are linked to self-rated political ideology and consciousness (Austin et al., 2021). Lastly, this also suggests the need to continuously invest in understanding the political consciousness of women, which seems to be undervalued and under-researched. The next section focuses on fear-driven acceptance/hesitancy

Fear-Driven Acceptance/Hesitancy

Fear is an essential driver of change or stagnation. This section shows how the same fear-driven adverts complexly engendered both acceptance and hesitancy among women from the community under consideration. The researchers noted that fear was a major factor that influenced women in HCPC to get vaccinated. The way the adverts were framed, instilled fear in women who in panic chose to vaccinate to protect their families. The participants noted that ZBC-TV advertisements on COVID-19 in general had made them aware of the effects and dangers of the virus. As data from questionnaires and interviews shows, participants indicated that fear of COVID-19 influenced them to get vaccinated. The MoHCC Weekly Update showed the death toll around the world and skits by ZBC-TV on the perceived impact of COVID left two interview and three questionnaire participants anxious. COVID-19 statistics from infomercials like the Weekly Update showed a strong motivation for the participants to get vaccinated. At the same time, most women were also hesitant due to fear. Most of them raised their concerns on how information about the vaccines were insufficiently conveyed. According to one female participant, BB, the vaccine advertisements left more questions than answers. Information inadequacy has been noted as a major setback promoting vaccine hesitancy – affecting the marginalized communities in Africa and abroad (see Chaudhuri et al., 2022). It is the role of women as mothers of a society to make decisions on behalf of their families. Women also come across as opinion leaders in the society. Information insufficiency induced hesitancy among women, because they feared that it would risk their lives and families. Below is an extract of BB's response as well as VG's, a questionnaire respondent. We chose VG's response because it was more eloquently articulated than other responses from the questionnaires.

These extracts demonstrate that not knowing the after-effects and side-effects of the vaccines raised fears amongst women. This relates to the theoretical contention, in the reasoned action model, that people weigh options and if options are not clear,

Box 11.4 9 January, HCPC

GRC: Did the advertisements you mentioned provide enough information about the vaccines?

BB: No (pause) the advertisements did not address the issue of side-effects and that is the right of every patient before a vaccine is administered to them. *Imwe mishonga inotonyorwa* (other meds are written) that you will feel drowsy or vomit etc. I understand that all even immune boosters administered to children have side-effects and a patient is told before *abaiwa* (partaking).

Box 11.5 Extract from a questionnaire

GRC: How did the vaccines aired on ZBC-TV influence or not influence you to get vaccinated?

VG: COVID-19 is a complex pandemic that shook the world and vaccines were manufactured world over. But in terms of marketing the vaccine there was justice. All we knew from the advertisements was the vaccine is safe but how safe? They should tell us why we should use Sinopharm. I need to acquire enough facts and all instead of statistics they cannot help me to fully understand why I should vaccinate.

some may not be motivated to adopt the action (vaccination) that the ZBC-TV health communicators want to promote.

Vaccine Abundance Question

The COVID-19 pandemic saw many countries worldwide manufacturing vaccines to curb and end the COVID-19. It was a drive that was meant to benefit the world. However, for women in HCPC, the abundance of the vaccines induced fear and hesitancy. All five interview participants noted that all vaccines were declared safe and reliable, but there was no justification through ZBC-TV advertisements as to why there were many vaccines on board. Several studies on COVID-19 vaccines also note that distrust or mistrust in vaccines can cause hesitancy compared with any other factor (see Matenga, 2022). Chirara (2022) notes that deficiently designed health communication on the abundance of vaccines has a significant negative impact on vaccine uptake and health-related attitudes, beliefs, and behaviours. Women are not risk-takers, hence vaccine hesitancy was experienced by some women in the context under consideration.

However, despite the abundance of the vaccines, one interview participant noted that the abundance of vaccines was a relief, because, with the shutdown, the world needed strong intervention to return to normalcy. Some participants commended the government and ZBC-TV advertisements for bringing various vaccine brands, since patients need a variety to choose on depending with their allergies and health statuses. The Weekly Update show was of great help to female participants as it elaborated that before getting vaccinated, one can seek advice from medical practitioners. For example, Mai Shalo (interview 2022) said that she supports the abundance of vaccines. She made it her assignment to research on the vaccines to understand them before vaccination.

Conclusion

This study has shown that there are various complex factors that influence vaccine acceptance and hesitancy. Although television is an effective medium of communicating and disseminating information on risks and pandemics, it requires transparency. The decisions of women to vaccinate or not vaccinate are influenced by complex personal, social, and political factors that include trust in the vaccines, trust in the media channel used, fear of the pandemic, as well as information adequacy. Hesitancy amongst participants was influenced by mistrust in vaccines and information source, interaction with social media, and information inadequacy. We have demonstrated how these variables relate to women's agencies and capabilities in media literacy, political consciousness, and gender identity politics, which then directly and indirectly inform the way the women accept or reject vaccines. These factors link with complex behavioural intentions and evaluative competencies of women. Hence, the safety of women in a pandemic will largely depend on how their media literacy, political and corporeal agencies, and capabilities are continuously reinforced before, during, and after a pandemic. These findings point to the need to scale up theory-based interventions in producing persuasive messages that can influence protective behaviour by women during pandemics.

Note

1 (Agnes), COVID-19 Chief Coordinator in the Office of the President, Government of Zimbabwe.

References

Ansah, P. O. (2022). COVID-19 dialogue on Facebook: Crisis communication relationship between Ghanaian authorities and citizens. *Journal of International Crisis Communication and Risk Communication Research,* 5(10): 57–86.

Austin, E. W., Borah, P., Domgaard, S. (2021). COVID-19 disinformation and political engagement among communities of colour: The role of the media literacy. *Harvard Kennedy School of Misinformation Review,* 1(1): 1–16.

Catalan-Matamoros, D., Peñafiel-Saiz, C. (2019). How is communication of vaccines in traditional media: A systematic review. *Perspectives in Public Health*, 139(1): 34–43. doi:10.1177/1757913918780142

Chaudhuri, K., Chakrabarti, A., Chandon, J. S., Bandyopadhyay, S. (2022). Covid-19 vaccine hesitancy in UK: A longitudinal household cross-sectional study. *BMC Public Health*, 3(6): 15. https://do.org/10.1186/s128801-021-12472-3

Chikonzo, A. C. (2018). The roles of social media in disseminating HIV/AIDS information to young people aged 18–24 in Zimbabwe. D.Phil. thesis. University of Pretoria. https://hdl.handle.net/2263/71049 (retrieved 25 May 2022).

Chirara, G. R. (2022). The manifestations of Covid-19 vaccination hesitancy and acceptance in Harare Central Prison Camp: A case of ZBC-TV vaccine advertisement campaigns. Undergraduation thesis, University of Zimbabwe.

Dzinamarira, T., Nachipo, B., Phiri, B., & Musuka, G. (2021). COVID-19 vaccine roll-out in South Africa and Zimbabwe: Urgent need to address community preparedness, fears and hesitancy. *Vaccines,* 9(2): 1–10.

Dzinamarira, T., Nachipo, B., Nyathi, M., Madziva, M., Herrera, H., Siegel, H., & Msasuka, G. (2022). The case to scale up edutainment as an effective public health communication intervention to combat the COVID-19 pandemic in Zimbabwe. *Health Promotion Perspectives,* 12(1): 34–36.

Fishbein, M., & Ajzen, I. (2010). *Predicting and Changing Behaviours: The Reasoned Action Approach*. New York: Psychology Press.

Kugarakuripi, J., & Ndoma, S. (2022). Lack of trust in government, reliance on social media may drive vaccine hesitancy in Zimbabwe. *Afrobarometer, Dispatch IJR 500* africaportal.org/publication (retrieved 22 January 2022).

Mackay, M., Calongeli, T., Gillis, D., McWhirter, A., & Papadopuulos, A. (2021). Examining social media crisis communication during early COVID-19, from public health and news media for quality, content and corresponding public sentiment. *International Journal of Environmental Research and Public Health*, 18(15), 7986. doi: 10.3390/ijerph18157986.

Makuyana, K. A. (2013). *The Role of ZBC-TV Programme Positive Talk in Informing and Educating on Health-related Issues*. Gweru: Midlands State University.

Matenga, T. F. L., Tullani, F., Zulu, J. M., Davis, L. M., & Chavula, M. P. (2022). Motivating factors for and barriers to the Covid-19 vaccine uptake: A review of social media data in Zambia. *Cogent Public Health*, 9(1): 1–17. https:/doi.org/10.1080/27707571.2022.205921

Muchetwa, K., Maruta, E., Jaka, H., Ruvado, J., & Chazireni, E. (2021). Health communication strategies employed by the media during the Covid-19 crisis: Case of Zimbabwe Broadcasting Corporation Television (ZBC-TV). *European Journal of Social Sciences Studies*, 6(6): 38–50. doi: http://dx.doi.org/10.46827/ejsss.v6i6.1132

Mudavanhu, S. L. (2015). A study of Radio Zimbabwe messages and audiences in a time of crisis. D.Phil. dissertation. University of Cape Town.

Mukenge, C. (2020). An exploration of the communicative efficacy of HIV/AIDS IEC materials among secondary school teenagers in Harare. *Journal of Creative Communications*, 15(3): 235–254. https://doi.org/10.1177/073258620952273

Murewanhema, G. Musuka, G., Gwanzura, C., Makurumidze, R., Chitungo, I., Chimene, M., Tungwarara, N., Dzinamarira, T., & Madzyire, M. G. (2022). Maternal sexual and reproductive health in marginalized areas: Renewing community's involvement strategies beyond the worst COVID-19 pandemic. *Environmental Research and Public Health,* 19(1): 1–12.

Muyambo, T., Sibanda, F., & Chitando, E. (Eds.). (2023). *Religion and COVID-19 Vaccination in Zimbabwe*. London: Routledge.

Penafiel-Saiz, C. (2019). Message analysis about vaccines in print press, television and radio characteristics and gaps in previous research. DOI:10.1080/17538065.2019.1614377 (retrieved 4 July 2022).

Piltch-Loeb, R., Savoia, E., Goldberg, B., Haughes, B., Verhey, T., Kayyem, J., Miller-Idriss, C., Testa, M., et al. (2021). Examining the effect of information channel on Covid-19 acceptance. *PLoS ONE,* 16(5): e0251095. https://doi.org/10.1377/journalpone.0251095 (retrieved 30 May 2022).

Piltch-Loeb, R., Mazibuko, L., Stanton, E., Mngomezulu, T., Gareta, D., Nxumalo, S., Kraemer, J. D., Herbst, K., Siedner, M. J., & Harling, G. (2023). COVID-19 vaccine uptake, confidence and hesitancy in rural KwaZulu-Natal, South Africa between April 2021 and April 2022: A continuous cross-sectional surveillance study. *PLOS Glob Public Health.* 3(6): e0002033. https://journals.plos.org/globalpublichealth/article?id=10.1371/journal.pgph.000203

WHO. (2020). *Risk communication and community engagement readiness and response to coronavirus disease (COVID-19)*. Geneva. COVID-19 Global Risk Communication and Community Engagement Strategy – interim guidance (who.int).

WHO. (2021). Report of the Sage working group on vaccine hesitancy. www.asset-scienceinsociety.eu/sites/default/files/sage_working_group_revised_report_vaccine_hesitancy.pdf

Yoda, T., & Katsuyama, H. (2021). Willingness to receive Covid-19 vaccination in Japan. *Vaccines (Basel).* 9(1): 48. doi: 103390/vaccines9010048; PMID: 33466675; PMCID: PMCI82881 (retrieved 12 July 2022).

Yzer, M. (2017). Reasoned action as an approach to understanding and predicting health message outcomes. *Oxford Research Encyclopaedias,* https:/doi.org/10.1093acrefore.9780190228613.013.255 (retrieved 2 May 2023).

12 Medical Experts on Religious Influencers' Framing of COVID-19 Risk Communication

Implications on Women

Denise Shorayi, Makomborero Allen Bowa and Nehemiah Chivandikwa

Introduction

This chapter examines selected Zimbabwean medical doctors' perspectives on religious influencers' framing of COVID-19 risk communication. Essentially risk communication is "… interactive and dynamic exchange of information, advice and opinions between experts and people facing threats to their health and social well-being …" (El-Gilany and Farrag, 2021: 228). The chapter, therefore, specifically focuses on the exchange of COVID-19 information between religious experts and the public more broadly, and women specifically. It interrogates the implications of these perspectives and frames in relation to the impact of religion and media on women's behaviour during the pandemic. In essence, the chapter interrogates the interface between religion and the COVID-19 pandemic by providing critical reflections on the ambivalent influence of religious influencers on risk communication in media during the COVID-19 pandemic. In a broad sense, the chapter critically interrogates the role of religion in nurturing and perpetuating conspiracy theories, which essentially had direct and indirect implications on vaccine acceptance and hesitancy among the constituency of women. The chapter is premised on the idea that the religious sector is a major stakeholder in community engagement and strategic agenda setting in the media, and thus religious influencers can directly influence societal perceptions and attitudes in the wake of a pandemic such as COVID-19. In turn, the chapter contributes to perspectives on women's mental health as well as security during pandemics. This will enhance pandemic preparedness and address diverse and less acknowledged forms of violence against women in future pandemics.

Statistics in Zimbabwe indicate that women occupy the highest percentage in religion and they take a great hold in the community (see Manyonganise, 2022). Accordingly, studies (Maponya, 2021; Simba and Ngcobo, 2020) show that religious leaders have greater influence on women than men, and media occasionally report on the manipulation, abuse and brain washing of women by religious leaders. It is precisely this reality that has prompted a considerable number of researchers

DOI: 10.4324/9781003494546-13

to empirically interrogate the impact of religious leaders on women's behaviour. Therefore, it is against this backdrop that the chapter advances the argument that religion or religious influencers negatively and positively shaped women's behaviours and attitudes during the pandemic through the use of the media, particularly television. Fundamentally, the chapter argues that there is a strong correlation between the projection of religious leaders on COVID-19 issues in the media and the behaviours of women towards the pandemic. Thus, this study interrogates the largely positive views of medical experts on the media use of religious influencers (in selected media sermons and news interviews) in framing COVID-19 risk communication. Overall, the study concludes that the perspectives of medical experts validate the correlation between religiosity and risk communication, noting that both the media and medical experts seem to underestimate some potentially negative implications of using religious influencers' framing of COVID-19 in risk communication among Zimbabwean women.

Theoretical and Methodological Considerations

This chapter draws insights from the agenda-setting theory and the framing theory. Thus, the chapter examines how aspects of pandemics, religion and gender intersect in the context of the media to produce poorer outcomes for women through these two theories. First, this chapter engages the agenda-setting theory which was developed by Lippman (1992). The theory states that the media gives prominence to an issue through coverage and the number of times it appears in the media shapes peoples' thoughts and perceptions (Zain, 2017; Mccombs and Shaw, 1972; Drew, 2022). What this essentially means is that there is often a correlation between what people think towards something and projections relating to the same prevalent in the media. Thus, the media or rather stories that are repeated and given illumination even in the main news segment influence how people think. Insights from this theory provide an important framework for analysing the impact of the perspectives of religious influencers projected in the media on COVID-19 risk communication among Zimbabwean women.

Second, the study draws from the framing theory which either informs or emphasises or do both to impact opinion on a given subject (Chong and Druckman, 2007; Vreese, 2005; Leeper and Slothuus, 2018; Scheufele, 1999). According to this theory, the media portrays information through various frames to communicate certain information – thus influencing the behaviours of the public. Framing implies drawing attention to certain attributes of the objects of news coverage and the objects themselves (Goffman, 1974). It occurs in two ways: "frame in communication or media frame," that is how an event/occurrence or topic is communicated by a speaker to an audience, and "frame in thought or an individual frame," that is how the audience perceives the communication (Chong and Druckman, 2007: 100–101). Thus, the frame in thought concept is relevant in bringing forth the views on how the doctors perceive the framing aspects of health communication on ZBC news in Zimbabwe. Information from the media should not be taken at face value, but requires critical analysis and interpretation. This is the reason why the views of the experts are important in highlighting the effective strategies used by ZBC news in health communication. In risk communication, news coverage should articulate the nature and extent of the pandemic in the country, including general information about the virus, provision of health services and challenges in the health delivery system (Bouder, 2022; El-Gilany and Farrag, 2021).

In terms of methodology, the researchers conducted interviews with selected medical experts as key informants based on their educational background, work experience and exposure to the medical fraternity. They had first-hand information on COVID-19 because of their daily encounters with the pandemic as frontline workers. They were working in hospitals during the pandemic which increased their knowledge about the pandemic. Their views are different because they had first-hand experience and they had an appreciation of the media's role in a pandemic. The researchers focused on getting detailed information on the efficient ways the media can influence positive behaviour in risk communication. The ZBC television news was specifically selected because it was one of the main sources of information for many people in Zimbabwe. For this study, the news stories were selected and retrieved from the ZBC news online YouTube channel. This YouTube page represents the visual and textual narrative of the television.

The researchers employed qualitative research approaches, particularly the case study research approach on the role of news in risk communication. Qualitative research is understood in this inquiry as "any kind of research that produces findings not arrived at by means of statistical procedures or other means of quantification" (Strauss and Corbin, 1990: 17). This reveals that in qualitative research results are not numerical data collected but an "in-depth and holistic understanding" (Punch, 2005: 242). The research used directed content analysis to analyse the relationship between the use of the text and visual meaning. It examines documents and communication artefacts, which might be pictures, text audio and video (Assarroudi et al., 2018). The researchers used the deductive approach because the study is grounded in the agenda-setting theory and risk communication which was the basis of the research. The research used a structured approach where the medical experts describe the way media attempts to influence people, and establish a hierarchy of news prevalence in a pandemic. Latent analysis (Kaarianen and Elo, 2019) includes both the researcher's interpretation and the participant's silences, comments, sighs and laughs to get a deeper understanding of the data under research. The researchers used a snowball approach by initially contacting a medical specialist, who was part of the frontline workers in the COVID-19 Task Force at Parirenyatwa Group of Hospitals in Harare.

Pandemics, Religion and the Emergence of Conspiracy Theories

The emergence of conspiracy theories in the wake of societal crisis situations such as pandemics has been prevalent throughout human history (Prooijen and Douglas, 2017: 323). There is consensus among experts that crisis situations breed and spread conspiracy theories, which in essence are peoples' attempts of coping with the uncertainty caused by crisis situations (Prooijen and Douglas,

2017: 325). Interestingly, most of the conspiracy theories emerge precisely from religious spheres. Thus, these conspiracy narratives are formulated and perpetuated by religious influencers. This has been the pattern in the context of the COVID-19 pandemic. Emerging evidence clearly demonstrates that since the outbreak of the COVID-19 pandemic, various conspiracy theories emerged and circulated, particularly through social media into public consciousness. As Fuchs (2021: 147) rightly points out, the emergence of COVID-19 gave momentum to the anti-vaccination movement that created and spread new conspiracy theories about the disease and COVID-19 vaccines. Religious leaders attempted to make sense of the COVID-19 crisis through the proliferation of various conspiracy theories. Consequently, the public space in Africa became characterised by multiple interpretations of the origin of the pandemic, its signification and routes of resolution (Sibanda et al., 2022: 11). Thus, most of the COVID-19-related conspiracy theories were entrenched in biblical interpretation. Ultimately, biblical fundamentalists and some mega-church leaders associated the COVID-19 pandemic with signs of the end times, and COVID-19 vaccines with the mark of the beast described in the apocalyptic *Book of Revelations*. As such, the devastating impact of COVID-19 pandemic, particularly in Southern Africa saw the retrieval and use of images of apocalypticism (Sibanda et al., 2022: 11). This puts into perspective Bodner et al.'s (2022:143) observation that some of the conspiracy theories circling during COVID-19 pertained to a New World Order and extra-biblical approaches to End Times, making a connection between vaccinations, contact-tracing and 'the Mark of the Beast' described in the *Book of Revelations*.

What emerges quite clearly from the analysis from COVID-19-related conspiracy theories is that such theories had direct and indirect implications on vaccine acceptance and hesitancy. Indeed, such conspiracy theories played a significant role in not only shaping the politics around COVID-19 vaccines but also in influencing how people, particularly women, experienced and responded to the pandemic in the Zimbabwe context (Sibanda et al., 2022: 13). McAbee et al. (2021: 2) define vaccine hesitancy as the delay in acceptance or refusal of vaccination despite availability of vaccination services. This puts into perspective Humbe (2022: 77) and Dzanamarira's (2021: 7) argument that the initial vaccination process in the Zimbabwean context was associated with high levels of complacency in embracing the vaccination drive due to the prevalence of confusing information. Thus, the provenance of COVID-19-related conspiracy theories emanating from religious spheres posed serious threats to public health in that they undermined all efforts to combat the spread of the pandemic. Generally, all efforts to reduce the burden of the COVID-19 pandemic through vaccination were further compounded by the emerging threat of vaccine hesitancy (McAbee et al., 2021: 2). Thus, the various conspiracy theories generated by religious leaders essentially downplayed the value of official public health guidance, and offering religious panaceas that have been detrimental to good public health practice (Sibanda et al., 2022: 6). This development retrogressively impacted on COVID-19 risk communication initiatives which were geared towards curbing the spread of the pandemic.

Conversely, McAbee et al. (2021: 2) observe that socio-cultural and religious beliefs also played a significant role in COVID-19 vaccine acceptance in Africa, as the majority of the population is religious. It is in this respect the role played by a substantial number of religious influencers in supporting the use of vaccines as a safe and effective way for curtailing the COVID-19 pandemic must be appreciated. Thus, such religious influencers provided religious backing on the use of vaccines through the biblical interpretation with the primary view of fostering vaccine acceptance in the broader Zimbabwean context. Ultimately, such religious leaders used biblical interpretation to defuse some of the conspiracy beliefs that fuelled vaccine hesitancy. Indeed, the messages of these religious influencers had far-reached implications on the acceptance of vaccines across the broader spectrum of society. Undoubtedly, perspectives emanating from these religious influencers informed people's behaviours and attitudes towards COVID-19 vaccines in the Zimbabwean context.

Framing the Issue: Religion, Women, TV News and the COVID-19 Pandemic

That the COVID-19 pandemic interfaced with religion and gender in a manner that retrogressively impacted on the experiences of women is not a farfetched argument. Generally, as history has demonstrated, crisis situations affect men and women differently. In fact, pandemics and catastrophic situations create and compound inequalities which often leave women in a more vulnerable position across the broad spectrum of society (Simba and Ngcobo, 2020: 2). This is exactly the pattern that was witnessed in the context of the COVID-19 pandemic. Within scholarship focusing on the effects of the pandemic, there has emerged a wealth of commentary on the gendered implications of the COVID-19 pandemic (Manyonganise, 2022: 222). Indeed, the gendered burden of COVID-19 has been clear and undeniable (Simba and Ngcobo, 2020: 3).

The pandemic magnified and exacerbated the challenges of the constituency of women, particularly in the context of developing countries such as Zimbabwe. Disaster risk is socially distributed in ways that reflect pre-existing inequalities in that some groups are more vulnerable and prone to economic loss in the wake of different hazards (Peek and Stough, 2010: 1261). Similarly, this pattern has been witnessed in the context of the experiences of women in the wake of the COVID-19 pandemic. The pandemic has disproportionately impacted on women. What this essentially entails is that circumstances associated with the pandemic have intensified pre-existing inequalities related to gender in the context of countries such as Zimbabwe. Interestingly, some of these pre-existing gender-related inequalities have emanated precisely from the sphere of religion (Maponya, 2021: 345). Hence the observation that the differences in how women have fared during the pandemic compared with men are largely due to long-existing inequalities and social disparities, which are exacerbated by the pandemic rather than biology (Simba and Ngcobo, 2020: 2). Indeed, women have been hardest hit by COVID-19 within the Zimbabwean context (Manyonganise, 2022: 222).

Bodner et al. (2022:246) argue that the social, economic and health crises brought on by the COVID-19 pandemic was exacerbated by conspiracy theories. Given that women constitute the highest percentage in Zimbabwe's population dynamics and occupy the highest percentage in religion, it therefore follows that their attitudes towards the COVID-19 pandemic and associated vaccines have been largely influenced by the religious fraternity. It is precisely in this respect that the COVID-19 pandemic, religion and gender have intersected. As such, this is the complexity that has characterised the interface between the COVID-19 pandemic, religion and gender in the Zimbabwean context, which further worsened the actual lived experiences of most women. Thus, any attempt to examine the impact of the pandemic on the experiences of women must take into account the role that religious influencers have played in shaping societal perceptions and responses towards the COVID-19 pandemic. More importantly, specific attention must be directed towards understanding how the perceptions emanating from the religious fraternity have affected COVID-19-related risk communication.

Television news is a critical window when the public is faced with a crisis as it is the only note they can read and hear to understand what is going on around them (Hirschfeld and Thielsch, 2021; Abrams and Greenhawt, 2020; Aelst et al., 2021; Bouder, 2022). African literature (Olatunji et al., 2020; Oberiri and Bahiyah, 2021; Kiptinness and Okoye, 2021; Ouma et al., 2020) explores the effectiveness of framing the pandemic through content analyses and audience reception of print news. Whereas Zimbabwean studies, including Mackworth-Young et al. (2021), Mhiripiri and Midzi (2021), Muchetwa et al. (2021), Dzobo et al. (2020), and Dzinamarira et al. (2022), explore the awareness rate of the COVID-19 pandemic through the television media and social media, the same literature also examines the translation of COVID-19 information into indigenous languages. The current research is cognisant of the fact that news not only has the authority to influence opinion but also has an emotional impact on its audience. Aelst et al. (2021) denote that news media is crucial in crisis as people highly depend on it as it serves to guide people to safety influencing positive behaviour change. This reveals that depending on accuracy, transparency and timely information, the news media has the power to shape and influence the minds and perceptions of people towards behaviour change in a crisis.

COVID-19 Frames from Religious Leaders

ZBC-TV deployed religious leaders to persuade citizens to accept vaccines, observe UN and government COVID-19 protocols, and to deploy scriptures to provide hope, comfort and guidelines to negotiate, mitigate and survive the COVID-19 pandemic. Five frames were clearly prominent in the interviews that the researchers watched, namely positive frame, fear appeal strategy frame, attribution of responsibility frame, *Bible*–science frame and the conflict frame (see Gesser-Edelsburg et al., 2022). The positive frame emphasised the potency and scriptural relevance of vaccines and lockdown protocols, as well as lauding government achievement in combating the COVID-19 pandemic. The fear appeal frame consisted of persuasive messages that instilled fear to dissuade any potential resistance to vaccines and the broad COVID-19 protocols. The attribution of responsibility frame was largely blaming violators of COVID-19 protocols and the unvaccinated, while the *Bible*–science frame was insistent and persistent that vaccines and lockdown protocols have biblical basis, and that they were the means through which God would protect his people during the pandemic. Lastly, the conflict frame specifically challenged religious conspiracy theories. Table 12.1 has some of the details on these frames.

Having outlined the views and frames from religious influencers, we present perspectives of medical doctors in the relevance, effectiveness and potential of religious influencers in health risk communication in the context of a pandemic.

Medical Doctors on Religious Opinion Leaders' Frames

This section presents the views of the medical experts, on the role of the opinion leaders, who were invited for interview on ZBC news coverage as an endorsement strategy of the adoption of the prevention measures, compliance to COVID-19 lockdown regulations and COVID-19 vaccination drive. The role of the opinion leader in health communication has proved to be a critical strategy in COVID-19 risk communication in most parts of the world (Sng et al., 2019; Borchers and Enke, 2021; Hatami et al., 2021). In Africa, religious leaders have been used as critical voices to impact behaviour change in media audiences (Okoye & Obulor, 2021; Tony Blair Institute for Global Change, 2020).

The findings highlighted that religious leaders are respected in society. Hence their presence in the news coverage has an impact. This is analysed through the concept of the communication persuasion matrix model, which states that elements of risk communication which are the source, message and channels influence the target audience. Story analysis revealed that the religious leaders were used as endorsement voices to the strategies taken by the government in the pandemic. The media shaped and selected the information they wanted the audience to hear, to influence intended behaviour change. Zimbabwe's population constitutes 86% Christians, 11% have no religious affiliation, and 1% Muslims, less than 2% strict traditional worshippers (International Religious Freedom Report, 2021). These statistics are crucial to interpreting the selection of opinion leaders in the news coverage as a force in influencing behaviour change to curb the COVID-19 pandemic. The extract mentioned further is the dialogue of the critical answers that came up on source credibility based on the criterion of the information source used in the news stories, which was an insight into the positive role and impact of the opinion leader on COVID-19 awareness and behaviour change. The research was based on a communication persuasive matrix, the interviews were held on 22 May 2022.

With regards to the aforementioned views, findings on the opinion leader strategy in communication persuasive matrix proved to be effective in endorsing

Table 12.1 A rundown of stories

Story title	*Story source – time frame*	*Brief description of story*
Church leaders on COVID-19	Reverend Andrew Wutawunashe – Founder and overseer of African Revival Family of God Churches (ARFGC) Sheikh Ishamael Duwa – President of Zimbabwe Islamic Council Rev Dr Kenneth Mtata – Secretary General of Zimbabwe Council of Churches	The church continues to affirm this programme, in fact we regard ourselves as the allies of the government in the vaccination programme; we also call upon all people and the people of the church in particular to remember that when you are vaccinated for COVID-19, you are not only protecting yourself, you are protecting your neighbour because Jesus says love thy neighbour. - As Muslims, that is a positive move as our *Quran* states that do not kill yourselves and save other people's lives, so if you are vaccinated and a God-fearing person, you can go and worship freely
Church leaders join the discussion of vaccination programmes in a bid to demystify the myths about the role out of vaccinations	Evangelist Amon Madawa – Apostolic Faith Mission Sheikh Ishmael Duwa – President of Zimbabwe Islamic Council Reverend Andrew Wutawunashe – Founder and overseer of African Revival Family of God Churches (ARFGC)	- Vaccines have always been produced mostly, which are for protecting kids from child-killer diseases and they have been produced since long ago. Christians whatever they do have to consider knowing the fact that these vaccines have been existing. He concluded that if the vaccine works for one, he should take it. - He held that we should be guided by the laws being established in Zimbabwe from the biblical view. Believers should work with the government and refer to the *Quran*. He quoted Chapter 4 vs. 42, which says that there is no disease that God can never cure. He holds that vaccines are the answers to our prayers. He explained it by referring to the story of the Israelites in the wilderness with Moses in the *Book of Exodus*, he holds that it's like a tree that God has told Moses to throw into water to make water sweet. He was arguing that people are using the *Bible* to criticise the vaccine, but themselves are vaccinated against child-killer diseases. He ensures the government takes all the necessary precautions. He also urges those responsible stakeholders to get the best vaccine for the people.

Box 12.1 Extract from one-on-one interview held on 22 May 2022

DS: You spoke on the dynamics of the audience's trust in the source can you highlight this further.

DR M: You know what .... There are people who trust more in their religious leader, friends, celebrities and politician more than in the doctor's view .... you see … . so the message makes an impact if they endorse what the doctor says they will quickly believe it. This is what l have seen

DS: Do you think we have such source credibility which made an impact on the pandemic?

DR M: As it did know the psychology of people this is why ZBC news did not only use the medical doctors as sources......... *waiona ma* traditional healer emphasising the need for caution, Pentecostal leaders, Apostolic faith leaders you can name it this because people they have certain people they believe in and what they say can influence their behaviours .... This happened with the Makandiwa[1] issue … when he first said he won't get vaccinated most of his people from his church that l know were resisting the vaccine. When he changed his mind and took back his words they were now saying prophet *vati* has said its okay that alone shows the impact of a source if its trusted by the receiver.

COVID-19 measures and dismissing fake news on the pandemic. The religious leader served as means of reaching out to religious congregants who trust in the information they disseminate. Christians use their leaders as confirmation of the medical reports given by the experts – hence the decision to obey or disobey is based on the response of the religious leaders. The medical doctors are unanimous that religious influencers played significant and positive roles in complementing efforts from science, the state and the United Nations. Essentially, the medical doctors acknowledge the socialising agency of religious leaders which may yield positive results in a pandemic such as influencing protective behaviour, hope, comfort and coping with effects of a pandemic and sustaining valued health behaviour.

Yet research in Africa (Okoye and Obulor, 2021; Tony Blair Institute for Global Change, 2020) states that religiosity may hinder audience adherence to COVID-19 prevention and mitigation strategies. This highlights religiosity as a barrier to health communication as is evident from the previous findings. For instance, in Zimbabwe the story of Prophet Emmanuel Makandiwa vaccination controversy has been raised. The prophet on social media, through his sermon, questioned the

Box 12.2 Extract interview with DR N and DR M, one-on-one interview held at Parirenyatwa Hospital, 10 May 2022

DS: What are views from this video we watched do your religious leaders can have an effective on their congregants?

DR N: They do have an impact on their congregants and them speaking on news encouraging vaccination acceptance affects the acceptance. If you take a closer look, even when the government announced that the churches will be open only for the vaccinated congregants, that alone increased the vaccination intake as people believe in their leaders and do not want anything that comes between them and their religion.

DR M: It's sad how many people have died due to their beliefs because most of the times the hospital is the last resort … . that's if the pastor, prophet or papa says "you can go to the hospital" … .. in as much we have believe, science is science… . when you get the symptoms rush to the hospital but some were spreading it in the community drinking holy water, using anointing oil and all sorts of prayers. By the time the patient gets worse they rush to the doctor when it already too late … .A life lost which could have been saved … this is the amount of power the church has, especially over women.

vaccine efficacy and labelling it as the mark of the beast. This largely impacted his congregants, triggering vaccination hesitancy. This shows the power of religiosity on the behaviour change of congregants.

The framing of religious leaders was engrossed in endorsing every decision raised by the government in curbing the pandemic. Prior research, especially in Africa (MAINA, 2022; Okoye and Obulor, 2021) has shown that people believe more in their religious leaders rather than scientific sources, because these are the custodians of people's daily life in communities. The frame of religious leaders in Zimbabwe has been a strategy with its roots in political coverage (Manyonganise, 2022; Kaulemu, 2010). Politicians tend to rely more on endorsement from religious leaders to get votes and its impact in political crisis. Their impact has either been overrated or underrated in influencing the audience in decision-making. Thus, more research needs to be conducted to unpack the dynamics which influence the followers' decision-making.

What is not evident, however, is how women are implicated in all these media-based forms of health risk communication in the COVID-19 pandemic, and in the concluding section, the researchers will attempt to initiate a discussion on this crucial theme.

Conclusion: Implications on Safety of Women in a Pandemic

The first challenge is that women's voices are missing from religious influencers' framing of COVID-19 and perhaps this emerges from the general gender imbalances in the media industry where women are generally invisible and silent. Clearly, there are three axes of power (patriarchy, religion and political power) here which silence women. As a critical institution, the media (particularly, in disaster contexts) should never renege on its watchdog role (see Gesser-Edelsburg et al., 2022), because this will expose women to more dangers arising from a health pandemic. Research (Pilch-Loeb et al., 2021) has shown that there are vaccines which have side-effects on women and such information was never broadcast on the news. Hence, there was need to provide objective and balanced information and keep a close eye on structural dynamics throughout the crisis and desist from passively broadcasting information from doctors, politicians and religious leaders. This has serious implications given that there are many religious organisations whose values and practices were never engaged during the crisis. For example, those white garments churches who do not allow their members to access modern medicine were conveniently left out of the list of religious influencers who were interviewed on the news. Clearly, ZBC subtly filtered and shaped news (Apuke and Omar, 2021) in ways that protected some churches that endangered the health of women, perhaps, because such churches have political links with the ruling party. As shown earlier, COVID-19 frames from religious leaders passively echoed government data and propaganda on COVID-19. Yet, there are too many structural defects which resulted in professional, social and physical losses to women (Manyonganise, 2022), which are yet to be sufficiently qualified and quantified. Women's health is endangered in such churches, given that women are invisible and silent in most churches. Their agency to articulate dissidence on such health-related matters is very limited.

Clearly, all the news items on religious influencers lacked sensitivity to gender inequalities which worsen the plight of women in health crises such as the COVID-19 pandemic. Religious, medical and political experts that dominated news, during the COVID-19 crisis hardly raised serious gendered information that could assist women to anticipate and cope with the many physical, psychological, social, bodily and economic challenges that were brought about by the COVID-19 pandemic – whose gendered dimensions are yet to be sufficiently unearthed.

Note

1 A prominent Pentecostal prophet-movement founder.

References

Abrams, E. M. & Greenhawt, M. 2020. Risk communication during COVID-19. *Journal of Allergy and Clinical Immunology: In Practice*, 8(6): 1791–1794. doi: 10.1016/j.jaip.2020.04.012.

Aelst Van, P., Toth, F., Stetka, V., De Vreese, C., Aalberg, T., Cardenal, A. S., Corou, N., Esser, F., Hopmann, D. N., Koc-Michalska, K., Matthes, J., Schemer, C., Sheafer, T., Splendore, S., Stanyer, J., Stepinska, A., Strömbäck, J., & Theocharis, Y. 2021. Does a crisis change news habits? A comparative study of the effects of COVID-19 on news media use in 17 European countries. *Digital Journalism*, 9(9): 1208–1238. https://doi.org/10.1080/21670811.2021.1943481

Apuke, O. D. & Omar, B., 2021. Social media affordances and information abundance: Enabling fake news sharing during the COVID-19 health crisis. https://doi.org/10.1177/14604582211021470

Assarroudi, A., Heshmati, F., Armat, M. R., Ebadi, A. & Vaismoradi, M. 2018. Directed qualitative content analysis: The description and elaboration of its underpinning methods and data analysis process. DOI: 10.1177/1744987117741667

Bodner, A., Ruhl, L., Barr, E., Shridhar, A., Skakoon-Sparling, S. & Card, K. G. 2022. The impact of working from home on mental health: A cross-sectional study of Canadian worker's mental health during the Third Wave of the COVID-19 pandemic. www.ncbi.nlm.nih.gov/pmc/articles/PMC9517068/

Bodner, J., Wendy Welch, Ian Brodie, Anna Muldoon, Donal Leech & Ashely Marshal. 2022. *Covid-19 Conspiracy Theories QAnon, 5G, the New World Order and Other Viral Ideas*. North Carolina: McFarland & Company, Incorporated Publishers.

Borchers, N. S. & Enke, N. 2021. Managing strategic influencer communication: A systematic overview on emerging planning, organization, and controlling routines. https://doi.org/10.1016/j.pubrev.2021.102041

Bouder, F. 2022. Principles and challenges of risk communication/crisis communication, specifically addressing issues relating to pandemics. Available at: https://coronakommissionen.com/wp-content/uploads/2022/02/underlagsrapport-principles-and-challenges-of-risk-communicationcrisis-communication.pdf

Chong, D. & Druckman, J. N. 2007. Framing theory. *Annual Review of Political Science*, 10(1): 103–126.

Drew, C. 2022. Agenda setting theory (definition, examples, & criticisms). Available at: https://helpfulprofessor.com/agenda-setting-theory/

Dzinamarira, T., Nachipo, B., Nyathi, A., Madziva, R., Herrera, H., Siegel, H. & Musuka, G. 2022. The case to scale up edutainment as an effective public health communication intervention to combat the COVID-19 pandemic in Zimbabwe. *Health Promotion Perspectives*, 12(1). DOI: 10.34172/hpp.2022.05

Dzobo, M., Chitungo, I. & Dzinamarira, T. 2020. COVID-19: A perspective for lifting lockdown in Zimbabwe. *Pan African Medical Journal*, 35(2): 13. doi: 10.11604/pamj.supp.2020.35.2.23059

El-Gilany, A.-H. & Farrag, N. S. 2021. Risk communication in COVID-19: A note for healthcare workers. *International Journal of Health & Allied Sciences* 10(3). researchgate.net.

Fuchs, C. 2021. *Communicating COVID-19: Everyday Life, Digital Capitalism, and Conspiracy Theories in Pandemic Times*. United Kingdom: Emerald Publishing Limited.

Gesser-Edelsburg, A., Hijazi, R. & Cohen, R. 2022. It takes two to tango: How the COVID-19 vaccination campaign was framed by the health ministry vs. the television news. *Frontiers in Public Health*, 10: 1–18. https://doi.org/10.3389/fpubh.2022.887579

Goffman, E. 1974. *Frame Analysis: An Essay on the Organization of Experience*. Cambridge: Harvard University Press.

Hatami, Z., Hall, M. & Thorne, N. 2021. Identifying early opinion leaders on COVID-19 on Twitter. https://doi.org/10.1007/978-3-030-90238-4_20

Hirschfeld, G. & Thielsch, M. 2021. Impact of crisis communication strategies on people's attitudes toward behavioral guidelines regarding COVID-19 and on their trust in local officials. www.ncbi.nlm.nih.gov/pmc/articles/PMC9340733/#:~:text=Abstract.%20Situational%20Crisis%20Communication%20Theory%20(SCCT)%20guides%20responses%20of%20corporations

Humbe, B. P. 2022. Living with COVID-19 in Zimbabwe: A religious and scientific healing response. In Sibanda, F., Muyambo, T. & Chitando E. (eds), *Religion and the COVID-19 Pandemic in Southern Africa.* London: Routledge.

International Religious Freedom Report, 2021. *Zimbabwe International Religious Freedom Report*. www.state.gov/wp-content/uploads/2022/04/ZIMBABWE-2021-INTERNATIONAL-RELIGIOUS-FREEDOM-REPORT.pdf

Kaulemu, D., 2010. Church responses to the crisis In Zimbabwe. DOI: 10.1080/15570271003707853

Keith F. Punch. 2005. *Introduction to Social Research–Quantitative & Qualitative Approaches*. London: Sage.

Kiptinness, E. M. & Okoye, J.-B. 2021. Media coverage of the novel Coronavirus (Covid-19) in Kenya and Tanzania: Content analysis of newspaper articles in East Africa. https://doi.org/10.1080/2331205X.2021.1956034

Kyngäs, H., Kääriäinen, M. & Elo, S. 2019. The trustworthiness of content analysis. DOI:10.1007/978-3-030-30199-6_5

Leeper, T. & Slothuus, R. 2018. How the news media persuades: Framing effects and beyond. https://s3.us-east-2.amazonaws.com/tjl-sharing/assets/HowTheNewsMediaPersuade.pdf

Lippmann, W. 1922. *Public Opinion*. New York, NY: Macmillan. Internet Archive.

Mangwaya, M. 2021, August 12. Churches should champion COVID-19 fight. Newsday. www.newsday.co.zw/local-news/article/26251/churches-should-champion-covid-19-fight#:~:text=CHURCH%20leaders%20have%20been%20urged%20to%20play%20a%20leading%20role

Manyonganise, M. 2022. 'When a pandemic wears the face of a woman': Intersections of religion and gender during the COVID-19 pandemic in Zimbabwe. In Sibanda, F., Muyambo, T. & Chitando, E. (eds.), *Religion and the COVID-19 Pandemic in Southern Africa*. London: Routledge, pp. 232–242.

Maponya, D. T. 2021. Religion, patriarchy and the prospect for gender equality in South Africa. *International Journal of Philosophy and Theology*, 82(4-5): 337–349. DOI: 10.1080/21692327.2021.200323

McAbee, L., Tapera, O. & Kanyangarara, M. 2021. Factors associated with COVID-19 vaccine intentions in eastern Zimbabwe: A cross-sectional study. *Vaccines*, 9(1109): 1–10.

McCombs, M. E. & Shaw, D. L. 1972. The agenda-setting function of mass media. *The Public Opinion Quarterly*, 36(2): 176–187. JSTOR, www.jstor.org/stable/2747787

Mhiripiri, N. A. & Midzi, R. 2021. Fighting for survival: Persons with disabilities' activism for the mediatisation of COVID-19 information. *Media International Australia*, 178(1): 151–167. https://doi.org/10.1177/1329878X20967712

Muchetwa, K., Maruta, E., Jaka, H., Ruvado, J. & Chazireni, E. 2021. Health communication strategies employed by the media during the Covid-19 crisis: Case of Zimbabwe Broadcasting Corporation Television (ZBC-TV). *European Journal of Social Sciences Studies*, 6(6): 38–50. http://dx.doi.org/10.46827/ejsss.v6i6.1132

Okoye, A. C. & Obulor, I. 2021. Religious organisations and fight against the spread of COVID-19 in NIGERIA. Journal of Sustainable Development in Africa, 23(1): 65–78. https://jsd-africa.com/Jsda/2021%20V23%20No%201%20Spring/PDF/Religious%20Organisations%20and%20the%20Fight%20against%20Spread%20of%20Covid%2019%20in%20Nigeria_Anthony%20Okoye.pdf#:~:text=The%20study%20argued%20that%20religious%20leaders%20and%20religious%20organizations%20contribute

Olatunji, O., Ayandel, O., Ashiruden, D. & Olaniru, O. 2020. Infordemic in a pandemic: COVID-19 conspiracy theories in an African country. www.researchgate.net/publication/344154568_Infodemic_in_a_Pandemic_COVID-19_Conspiracy_Theories_in_an_African_Country#:~:text=Original%20Article.%20%E2%80%9CInfodemic%E2%80%9D%20in%20a%20Pandemic:%20COVID%E2%80%9019%20Conspiracy%20Theories%20in

Oberiri, D. A. and Bahiyah O. 2021. Television news coverage of COVID-19 pandemic in Nigeria: Missed opportunities to promote health due to ownership and politics. DOI:10.1177/21582440211032675

Ouma, P. N., Masai, A. N. & Nyadera, I. N. 2020. Health coverage and what Kenya can learn from the COVID-19 pandemic. DOI: 10.7189/jogh.10.020362

Peek, L. & Stough, L. 2010. Children with disabilities in the context of disaster: A social vulnerability perspective. *Child Development*, 81(4): 1260–1270.

Pilch-Loeb, R., Savoia, E., Goldberg, B., Haughes, B., Verhey, T., Kayyem, J., Miller-Idriss, C., Testa, M., et al. 2021. Examining the effect of information channel on Covid-19 acceptance. *PLoS ONE*, 16(5): e0251095. https://doi.org/10.1377/journalpone.0251095 (retrieved 30 May 2022).

Prooijen, J. & Douglas, K. M. 2017. Conspiracy theories as part of history: The role of societal crisis situations. *Memory Studies*, 10(3): 323–333.

Scheufele, D. A. 1999. Framing as a theory of media effects. *Journal of Communication*. 49(1): 103–122. https://doi.org/10.1111/j.1460-2466.1999.tb02784.x

Sibanda, F., Muyambo, T. & Chitando, E. 2022. Introduction: Religion and public health in the shadow of COVID-19 pandemic in Southern Africa. In Sibanda, F., Muyambo, T. & Chitando, E. (eds.), *Religion and the COVID-19 Pandemic in Southern Africa*. London: Routledge, pp. 1–24.

Simba, H. & Ngcobo, S. 2020. Are pandemics gender neutral? Women's health and COVID-19. *Frontiers in Global Women's Health*, 1: 570666. doi: 10.3389/fgwh.2020.570666

Sng, K., Au, T. Y. & Pang, A. 2019. *Social Media Influencers as a Crisis Risk in Strategic Communication: Impact of Indiscretions on Professional Endorsements*. DOI:10.1080/1553118X.2019.1618305

Strauss, A. L. & Corbin, J. 1990. *Basics of Qualitative Research: Grounded Theory Procedures and Techniques*. Thousand Oaks, CA: Sage.

Tony Blair Institute for Global Change, 2020. Covid-19: Guidelines for governments working with religious leaders to support. https://institute.global/insights/public-services/tony-blair-institute-insight-and-expert-analysis-tackling-covid-19

Vreese, C. 2005. News framing: Theory and typology. *Information Design Journal + Document Design*, 13(1): 51–62.

Zain, N. R. B. M. 2017. Agenda setting theory. researchgate.net.

13 Pandemics as Disability

Reflections on the Feminisation of Care during Pandemics in Zimbabwe

Tsiidzai Matsika

Introduction

Pandemics are a disability to all. Like disability, they are characterised by helplessness, isolation, loss of control, having decisions made for you and dependence. In pandemics just like with disability – many are thrust into the role of care without warning, and find themselves groping in the dark. The post-2019 Zimbabwean period presented a complex terrain characterised by a serious COVID-19-induced socio-economic meltdown. The feminisation of disability refers to how women are disproportionately affected by pandemics, and the socio-economic factors which make them more vulnerable. Women account for the duty of caring for sick in Zimbabwe. Where the duty of caring for sick is concerned, it has intersected with gender inequality. Pandemic issues expose the intersections of gender inequalities and the violation of women's human rights. Care duties weigh heavily on the shoulders of women and the impact of any pandemic is more overt on them. Women's mental health, emotional, spiritual, social and economic dimensions are all threatened as care remains largely their responsibility. The structural elements of cultural, economic and social inequalities significantly push discrimination and disenfranchisement of women. Models of free 'independent' male breadwinners and 'dependent' wives and mothers providing unpaid care are deeply entrenched in social and cultural attitudes and choices that people make. These attitudes are discussed in this chapter using Charamba and Hwede's (2009) *In the Wake of Our Shadows,* a collection of women's experiences in caring for children with disabilities. Almost all the women described in the stories struggle with the children alone, while the fathers hardly take responsibility for their children. Ironically, even when the fathers are not even working, they are unfettered by care duties.

In the Wake of Our Shadows is a collection of stories of mothers and grandmothers narrating the difficulties they face raising children with disability (representing the sick during pandemics) within the Zimbabwean context. When a country is hit by a pandemic or is in a crisis, facing a socio-economic meltdown, certain groups of people suffer the most due to certain handicaps. In the context of this discussion, disability will be used as a metaphor describing the physical conditions of

DOI: 10.4324/9781003494546-14

being physically impaired, pandemics and the depiction of the disabling environment. According to Hunt (1966), disability can be described as a situation caused by social conditions, which require its elimination and that no one aspect such as income, mobility or institutions, is treated in isolation.

In highlighting the complexity of care, Shakespeare (2006) notes that it is vital to situate particular care arrangements within the broader social and political contexts. He elucidates that "care has often been the site of oppression and disempowerment" (Shakespeare, 2006, p. 135). In *In the Wake of Our Shadows* (ITWOS), the face of disability that we see is the face of women as "the brunt of the burden of care continues to rest largely with women, and scaling up male involvement remains an area screaming for the broader society's attention" (ITWOS, p. 3). The connection between gender, disability and care work is imminent. The feminisation of the pandemics is widespread and it will only get worse, with women solely bearing the burden if attention is not given to their ultimate victimisation in relation to gender. In *In the Wake of Our Shadows*, women are a marginalised group and the narrations focus on the lineaments of disability and the experiences they have. The text reflects the relationships and rampant (not so-called universal) transcendent, normative attitudes which are both cultural and temporal when it comes to care. The focus is to revisit how to represent our cultures in a way that avoids 'mastering' or 'appropriating' it to naturalise women as caregivers. Generally, negative attitudes and misconceptions are the basis of discrimination and a barrier to equal socio-economic participation. They are also the source of gender-based violence (GBV) which is widespread in Zimbabwe.

Methodology

This chapter will deploy a critical literary analysis of the selected text, *In the Wake of Our Shadows*. Literary analysis focuses on interpreting works of literature, such as novels, poetry and plays. The analysis involves examining the literary devices used in the work, such as symbolism, imagery and metaphor, and how they contribute to the overall meaning of the work. Critical literary analysis is a qualitative research method which examines a piece of work or an idea in a systematic, objective and analytical way. It involves breaking down complex ideas, concepts or arguments into smaller, more manageable parts to understand them better. It illuminates the taken-for-granted notions like how the duty of care in times of crisis, such as in pandemics, largely falls heavily on the shoulders of women.

Theoretical Framework

The overarching theoretical framework in this paper is Fineman's vulnerability theory. This theory highlights people as susceptible to multiple dimensions of stressors and shocks which are accentuated by factors such as abuse, social exclusion and natural hazards. Generally, the concept of vulnerability is used to define groups of marginalised and stigmatised subjects, designated as 'populations'.

Vulnerability is typically associated with victimhood, deprivation, dependency or pathology. It is fuelled mainly by the inherent social interactions, institutions and systems of cultural values, as evident in *In the Wake of Our Shadows*. According to Fineman (2004), vulnerability is a universal aspect of the human condition, arising from our embodiment and our location within society and its institutions. As embodied beings, people are universally and individually constantly susceptible to pandemics, injury, harm and dependency over their life course. Though disability might be a biological and natural phenomenon, anyone can easily be a victim of disability, anytime, due to accidents or illnesses. As evident with the COVID-19 pandemic, everyone became susceptible.

Pandemics and Disability

This chapter will refer to *In the Wake of Our Shadows* as well as COVID-19 experiences to illuminate issues and theorise disability in relation to care in the context of pandemics. The issue of vulnerability in the context of pandemics is evident in the COVID-19 case. According to Barbarin (2020), "COVID-19 is a mass disabling event". Unexpectedly, the whole world was grounded by the pandemic, and everyone was susceptible to the epidemic as it affected people across all divides, affecting everyone, the poor and the rich unsparingly. As the *Spotlight on Sustainable Development* (2021, p. 8) report highlights, "the scourge of Covid-19 struck an already stark reality of multiple inequalities – in households, across communities, in national context, and among countries. Its waves of devastation … exacerbated pre-existing conditions and disparities as well as creating new ones". As Linton (1998, p. 118) puts it, studying disability is "a prism through which one can gain a broader understanding of society and human experience". She elucidates that

> It deepens our understanding of gender and sexuality, individualism and equality, minority group definitions, autonomy, wholeness, independence, dependence, health, physical appearance, aesthetics, the integrity of the body, community, and ideas of progress and perfection in every aspect of cultures.
>
> (Linton, 1998, p. 118)

Understanding how disability operates as an identity category and cultural concept will enhance how we understand what it is to be human, our relationships with one another and the experience of embodiment. It illuminates the vulnerability of human beings. As Fineman (2004, p. 79) expounds:

> Often narrowly understood as merely openness to physical or emotional harm, vulnerability should be recognized as the primal human condition. Understanding vulnerability begins with the realization that many such events are ultimately beyond human control … The inevitability of vulnerability means that there is no position of invulnerability; there is only the possibility of resilience. We gain resilience when we have accumulated sufficient resources to allow us to adapt to, ameliorate, compensate for, or contain our vulnerability.

Thus, individuals can attempt to lessen the risk or mitigate the impact of such events, but they cannot eliminate their possibility. Recognition of embodied vulnerability and the social production of resilience reveals that far from being autonomous and independent beings imagined in liberal theory, humans are inescapably embedded in society – dependent on its institutions, conventions and cultures. In this sense, "human vulnerability should be understood as the precursor for social and familial institutions and relationships, which are the positive manifestations of embodiment" (Fineman, 2004, p. 79). These assertions highlight the importance of having supportive relationships and functional systems and structures in societies. So, when these systems are supportive, it becomes easier to deal with issues such as disability and navigate in times of pandemics.

Spinney (2022) asserts that it is particularly deadly if we do not frame COVID-19 as a disability issue. During the pandemic, it was highlighted that people with pre-existing conditions were more vulnerable. 'Pre-existing condition' was a way of not saying 'disability'. Zimbabwe itself as a nation had pre-existing conditions. The context itself was more disabling, and the nation was disabled to deal effectively with the demands of a pandemic like COVID-19. Macha (2007) explains disability as a result of consequences of barriers external to the individual, making it a social and political issue, influencing the problems disabled people face squarely within society's perceptions and settings. So, more pressing than the condition of being disabled itself is the disabling environment that worsens the condition. This includes, among other things, failure to provide appropriate social services and articulate different needs of people with disability. In *In the Wake of Our Shadows*, almost all the testimonies illuminate the economic and political challenges characterising the post-2000 Zimbabwean nation. The nation is characterised by a lack of resources which worsens the burden of having to care for children with special needs. Most women in the testimonies are disadvantaged because they do not have enough education to earn them any form of formal employment and decent earning jobs that would enable them to fend for their families. Due to economic hardships, the men on their own cannot afford providing for the families too. In her testimony, Grace Chimuti, who looks after her grandchild with disability, says

> The major problem I have is food. Her requirements are difficult to find and the prices of basics has soared. I used to get milk and beat it together with raw eggs and that helped give her more energy but now life has gotten more difficult. Food is difficult to find.
>
> (p. 21)

As Tapureta (2014) understands, "when a country faces crisis, there are certain special groups of people that suffer most". One group is that of people with disability. One wonders, for example, how the economically marginalised and those without adequate resources cope or are expected to cope caring for people with disability and in situations such as lockdowns. During lockdowns, people were expected to adhere to World Health Organization (WHO) protocols such as washing hands often under running water and maintaining social distancing.

Care is an arduous task that demands economic, emotional and other varying resources. As Fineman (2015) advocates, people and organisations have to find ways of supporting care work and recognise that care has cost. In representing the people with disability, the testimonies in *In the Wake of Our Shadows* illuminate the socio-economic challenges of women living with children with disabilities. In caring for children with disability, lack of resources, inflation, poverty and isolation coupled with having to deal with psychological and social stigmas become a source of anguish for women and become a yoke that sinks heavily on their shoulders.

Disability issues reflect the complex web of social ideals which include gender relations, institutional structures and government policies. Talking on the politics of care and how it is gendered, marginalising women requires a wholesale re-evaluation of how we understand relations, power dynamics, causes of inequalities and how 'othering' is underpinned by the pervasive devaluing of people with differences. As reflected in *In the Wake of Our Shadows*, children with disability and women with children with special needs strive under demeaning circumstances. Issues about perceptions, mobility, access to resources and spaces are all problematic. Exploring these issues through gender lenses and how bodies in their variations are identified, defined, valued, devalued, normalised and (ab)normalised is central to disability as it is within the social ideals, prejudices and ideologies that marginalise people with differences to the extent that they are relegated to the peripheries. People with disabilities are debased and are not accorded the opportunity to live their lives to the fullest but always have to wallow in the 'shadows' of their lives. Shadows in the selected text represent the ever-present gloominess and darkness characterising the lives of children with disabilities and those caring for these children.

To understand the embodied social constructions at the centre of gender and disability issues, it is imperative to examine how people make sense of patterns between individuals and groups in society. People have to question consistencies and inconsistencies that are perceptible in our society, such as, how women are affected by the disability and how different people are affected by different pandemics. Societal institutions ranging from the family, the community, civic societies and the government must share responsibility for not 'privatising dependency' to a certain group or individuals. For example, caring for children should be the responsibility of both parents but, as evident in *In the Wake of our Shadows*, men are taking the back seat or are nowhere to be seen. People with disabilities often become departmentalised and become mainly women's sole responsibility, no longer a family or a community network which could be maintained or supported in mainstream society. It is naturalised through gender stereotypes and biases that assume it is the role of women to take care of the children and that women have maternal instincts. However, in some instances, some parents run away from the responsibility of taking care of their own biological disabled children, as evident in *In the Wake of Our Shadows*. In Sarudzai Butau's narration, her son and daughter-in-law just dumped their child on her. She says, "I keep wondering how my son and his wife can be so quiet. They have another child whom they live with …"

(ITWOS, p. 14). This scenario of grandmothers being burdened with taking care of disabled grandchildren is recurrent in many of the testimonies.

In analysis of women's plight as well as in the context of pandemics, it is critical to examine differences within people and how people treat those differences as individuals and as societies. These have consequences in our societies. People have to question where those differences come from and analyse their pervading attitudes and what they do about such differences. In narrating their experiences as women with children with disabilities, the narrators offer authority and authenticity of the marginal experience. This chapter investigates how the emphasis on inclusion and non-indiscrimination in pandemics and disability issues involves a process of understanding the ethics of universal care in relation to the gendered experience. The narratives manifest an anxious awakening to the inadequacy and shallowness in negotiating the complex spatial reality of women and care work in Zimbabwe.

The illumination of economic hardships in *In the Wake of Our Shadows* and during COVID-19 is not coincidental. It intersects with the fact that women are synonymous with putting food on the table. At the individual level, vulnerability refers to the ever-present possibility of harm, injury, biological impairment or limitation. As human creations, institutions are also vulnerable to confinement, bureaucracy, co-optation and corruption. Vulnerability also has to be understood as generative, as it presents opportunities for innovation and growth, creativity and fulfilment. As embodied and vulnerable beings, people experience, express, need and strive for things such as love, care, respect, support and happiness. They have desires that make them reach out to others, form relationships and build institutions. Fineman (2015) explains that the vulnerability approach does not rely on abstract and inevitably contested legal principles, such as liberty or dignity to define what it means to be human or have legal subjectivity. Rather, it brings bodily, material and institutional contexts into discussion by focusing on vulnerability and dependency, which are posited as universal and inherent in the human condition.

In the Wake of Our Shadows takes a closer look 'at the burden of care' and advocates the role of institutions, especially academic institutions, in effecting the transformation of public perception in pandemics and on disability issues. Within the rubric of gender and disability, the multi-layered approach probes questions on the national movements, societal biases, prejudices, attitudes, critical paradigms, identity discourses and institutional practices towards the subordinated, disenfranchised groups, women and disabled children. In the context of the text under analysis, most of the women and the children did not have the opportunity to be educated so that they could improve or live their lives as empowered individuals. Predominantly, the existing social setup and hierarchy automatically ties the women and the children to be homebound as their praxis is strictly domestic. Their welfare is characterised by a lack of resources that makes it difficult for them to attain the basics that they need in their lives. This study takes into account the expressed, silenced, deferred, as well as negotiated subjectivities across the spaces and dynamics of power relations and examines notions and politics of care.

Ableism is pervasive in disability issues and was a glaring feature during the COVID-19 pandemic as it makes assumptions on people's abilities and capacities. The social and cultural systems relativise motherhood; giving birth to an able-bodied child becomes a privilege and defines one's life in terms of expectations, assumptions and impressions. There is a mismatch between the perceived pressures on the individual, which ends up stressing the women or individuals, making it difficult for them to cope. In the context of women and disability, there is an overarching tendency to assume centrist positions of ableism, and it is critical to examine how we can accommodate differences without appropriating the 'other', whether that 'other' is female or disabled. What is evident is that this oft-invoked 'other' becomes a subjugated group, designated roles based on bodily features. People judge them based on stereotypes and biased processes of constituting difference as though it is transfixed. Bhabha (1994) highlights that the marginal or minority is not the space of a celebratory, or utopia, self-marginalisation; it is a much more substantial intervention into those justifications of modernity, progress, homogeneity and cultural organicism that rationalise the normalising tendencies within culture.

The notion of ableism is evident in how WHO guidelines were enforced within the Zimbabwean context. While some of the COVID-19 guidelines were universal, others required a response tailored to specific contexts. WHO provided decision-makers with the information to make the best decisions for and with their people. In Zimbabwe, meeting even the basic guidelines which were universal, like washing hands and maintaining distance, staying home for lockdowns, was not very possible. Incessant challenges within the context such as lack of basic commodities such as food and functional service delivery system made it impossible to adhere to WHO guidelines. Water was one of the major factors that forced people not to adhere to WHO regulations and lockdown restrictions. Failure by the Harare City Council to regularly supply water, ranging to some days to many years, forced residents to queue up at public boreholes (Mutanda, 2022). There would be queues in banks and for public transport, ZUPCO. In addition,

> [T]he shortage of basic commodities such as maize meal in particular forced people to queue up for these things. Lockdown restrictions and social distancing rules ended up being disregarded and difficult to enforce because what was at stake was access to food. Some people in urban areas travelled to nearby farms where basic needs such as maize grain could be found.
>
> (Mutanda, 2022, p. 5)

In the case of Zimbabwe, *In the Wake of Our Shadows* and experiences from the COVID-19 pandemic expose challenges inherent in the Zimbabwean socio-economic terrain. Unemployment, technocratic policies, inadequate social welfare programmes, lack of health services and lack of government commitment to service delivery made life unbearable to vulnerable communities. The experiences illuminate the need for considerate policies, sensitive to the socio-economic, religious and political environment. Policies need to be inclusive and address challenges and inequalities within their socio-economic and political settings.

As reflected in *In the Wake of Our Shadows*, the women tell their life stories, highlighting their experiences living with children with disabilities and their quest to give them a normal life. Thus reconsidered, vulnerability raises new issues, poses different questions and opens up new avenues for critical exploration of taken-for-granted notions and biases that shape social, political and cultural significances. Fineman (2015) stresses that conceiving vulnerability in this way renders it valuable in constructing critical perspectives on political and societal institutions, including the law. A vulnerability analysis demands that in designing and implementing rules the state be responsive to the needs of a subject who is both an embodied being and embedded in social relations. This requires recognition and monitoring of the operation of social institutions and relationships. Attention should also be directed to how privileges and disadvantages are fashioned within the social paradigms. Fineman (2015) clarifies that people, in this case, women, the poverty-stricken and the disabled, are positioned differently within a web of economic and institutional relationships. Their vulnerabilities range in magnitude and potential at the individual level. Undeniably, pandemics' impact on. vulnerability engendered by disability is particularly experienced uniquely by different individuals and sexes. Experiences are greatly influenced by the quality and quantity of resources one possesses or can command.

As Enríquez (2021) illuminates, human beings are vulnerable and interdependent. She explains that "throughout their lifecycle, people need to be cared for when they are young, when they are old, when they are sick, when they are pregnant, when they are temporarily or permanently disabled" (Enríquez, 2021, p. 87). Accordingly, systems of care need to be enabling. The quality of support networks and systems makes it easier for people to cope during pandemics.

Some Lessons from COVID-19

Pandemics disable people but there are critical lessons from the COVID-19 experience that policy-makers should not ignore, especially in the context of care. During the COVID-19 pandemic, it could no longer be business as usual in homes, workplaces and in nation-states. People were forced to recognise and give the pandemic serious attention. People worked together in their respective capacities and beings to mitigate and survive the pandemic. In the heat of the pandemic, those lines that divide people such as race, class, gender and religion were transcended as all were vulnerable. The lessons can actually be incorporated into lived experiences, policies and protocols.

Like disability in general, COVID-19 demanded people to re-evaluate their priorities and see what mattered. Spinney (2022, p. 385) asserts that:

> Two years in, the debilitating tail of the pandemic has revealed itself in the form of tens of millions of people living with long Covid-19. It is high time to ask whether attitudes to disability will change as a result. Will society grasp that the body can be altered for a long period – even permanently by infectious disease, just as it seems to have accepted that the body politic will never be the same again? And will it make the necessary accommodations?

The questions that Spinney (2022) poses call to us to think through some things that we take for granted, especially in the context of disability and in times of pandemics. As was evident during the COVID-19 pandemic, it could not be business as usual as people had to depart from 'normal' ways of thinking and doing things. People had to embrace the new normal. Spinney (2022) points out that, "during the lockdowns triggered by the present pandemic, accommodations that disabled people had long campaigned for – remote working, and flexibility in working hours, communication format and metrics of productivity – were universally adopted". Spinney (2022) worries that the new approaches will be dropped in some futile quest to return to a pre-pandemic 'normal'. The extent to which some conditions are disabling is largely determined by society's cultural norms, people's choices and willingness to adapt.

It has tragically taken a worldwide pandemic to remind us of just how care should be everyone's business. COVID-19 compelled everyone to think of the pandemic and adopt new forms of taking care of others and ourselves. Issues of care were no longer only relegated to women, as it became everyone's business. To some extent, COVID-19 pushed aside individualised notions of resilience and wellness which relegates care to something people have to think on a personal basis. People have not been compelled to care for each other, especially the vulnerable, the poor and the weak during the COVID-19 pandemic. As Chatzidakis et al. (2020, p. 2) put it, "rhetorically at least, governments worldwide have responded, and in sharp contrast to 2019, talk of care is currently everywhere. Even the least likely have rolled out major economic aid packages in the name of care for the nation".

During the COVID-19 pandemic, people experienced living in an accelerating social system of organised isolation. People were encouraged to care for themselves as a way of caring for others. To thrive during the pandemic there was need to think about one's safety relative to the safety of those people around him/her. From the positive and negative experiences, there were lessons that for people to thrive in their environments they need to support each other and generate networks of support. It became apparent that there is a need for conditions that enable people to create communities that support abilities and nurture people's interdependencies. This is because:

> [I]ssues of care are not just bound up with the intimacy of very close relationships, such as family and kinship. They also take shape in the environments we inhabit and move through – in local communities, neighbourhoods, libraries, schools and parks, in our social networks, and the groups we belong to.
>
> (Chatzidakis et al., 2020)

It is critical to think how best people can create the kind of caring communities that make lives better and happier for everyone. As much as care is also a duty of love, it becomes problematic when it burdens some people and creates inequalities accentuated by gender biases. People have to think of infrastructures that are necessary to create communities that care, are inclusive and enabling.

Conclusion

It is critical to understand that vulnerability is part of the human condition and unpredictable as evident with the COVID-19 pandemic. Marginalisation of women and accentuation of disability results from the interplay of individual, cultural and contextual factors. Issues of gender and disability go beyond being physical and biological as "people are disabled by society and by their bodies" (Shakespeare, 2006, p. 2). Care arrangements are basically about choices made by families, communities, institutions, policies and governments. Williams (2001, p. 487) enunciates that "care should not be fixed in a role, it is an activity that binds us all". Reconciling disability and womanist ethic approaches represents the way forward for understanding and improving the social relation of care (Hughes et al., 2005). There is a need to strive for "systems of care and support which maximise independence and choice and minimise abuse, neglect and paternalism". From some testimonies in *In the Wake of Our Shadows* and the COVID-19 pandemic experiences, it is evident that society can, and does mediate, compensate and lessen our vulnerability through programmes, institutions and inclusive structures. The women's testimonies highlight how the burden is made easier when they get support from these systems. Personal and collective social lives are marked and shaped by vulnerability therefore advocacy for inclusivity must look into both individual and institutional components. As the report on *Spotlight on Sustainable Development* (2021) notes, the post-COVID-19 society and economy need national policies that reduce inequalities manifest in multiple ways, such as through income, gender, disability, religion and race. Policies are needed to revalue care work and reorient global value chains towards domestic priorities and jobs, both in developing and developed countries. Care is a critical issue which cuts across all the Sustainable Developmental Goals. As care is important to achieving gender equality, there is a need for recognition and value of unpaid care and domestic work through the provision of public services, infrastructure and social protection policies and the promotion of shared responsibility within the household and the family as nationally appropriate.

References

Barbarin, I. 2020. Tiktoker and disability justice advocate Imani Barbarin (@crutches_and_spice) stitched a TikTok.

Bhabha, H. 1994. *The Location of Culture*. Routledge: London.

Charamba, A., and Hwede, E. (ed.). 2009. *In the Wake of Our Shadows*, Zimbabwe Women Writers: Harare.

Chatzidakis, A., Hakim, J., Littler, J., Rottenberg, C., and Lynne Sega, L. 2020. *The Care Manifesto: The Politics of Interdependence*. The Care Collective. Verso: London.

Enríquez, R. C. 2021. Development alternatives with women for a new era. *Spotlight on Sustainable Development*. DAWN.https://gadnetwork.org/global-database-feminists-working-on-macroeconomic-issues/dawn

Fineman, M. A. 2004. *The Autonomy Myth: A Theory Dependency*. New Press: New York.

Fineman, M. A. 2015. Understanding vulnerability theory. https://newlegalrealism.wordpress.com/2015/11/30/fineman-on-vulnerability-and-law/ (accessed 01 August 2017).
Hughes, B., McKie, L., Hopkins, D., and Watson, N. 2005. Loves labour lost? Feminism, the disabled people's movement and an ethic of care. *Sociology International Journal of Disability, Community & Rehabilitation*, 39(2), 259–275.
Hunt, P. (ed.) 1966. *Stigma*. Geoffrey Chapman Publishing: London.
Linton, S. 1998. *Claiming Disability*. New York University: New York.
Macha, E. 2007. Disabled people and discrimination: a global overview. Echoes. http://wcc-coe.org/wcc/what/jpc/echoes/echoes-19-02.html
Mutanda, D. 2022. Challenges and opportunities for Zimbabwe's responses to Covid-19. *Cogent Social Sciences*, 8(1), Taylor and Francis Online, www.tandfonline.com/doi/full/10.1080/23311886.2022.2084890
Shakespeare, T. 2006. *Disability Rights and Wrongs Revisited*. Routledge: London.
Spinney, L. 2022. Pandemics disable people – The history lesson that policymakers ignore, *Nature*, 602, 383–385.
Spotlight on Sustainable Development. 2021. Demanding justice beyond rhetoric. https://geneva.fes.de/e/spotlight-report-on-sustainable-development-2021.html.
Tapureta, B. 2014. Book reveals plight of disabled children. *The Herald,* 4 June 2014. http://theconversation.com/its-time-fix-power-dynamics-that-allowed-the-abuse-of-people-with-disabilities, Senate Report by Senator Claire Moore (2015) (accessed 10 August 2017).
Williams, F. 2001. In and beyond New Labour: Towards a new political ethics of care. *Critical Social Policy*, 21(4), 467–493. https://journals.sagepub.com/doi/10.1177/026101830102100405

Conclusion

Isaiah Munyiswa, Pauline Mateveke and Ezra Chitando

Narrations of women's experiences during pandemics highlight the need for immediate social change and a raft of legal changes in Zimbabwe. Almost all chapters in this volume show that pandemics intensify violence against women, with culture, religion and some traditional practices acting as catalysts. Gender-based violence (GBV) during pandemics has been analysed with a view to find effective remedies for the present and the future. The authors are realistic about the problem at hand but they are not completely hopeless. Each chapter begins by chronicling the reality on the ground and ends up proposing some possible solutions. To this end, we contend that the discourse has shifted from lament/ing (which remains important) to constructive engagement. It is also reassuring for us that indigenous male scholars have joined the quest for women's full liberation and have provided valuable insights (see, e.g., Isike, 2022; Chitando, Mlambo, Mfecane and Ratele, 2024 for the importance of male engagement).

The reflections provided in this volume are critical for pandemic preparedness. Whereas HIV and AIDS and COVID-19 caught the world by surprise, it would be unforgivable if the next pandemic caught the world napping. Contributors to this volume have offered penetrating insights into the urgency of embracing gendered, Africa-centred and adaptable interventions when facing pandemics in African contexts. There is an urgent need to decolonise policies and interventions and make them relevant to African realities (see, e.g., Atuire and Rutazibwa, 2021). Further, there must be a continuous interrogation of the choices and options that African bureaucrats settle for, particularly from a gender perspective. This volume, however, missed the multiple initiatives and strategies where Zimbabwean women deployed their capabilities and agency to negotiate their survival in the face of pandemics. There is, therefore, the need for a complementary volume that also provides reflections on women's and men's agency to remain afloat during pandemics (see, e.g., Nyanga, Zirima and Mashavira, 2020).

Observations running through the chapters are that during pandemics in Zimbabwe (and elsewhere), the burden of hardship often falls disproportionately on women owing to the fact that they are to some extent regarded as second-class citizens. Most authors are directly or indirectly laying the blame on the Zimbabwean culture which seems to deny women full and equal citizenship. Some statistics

DOI: 10.4324/9781003494546-15

confirm the authors' observations. For instance, according to UNAIDS (2016), in Zimbabwe, about one in three women aged 15–49 years have experienced physical violence, and about one in four women have experienced sexual violence since the age of 15 years. Such statistics are an indication that, in contexts such as Zimbabwe, women do not command respect as equal citizens, and this lack of respect undermines both their safety and bodily integrity, as well as their confidence to freely participate in the civic life of society (see Munyiswa, 2018). Cultural change is in this case a possible remedy. Both men and women need to take a second look at some of their beliefs and practices and revise where there is need.

Other suggested measures to end GBV apart from cultural and behavioural change include policy changes that are aimed at making women equal citizens. It is possible to argue that while being a citizen of a state is, per definition, to have the same membership status as every other citizen of that state, throughout most of human history and in all regions of the globe, women of all classes, races, ethnicities and religions have been, and often continue to be, denied full membership status, and hence full citizenship (Friedman, 2005). So exclusively male has this status been for nearly all of human history that substantial numbers of women do not yet have a status equal to that of their male counterparts in any given state, and even today, women and men are likely to differ in the political rights and privileges of citizenship that affect them, and differ in ways that are linked systematically to gender categories. This exclusion of women means they are excluded from full enjoyment of the different elements of citizenship, to the detriment of their autonomy, health, education, employment, in short, well-being (Lister, 2008). According to the UNDP (2015), even though a lot of progress has been made over the years in reducing disparities between men and women and although some convergence has occurred in capabilities between them, there is still some ground to cover as women remain unable to fully function and are still unable to exercise the same choices and realise their potential. These disparities generate unequal achievements, and, as a result, the full potential of many women's lives cannot be realised. In this regard, ending gender inequality requires the expansion of political, social and economic citizenship rights to fully include women. As long as women are accorded fewer platforms for exercising their capabilities relative to men, they are in effect deprived of equal freedoms and are easily exploited as witnessed during pandemics.

For the avoidance of doubt, researchers in this volume are calling out that for GBV to be eliminated in and out of pandemics, there is a need for behavioural and cultural change by all citizens of Zimbabwe. Additionally, there is a need to change current perceptions and conceptions about women. Women are no more care-givers than men. The dangerous duties assigned to women during pandemics citing culture and tradition have to be re-evaluated. Women, on the other hand, need to be further empowered about their actual, and not the socially constructed, status in society. That is where the media and the rest of civil society should come in – to remind and to empower. More focus should be on women in rural areas where most women are seriously disempowered and where some traditional customs are religiously adhered to regardless of their consequences. There is also a need to have more women in government, holding some cabinet positions. This allows them to influence policy changes at that level. The current cabinet at the time of writing had very few women and most of them were heading ministries that did not deal directly with women's issues. It is, however, noteworthy that the government in 2022 raised the age of consent from 16 to 18 years. Having sexual intercourse with a girl below 18 years has been criminalised. It remains to be seen whether this law will be fully enforced. Child marriages involving girls as young as nine years have been reported in some indigenous churches that strongly support the ruling ZANU-PF party. This raises doubt when it comes to law enforcement.

Lastly, chiefs and village heads who are the so-called custodians of culture need to have their capacity enhanced from time to time through workshops on women's rights, including the rights of women during pandemics. These traditional leaders are the ones heading communities in which cases of GBV are highest. It is, therefore, our hope that this book prompts action by policy-makers and civil society, including the media. In the event of pandemics in future, we hope cases of GBV will be much lower and women will not be the ones to be assigned risky roles that have the potential to harm their health, integrity and well-being.

References

Atuire, C. A. and Rutazibwa, O. U. 2021. Comment: An African reading of the Covid-19 pandemic and the stakes of decolonization. Available at https://law.yale.edu/sites/default/files/area/center/ghjp/documents/atuire_rutazibwa_commentary_v2.pdf, accessed on 10 June 2024.

Chitando, E., Mlambo, O. B., Mfecane, S. and Ratele, K. (eds.) 2024. *The Palgrave Handbook of African Men and Masculinities*. Cham: Palgrave Macmillan.

Friedman, F. 2005. *Women and Citizenship*. Oxford: Oxford University Press.

Isike, C. 2022. The value of re-socializing boys and men for positive gender relations to curb gender-based violence and femicide in South Africa, in K. Fontaine-Skronski, V. Thool, and N. Eschborn (eds.), *Does the UN Model Still Work? Challenges and Prospects for the Future of Multilateralism*. Amsterdam: Brill, pp. 266–286.

Lister, L. 2008. Inclusive citizenship, gender and poverty: Some implications for education for citizenship. *Citizenship Teaching and Learning*, 4(1), 4–19.

Munyiswa, I. 2018. *Citizenship as a Human Well-being Capability*. Stellenbosch: Stellenbosch University.

Nyanga, T., Zirima, H. and Mashavira, N. 2020. Withering [the] COVID 19 storm: Survival strategies employed by informal traders in Masvingo Urban, Zimbabwe. *Management Dynamics* 20(1), 1–9. Article 1. DOI: https://doi.org/10.57198/2583-4932.1012

UNAIDS. 2016. United Nations Population Fund (UNFPA) Unified Budget Results and Accountability Framework (UBRAF) 2016-2021. UNFPA_organizationalreport_final_tmp.pdf (unaids.org)

UNDP. 2015. Human Development Report 2015 | United Nations Development Programme (undp.org).

Index

Note: Entries in **bold** refer to tables. Entries refer to Zimbabwe unless otherwise stated.

Kolibri 360 GmbH
Ferdinand-Jühlke-Straße 7
99095 Erfurt, Deutschland
produktsicherheit@kolibri360.de